English Brushup

Fourth Edition

Annotated Instructor's Edition

John Langan
Atlantic Cape Community College

Janet M. Goldstein

Boston   Burr Ridge, IL   Dubuque, IA   Madison, WI   New York   San Francisco   St. Louis
Bangkok   Bogotá   Caracas   Kuala Lumpur   Lisbon   London   Madrid   Mexico City
Milan   Montreal   New Delhi   Santiago   Seoul   Singapore   Sydney   Taipei   Toronto

The McGraw·Hill Companies

Mc Graw Hill Higher Education

Published by McGraw-Hill, an imprint of The McGraw-Hill Companies, Inc., 1221 Avenue of the Americas, New York, NY 10020.

This book is printed on acid-free paper.

1 2 3 4 5 6 7 8 9 0 DOC/DOC 0 9 8 7 6

ISBN-13 (Student Edition):	978-0-07-312376-9
ISBN-10 (Student Edition):	0-07-312376-5
ISBN-13 (Instructor's Edition):	978-0-07-312377-6
ISBN-10 (Instructor's Edition):	0-07-312377-3

Editor in Chief: *Emily Barrosse*
Publisher: *Lisa Moore*
Sponsoring Editor: *John Kindler*
Marketing Manager: *Lori DeShazo*
Project Manager: *Christina Gimlin*
Manuscript Editor: *Margaret Moore*
Art Director: *Jeanne Schreiber*
Design Manager: *Cassandra Chu*
Text Designer: *Rick Soldin*
Cover Designer: *Glenda King*
Cover Illustration: *Paul Turnbaugh and Judith Ogus*
Production Supervisor: *Janean Utley*
Composition: *11/13 Times Roman by Electronic Publishing Services, Tennessee*
Printing: *PMS 286, 45# NewEra Matte, RR Donnelley Crawfordsville*

Library of Congress Cataloging-in-Publication Data

Langan, John, 1942–
    English brushup / John Langan, Janet M. Goldstein.—4th Ed.
        p. cm.
    Includes index.
    ISBN-13: 978-0-07-312376-9 (acid-free paper)
    ISBN-10: 0-07-312376-5 (acid-free paper)
        1. English language—Rhetoric—Problems, exercises, etc. 2. English language—Grammer—Problems, exercises, etc. I. Goldstein, Janet M., 1940– II. Title.

PE1413.L28 2006
428.2—dc22   2006041936

www.mhhe.com

Contents

Part Two: Extending the Skills   185

Part Three: Applying the Skills   229

four additional mastery tests for each of the skills in Part One of the book. The instructor has permission to make unlimited copies of these letter-sized, easily-scorable tests. To provide for a range of student needs, the first two tests are relatively easy, and the second two are more difficult.

Other features of the book include the following:

- A clear, inviting two-color design.
- Simple language rather than traditional grammatical terminology.
- Examples and practice materials that are "real-life," high-interest, sometimes amusing, and always *adult.*
- An insistence that students play an active role in the learning process, not just "correcting," as in so many grammar books, but actually *writing out* corrections.

In short, *English Brushup* offers a combination of appealing features not found in other texts. A focus on important skills, a self-teaching approach, a reasonable size, outstanding supplements—all these may prompt you to decide that *English Brushup* is the grammar book best suited to the needs of today's students.

Changes in the Fourth Edition

- A new chapter, "Parts of Speech: A Review," has been added to Part Two. Instructors can use this chapter either as an introduction to the grammar skills covered in Part One or as a reference at any point in the course.
- Five new editing tests, consisting of ten items each, have been added to Part Three, "Applying the Skills." In addition, all the combined mastery tests in this section now contain ten items.
- To provide additional practice on the skills taught in Part Two, many of the practice exercises have been expanded to ten items.
- Finally, practice items throughout the book have been revised and updated to ensure that each activity and test works as clearly and effectively as possible.

Acknowledgments

For assistance with the first and second editions of *English Brushup,* we are grateful to Kent Smith and Carole Mohr. In particular, our thanks go to Beth Johnson for her invaluable role in helping develop the examples and practice materials for the earlier editions of the book.

John Langan
Janet M. Goldstein

To the Instructor

English Brushup is a quick and practical guide to the grammar, punctuation, and usage skills that students most need to know. The book contains features that distinguish it from other grammar texts on the market:

1   *Three-part format.*   In order to highlight the most vital skills, the book is divided into three parts. Part One presents primary information about sixteen key skills. Part Two includes secondary information about these skills and also covers topics not discussed in Part One. Part Three tests students' mastery of the skills taught in Part One.

2   *Self-teaching approach.*   The *first page of every chapter* in Part One begins with an informal test—and then provides the answers and explanations. Students can quickly see what they know and don't know about the skill in question. In some cases, they may learn what they need to know about the skill without going any further in the chapter.

   The *next three to five pages* of each chapter present the basics about the skill. Lively examples and brief exercises give students the chance to practice the grammatical principle involved. Answers at the back of the book allow students to correct their own work, teaching themselves as they go.

   The *last six pages of each chapter* consist of six tests on the skill. Half of the items in Tests 1, 3, and 5 are accompanied by *hints*—shown in a second color—which are designed to guide students in thinking through each kind of correction. More self-teaching is therefore ensured.

   In addition, as students work through the tests, they master the skills in progressively longer passages. In Tests 1 and 2, students practice the skills in sentences; in Tests 3 and 4, they work with short passages; finally, in Tests 5 and 6, they apply the skills to entire paragraphs. Step by step, then, their mastery of the skills advances from the sentence to the paragraph level.

3   *Manageable size.*   The book's compact size and short chapters will not overwhelm students. In addition, *English Brushup* does not discourage or confuse students by offering an equal amount of coverage for every grammar rule. Instead, Part One of the book presents only those rules that students actually *need to know* to write well. Additional useful information about many skills appears in Part Two.

4   *Invaluable supplements.*   An *Instructor's Edition* consists of the student text, as well as answers to all the practices and tests. An *Instructor's Manual and Test Bank* contains a diagnostic test and an achievement test as well as

Introduction

WHY BRUSH UP YOUR ENGLISH?

Suppose you read the following paragraph in a job application:

> This June I will graduate. With twenty-four hours of courses in accounting. I have alot of previous experience. One was as a clerk in the school bookstore, the other doing data entry for ryder truck rental.

... or read the following line in a student's history paper:

> The soldiers in the civil war often wore rags, on there feet that were torn from scraps of old clothing.

... or read the following sentence in a business memo:

> The profit's at the company has tripled in the passed 3 months its been our best performance at the company in several yrs.

... or saw the following sign:

> Please dont put children in our shopping carts, they are unstable. And can fall over easily.

Chances are that the writers of the above lines felt vaguely uneasy about their sentences. They may have had doubts about whether their English was correct and clear. However, they went ahead because their work or school situation required them to put words on paper.

If you were uncertain about the corrections needed for the above sentences, then this book is for you. *English Brushup* is a guide to the essentials of English: the grammar, punctuation, and usage skills that you most need to write clearly and effectively.

HOW *ENGLISH BRUSHUP* WORKS

Here is one way to use the book:

1 **Look at the table of contents.** You'll see that *English Brushup* is divided into three parts. Part One presents sixteen key skills you need to write well. Part Two includes more information about some of the skills in Part One; it also covers some areas not included in Part One. Part Three contains a series of tests you can take after you have studied the skills in Part One.

2 **Turn to the first page of any chapter in Part One.** Take the "Seeing What You Know" test. Then check your answers. If you have a problem with the skill, you'll know it right away. In some cases, you may learn what you need to know about the skill without going any further in the chapter.

3 **Work through the rest of the chapter.** The next three to five pages of each chapter present the basics of the skill. The examples and brief exercises will give you the chance to practice the skill. The answers at the back of the book will allow you to correct your own work, teaching yourself as you go.

4 **Test yourself.** The last six pages of each chapter contain six tests on the skill. Tests 1, 3, and 5 usually include hints that will help you understand and answer half of the items on the tests. Be sure to take advantage of these hints to increase your mastery of the skill. You will find additional tests in Part Three, "Applying the Skills."

5 **Use the book as a reference tool.** Following the above sequence, work your way through the book. In Part Two, pay special attention to the section on paper format on pages 187–188. Refer to other sections of Part Two as needed or as your instructor suggests. To help you find your way around the book, use the table of contents at the front, the index at the back, and the correction symbols and page references on the inside front cover.

AN INTRODUCTION TO WRITING

Here in a nutshell is what you need to write effectively.

WHAT IS A PARAGRAPH?

A **paragraph** is a series of sentences about one main idea, or point. A paragraph typically starts with a point, and the rest of the paragraph provides specific details to support and develop that point.

Consider the following paragraph, written by a student named Gary Callahan.

Returning to School

Starting college at the age of twenty-nine was not easy for me. For one thing, I did not have much support from my parents and friends. My father asked, "Didn't you get dumped on enough in high school? Why go back for more?" My mother worried, "Where's the money going to come from?" My friends seemed threatened. "Hey, there's the college man," they would say when I approached. Another reason that starting college was difficult was that I had bad memories of school. I had spent years of my life sitting in classrooms completely bored, watching clocks tick ever so slowly toward the final bell. When I was not bored, I was afraid of being embarrassed. Once a teacher called on me and then said, "Ah, forget it, Callahan," when he realized I did not know the answer. Finally, I soon learned that college would give me little time with my family. After work every day, I have just an hour and ten minutes to eat and spend time with my wife and daughter before going off to class. When I get back, my daughter is in bed, and my wife and I have only a little time together. Then the time on weekends goes by quickly, with all the homework I have to do. I am going to persist, though, because I believe a better life awaits me with a college degree.

The paragraph above, like many effective paragraphs, starts by stating a main idea, or point. In this case, the point is that starting college at age twenty-nine was not easy. A **point** is a general idea that contains an opinion.

In our everyday lives, we continually make points about all kinds of matters. We express such opinions as "That was a terrible movie" or "My psychology instructor is the best teacher I have ever had" or "My sister is a generous person" or "Eating at that restaurant was a mistake" or "That team should win the play-off game" or "Waitressing is the worst job I ever had" or "Our state should allow the death penalty" or "Cigarette smoking should be banned everywhere." In *talking* to people, we don't always give the reasons for our opinions. However, in *writing*, we *must* provide reasons to support our ideas. Only by supplying solid evidence for any point that we make can we communicate effectively with readers.

An effective paragraph, then, not only must make a point but also must support it with **specific evidence**—reasons, examples, and other details. Such specifics help prove to readers that the point is reasonable. Even if readers do not agree with the writer, at least they have in front of them the evidence on which the writer has based his or her opinion. Readers are like a jury: they want to see the evidence so that they can make their own judgments.

WHAT ARE THE GOALS OF EFFECTIVE WRITING?

Now that you have considered an effective student paragraph, it is time to look at four goals of effective writing:

Goal 1: Make a Point.

It is often best to state your point in the first sentence of your paper, just as Gary did in his paragraph about returning to school. The sentence that expresses the main idea, or point, of a paragraph is called the **topic sentence.**

Goal 2: Support the Point.

To support your point, you need to provide specific reasons, examples, and other details that explain and develop it. The more precise and particular your supporting details are, the better your readers can "see," "hear," and "feel" them.

Goal 3: Organize the Support.

You will find it helpful to learn two common ways of organizing the support in a paragraph—listing order and time order. Signal words, also known as **transitions,** increase the effectiveness of each method.

Listing Order   The writer organizes the supporting evidence in a paper by providing a list of two or more reasons, examples, or details. Often the most important or interesting item is saved for last because the reader is most likely to remember the last thing read.

Transition words that show listing order include the following:

one	second	also	next	last of all
for one thing	third	another	moreover	finally
first of all	next	in addition	furthermore	

The paragraph about starting college uses listing order: It lists three reasons why starting college at twenty-nine is not easy, and each of those three reasons is introduced by one of the above transitions. In the spaces below, write in the three transitions:

   For one thing   Another   Finally

The first reason in the paragraph about starting college is introduced with *For one thing,* the second reason by *Another,* and the third reason by *Finally.*

Time Order   Supporting details are presented in the order in which they occurred. *First* this happened; *next* this; *after* that, this; and so on. Many paragraphs, especially those that tell stories or give a series of directions, are organized in time order.

Transition words that show time relationships include the following:

first	before	after	when	then
next	during	now	while	until
as	soon	later	often	finally

Read the paragraph below, which is organized in time order. See if you can underline the six transition words that show the time relationships.

Della had a sad experience <u>while</u> driving home last night. She traveled along the dark, winding road that led toward her home. She was only two miles from her house <u>when</u> she noticed a glimmer of light in the road.

The <u>next</u> thing she knew, she heard a sickening thud and realized she had struck an animal. The light, she realized, had been its eyes reflected in her car's headlights. Della stopped the car and ran back to see what she had hit. It was a handsome cocker spaniel, with blond fur and long ears. <u>As</u> she bent over the still form, she realized there was nothing to be done. The dog was dead. Della searched the dog for a collar and tags. There was nothing. <u>Before</u> leaving, she walked to several nearby houses, asking if anyone knew who owned the dog. No one did. <u>Finally</u> Della gave up and drove on. She was sad to leave someone's pet lying there alone.

The main point of the paragraph is stated in its first sentence: "Della had a sad experience while driving home last night." The support for this point is all the details of Della's experience. Those details are presented in the order in which they occurred. The time relationships are highlighted by these transitions: *while, when, next, as, before,* and *finally.*

Goal 4: Write Error-Free Sentences.

If you use correct spelling and follow the rules of grammar, punctuation, and usage, your sentences will be clear and well-written. However, you do not need to have all that information in your head. Even the best writers use reference materials to be sure their writing is correct. So, when you write your papers, keep a good dictionary and grammar handbook nearby.

In general, however, do not refer to them until you have put your ideas firmly down in writing. As you will learn on the pages ahead, there will be time enough to make the needed corrections.

HOW DO YOU REACH THE GOALS OF EFFECTIVE WRITING?

Even professional writers do not sit down and automatically, in one draft, write a paper. Instead, they have to work on it a step at a time. Writing a paper is a process that can be divided into the following steps:

Step 1:   Getting Started through Prewriting

Step 2:   Preparing a Scratch Outline

Step 3:   Writing the First Draft

Step 4:   Revising

Step 5:   Proofreading

These steps are described on the following pages.

Step 1: Getting Started through Prewriting

First, you need to learn strategies for working on a paper. These strategies will help you do the thinking needed to figure out both the point you want to make and the support you have for that point.

There are several **prewriting strategies** that you can use before writing the first draft of your paper.

- **Freewriting** is just sitting down and writing whatever comes into your mind about a topic. Do this for ten minutes or so. Write without stopping and without worrying at all about spelling, grammar, or the like. Simply get down on paper all the information about the topic that occurs to you.

- **Questioning** means that you think about your topic by writing down a series of questions and answers about it. Your questions can start with words like *what, when, where, why,* and *how.*

- **Clustering** (also known as **diagramming** or **mapping**) is another strategy that can be used to generate material for a paper. It is helpful for people who like to do their thinking in a visual way. In clustering, you begin by stating your subject in a few words in the center of a blank sheet of paper. Then, as ideas come to you, put them in ovals, boxes, or circles around the subject, and draw lines to connect them to the subject. Put minor ideas or details in smaller boxes or circles, and use connecting lines to show how they relate as well. Keep in mind that there is no right or wrong way of clustering. It is a way to think on paper about how various ideas and details relate to one another.

- In **list making,** a strategy also known as **brainstorming,** you make a list of ideas and details that could go into your paper. Simply pile these items up, one after another, without worrying about putting them in any special order. Accumulate as many details as you can think of.

It is natural for a number of such extra or unrelated details to appear as part of the prewriting process. The goal of prewriting is to get a lot of information down on paper. You can then add to, shape, and subtract from your raw material as you take your paper through the series of writing drafts.

Important Notes about Prewriting Strategies   Some writers may use only one of the prewriting strategies. Others may use bits and pieces of all four. Any one strategy can lead to another. Freewriting may lead to questioning or clustering, which may then lead to a list. Or a writer may start with a list and then use freewriting or questioning to develop items on the list. During this early stage of the writing process, as you do your thinking on paper, anything goes. You should not expect a straight-line progression from the beginning to the end of your paper.

Instead, there probably will be a continual moving back and forth as you work to discover your point and just how you will develop it.

Finally, remember that you are not ready to begin writing a paper until you know your main point and many of the details that can be used to support it. Don't rush through prewriting. It's better to spend more time on this stage than to waste time writing a paragraph for which you have no solid point and too little interesting support.

Step 2: Preparing a Scratch Outline

A **scratch outline** is a brief plan for the paragraph. It shows at a glance the point of the paragraph and the main support for that point. It is the logical framework upon which the paper is built.

This rough outline often follows freewriting, questioning, clustering, or list making. Or it may gradually emerge in the midst of these strategies. In fact, trying to outline is a good way to see if you need to do more prewriting. If a solid outline does not emerge, then you know you need to do more prewriting to clarify your main point or its support. Once you have a workable outline, you may realize, for instance, that you want to do more list making to develop one of the supporting details in the outline.

Below is the scratch outline that Gary Callahan, after doing a good deal of preliminary writing, prepared for his paragraph on returning to school:

Example of a Scratch Outline

Starting college at age twenty-nine isn't easy.
1.   Little support from parents and friends
2.   Bad memories of high school
3.   Not enough time to spend with family

This helpful outline, with its clear point and solid support, became the foundation of Gary's paragraph.

Step 3: Writing the First Draft

When you do a first draft, be prepared to put in additional thoughts and details that didn't emerge in your prewriting. And don't worry if you hit a snag. Just leave a blank space or add a comment such as "Do later" and press on to finish the paper. Also, don't worry yet about grammar, punctuation, or spelling. You don't want to take time correcting words or sentences that you may decide to remove later. Instead, make it your goal to develop the content of your paper with plenty of specific details.

Step 4: Revising

Revising is as much a stage in the writing process as prewriting, outlining, and doing the first draft. **Revising** means that you rewrite a paper, building on what has been done to make it stronger and better. You might decide to use a thesaurus to find the best word choices for what you want to say. You'll try to add more supporting details—or more convincing supporting details. You'll look for pertinent quotations to include as support for your points. One writer has said about revising, "It's like cleaning house—getting rid of all the junk and putting things in the right order." A typical revision means allowing enough time to write at least one or two more drafts.

Step 5: Proofreading

Proofreading, the final stage in the writing process, means checking a paper carefully for spelling, grammar, punctuation, and other errors. You are ready for this stage when you are satisfied with your choice of supporting details, the order in which they are presented, and the way they and your topic sentence are worded.

Use a grammar handbook to be sure about your grammar, punctuation, and usage. Also, read through the paper carefully, looking for typing errors, omitted words, and any other errors you may have missed before. Such proofreading is often hard to do—students have spent so much time with their work, or so little, that they want to avoid proofing. However, if done carefully, this important final step will ensure that your paper looks as good as possible.

Hints for Proofreading

1   One helpful trick at this stage is to read your paper out loud. You will probably hear awkward wordings and become aware of spots where the punctuation needs to be improved. Make the changes needed for your sentences to read smoothly and clearly.

2   Another helpful technique is to take a sheet of paper and cover your paragraph so that you can expose and check carefully just one line at a time.

3   A third strategy is to read your paper backward, from the last sentence to the first. Doing so helps keep you from getting caught up in the flow of the paper and missing small mistakes, which is easy to do, since you're so familiar with what you meant to say.

WHAT IS AN ESSAY?

An essay does the same thing a paragraph does: It starts with a point, and the rest of the essay provides specific details to support and develop that point. However, while a paragraph is a series of *sentences* about one main idea or point, an **essay** is a series of *paragraphs* about one main idea or point—called the **central idea** of the essay. Since an essay is much longer than one paragraph, it allows a writer to develop a topic in more detail. Despite the greater length of an essay, the process of writing it is the same as that for writing a paragraph: prewriting, preparing a scratch outline, writing and revising drafts, and proofreading.

Here are the major differences between a paragraph and an essay:

Paragraph	Essay
Made up of sentences.	Made up of paragraphs.
Starts with a sentence containing the main point of the paragraph (**topic sentence**).	Starts with an introductory paragraph containing the central idea of the essay, expressed in a sentence called the **thesis statement** (or **thesis sentence**).
Body of paragraph contains specific details that support and develop the topic sentence.	Body of essay contains paragraphs that support and develop the central idea. Each of these paragraphs has its own main supporting point, stated in a topic sentence.
Paragraph often ends with a closing sentence that rounds it off.	Essay ends with a concluding paragraph that rounds it off.

Later in his writing course, the student Gary Callahan was asked to expand his paragraph into an essay. Here is the essay that resulted:

For a typical college freshman, entering college is fun and an exciting time of life. It is a time not just to explore new ideas in classes but to relax on the lawn chatting with new friends, to sit having soda and pizza in the cafeteria, or to listen to music and play cards in the student lounge. I see the crowds of eighteen-year-olds enjoying all that college has to offer, and I sometimes envy their freedom. Instead of being a typical freshman, I am twenty-nine years old, and beginning college has been a difficult experience for me. I have had to deal with a lack of support, bad memories of past school experiences, and too little time for my family.

Few people in my life are supportive of my decision to enter college. My father is especially bewildered by the choice I have made. He himself quit school after finishing eighth grade, and he assumes that I should hate school as much as he did. "Didn't you get dumped on enough in high school?" he asks me. "Why go back for more?" My mother is a little more understanding of my desire for an education, but the cost of college terrifies her. She has always believed that college was a privilege only the rich could afford. "Where in the world will all that money come from?" she says. Also, my friends seem threatened by my decision. They make fun of me, suggesting that I'm going to think I'm too good to hang around with the likes of them. "Ooooh, here comes the college man," they say when they see me approach. "We'd better watch our grammar."

I have had to deal not only with family and friends but also with unhappy memories of my earlier school career. I attended an enormous high school where I was just one more faceless kid in the crowd. My classes seemed meaningless to me. I can remember almost none of them in any detail. What I do remember about high school was just sitting, bored until I felt nearly brain-dead, watching the clock hands move ever so slowly toward dismissal time. Such periods of boredom were occasionally interrupted by moments of acute embarrassment. Once an algebra teacher called on me and then said, "Oh, forget it, Callahan," in a disgusted tone when he realized I didn't know the answer. My response, of course, was to shrink down in my chair and try to become invisible for the rest of the semester.

Furthermore, my decision to enter college has meant I have much less time to spend with my family. I work eight hours a day. Then I rush home and have all of an hour and ten minutes to eat dinner and spend time with my wife and daughter before I rush off again, this time to class. When I return from class, I am dead tired. My little girl is already asleep. My wife and I have only a little time to talk together before I collapse into bed. Weekends are a little better, but not much. That's when I try to get my papers written and catch up on a few chores around the house. My wife tries to be understanding, but it's hard on her to have so little support from me these days. And I'm missing out on a lot of special times in my daughter's life. For instance, I didn't realize she had begun to walk until three days after it happened.

Why, then, do I put myself through all these difficulties? Despite a lack of support, bad memories, and little family time, I dream about a different kind of future. I believe that I will benefit financially and become a better provider for my family. I also feel that I will become a more rounded human being as a result of achieving my goal of obtaining a college degree.

WHAT ARE THE PARTS OF AN ESSAY?

When Gary decided to expand his paragraph into an essay, he knew he would need to write an introductory paragraph, several supporting paragraphs, and a concluding paragraph.

Each of these parts of the essay is explained below.

Introductory Paragraph

A well-written introductory paragraph will often do the following:

1 *Gain the reader's interest.* On pages 12–13 are several time-tested methods used to draw the reader into an essay.

2 *Present the thesis statement.* The thesis statement expresses the central idea of an essay, just as a topic sentence states the main idea of a paragraph. Here's an example of a thesis statement:

> A vacation at home can be wonderful.

An essay with this thesis statement would go on to explain some positive things about vacationing at home.

- What is the thesis statement in Gary's essay? Find that statement on page 9 and write it here:

> I am twenty-nine years old, and beginning college has been a difficult
>
> experience for me.

You should have written down the next-to-last sentence in the introductory paragraph of Gary's essay.

3 *Lay out a plan of development.* The **plan of development** is a brief statement of the main supporting details for the central idea. These supporting details should be presented in the order in which they will be discussed in the essay. The plan of development can be blended into the thesis statement or presented separately.

Blended into a thesis statement: A vacation at home can be wonderful because you can avoid the hassles of travel, make use of your knowledge of the area, and indulge in special activities.

Presented separately: A vacation at home can be wonderful. At home you can avoid the hassles of travel, make use of your knowledge of the area, and indulge in special activities.

Note that some essays lend themselves better to a plan of development than others do. Some essays do not include a plan of development at all. At the least, however, your introductory paragraph should gain the reader's interest and present the thesis statement.

- What is the plan of development in Gary's essay? Find the sentence on page 9 that states Gary's plan of development and write it here:

  I have had to deal with a lack of support, bad memories of past school

  experiences, and too little time for my family.

You should have written down the last sentence in the introductory paragraph of Gary's essay.

Four Common Methods of Introduction

1   *Begin with a broad statement and narrow it down to your thesis statement.* Broad statements can capture your reader's interest while introducing your general topic. They may provide useful background material as well. The writer of the introductory paragraph below begins with a broad statement about her possessions. She then narrows the focus down to the three possessions that are the specific topic of the paper.

> I have many possessions that I would be sad to lose. Because I love to cook, I would miss several kitchen appliances that provide me with so many happy cooking adventures. I would also miss the wonderful electronic equipment that entertains me every day, including my large-screen television set and my DVD player. I would miss the two telephones on which I have spent many interesting hours chatting in every part of my apartment, including the bathtub. But if my apartment were burning down, I would most want to rescue three things that are irreplaceable and hold great meaning for me—the silverware set that belonged to my grandmother, my mother's wedding gown, and my giant photo album.

2   *Present an idea or situation that is the opposite of what will be written about.* One way to gain the reader's interest is to show the difference between your opening idea or situation and the one to be discussed in the essay.

> When I was a girl, I never argued with my parents about differences between their attitudes and mine. My father would deliver his judgment on an issue, and that was usually the end of the matter. Discussion seldom changed his mind, and disagreement was not tolerated. But the situation is different with today's parents and children. My husband and I have to contend with radical differences between what our children think about a given situation and what we think about it. We have had disagreements with all three of our daughters, Stephanie, Diana, and Giselle.

3   *Tell a brief story.* An interesting incident or anecdote is hard for a reader to resist. In an introduction, a story should be no more than a few sentences, and it should relate meaningfully to—and so lead the reader toward—your central idea. The story you tell can be an experience of your own, of someone you know, or of someone you have read about. For instance, in the following introduction, the writer tells a simple personal story that serves as background for his central idea.

> The husky man pushes open the door of the bedroom and grins as he pulls out a .38 revolver. An elderly man wearing thin pajamas looks at him and whimpers. In a feeble effort at escape, the old man slides out of his bed and moves to the door of the room. The husky man, still grinning, blocks his way. With the face of a small, frightened animal, the old man looks up and whispers, "Oh, God, please don't hurt me." The grinning man then fires four times. The television movie cuts now to a soap commercial, but the little boy who has been watching the set has begun to cry. Such scenes of direct violence on television must surely be harmful to children for a number of psychological reasons.

4   *Ask one or more questions.* The questions may be ones that you intend to answer in your essay, or they may show that your topic relates directly to readers. In the following example, the questions are designed to gain readers' interest and convince them that the essay applies to them.

> Does your will to study collapse when someone suggests getting a pizza? Does your social life compete with your class attendance? Is there a huge gap between your intentions and your actions? If the answers to these questions are *yes, yes,* and *yes,* read on. You can benefit from some powerful ways to motivate yourself: setting goals and consciously working to reach them, using rational thinking, and developing a positive personality.

- Which of the four methods of introduction described above does Gary use in his essay?

  Present an idea that is the opposite of what will be written about.

  _____

Gary begins with an idea that is the opposite of what he is writing about. His essay is about his difficulties with college life, but he begins with the idea that college "is fun and an exciting time" for some students.

Supporting Paragraphs

The traditional college essay has three supporting paragraphs. However, some essays will have two supporting paragraphs, and others will probably have four or more. Each supporting paragraph should have its own topic sentence, which states the point to be developed in that paragraph.

Notice that each of the supporting paragraphs in Gary's essay has its own topic sentence. For example, the topic sentence of his first supporting paragraph is "Few people in my life are supportive of my decision to enter college."

- What is the topic sentence of Gary's second supporting paragraph?
  I have had to deal not only with family and friends but also with unhappy memories of my earlier school career.

- What is the topic sentence of Gary's third supporting paragraph?
  Furthermore, my decision to enter college has meant I have much less time to spend with my family.

In each case, Gary's topic sentence is the first sentence of the paragraph.

Concluding Paragraph

The concluding paragraph often summarizes the essay by briefly restating the thesis and, at times, the main supporting points. It may also provide a closing thought or two as a way of bringing the paper to a natural and graceful end. Look again at the four sentences that conclude Gary's essay:

> Why, then, do I put myself through all these difficulties? Despite a lack of support, bad memories, and little family time, I dream about a different kind of future. I believe that I will benefit financially and become a better provider for my family. I also feel that I will become a more rounded human being as a result of achieving my goal of obtaining a college degree.

- With what sentence (*first, second, third,* or *fourth*) does he briefly summarize the essay? *second*

- With what sentence or sentences does he provide a closing thought or two?
  third and fourth

Activity

Answer each of the following questions by filling in the blank or circling the answer you think is correct.

1. An effective paragraph or essay
   a. makes a point.
   b. provides specific support.
   (c.) makes a point and provides specific support.
   d. does none of the above.

2. The sentence that states the main idea of a paragraph is known as the _____topic_____ sentence; the sentence that states the central idea of an essay is known as the _____thesis_____ statement.

3. Prewriting can help a writer find
   a. a good topic to write about.
   b. a good main point to make about the topic.
   c. enough details to support the main point.
   (d.) all of the above.

4. *True or false?* ___T___ During the freewriting process, you should not concern yourself with spelling, punctuation, or grammar.

5. One step that everyone should use at some stage of the writing process is to prepare a plan for the paragraph or essay. The plan is known as a(n) __scratch outline__.

6. When you start writing, your first concern should be
   a. spelling.
   (b.) content.
   c. grammar.
   d. punctuation.

7. Two common ways of organizing a paragraph are _____listing_____ order and _____time_____ order.

8. A thesis statement
    a.   is generally part of an essay's introduction.
    b.   states the central idea of the essay.
    c.   can be followed by the essay's plan of development.
    d.   all of the above.

A FINAL WORD

English Brushup has been designed to benefit you as much as possible. Its format is straightforward, its explanations are clear, and its practices and tests will help you learn through doing. *It is a book that has been created to reward effort,* and if you provide that effort, you can make yourself a competent and confident writer.

John Langan
Janet M. Goldstein

Part One

Sixteen Basic Skills

Preview

Part One presents basic information about sixteen key grammar, punctuation, and usage skills:

To the Instructor   Additional information about and practice with many of these skills appears in Part Two, starting on page 185.

1 Subjects and Verbs

Seeing What You Know

In each blank, insert a word that seems appropriate. Then read the explanations below.

Answers will vary.

1. The _____ accidentally _____ onto the floor.

2. My _____ often _____ at the mail carrier.

3. A _____ in the corner _____ loudly to the waitress.

4. _____ should never have _____ to study all night for the test.

Understanding the Answers

If your completed sentences make grammatical sense, the word in the first blank of each sentence will be its **subject,** and the word in the second blank will be the **verb.** Here are some completed versions of the sentences, with the subjects and verbs labeled:

1. The **knife** *(subject)* accidentally **fell** *(verb)* onto the floor.
   The *knife* is what the sentence is about. *Fell* is what the knife did.

2. My **cat** *(subject)* often **meows** *(verb)* at the mail carrier.
   The *cat* is the one the sentence is about. *Meows* is what the cat does.

3. A **customer** *(subject)* in the corner **shouted** *(verb)* loudly to the waitress.
   A *customer* is performing an action. *Shouted* is the action.

4. **Anita** *(subject)* **should** never **have tried** *(verb)* to study all night for the test.
   Anita is the person doing something. *Should [never] have tried* is what the sentence says about her. *Never* is not part of the verb.

Subjects and verbs are the basic parts of sentences. Understanding them will help you with most of the other skills in this book.

FINDING THE SUBJECT

Look at the following sentences:

> Eric tripped on the steps.
>
> The brakes on my car squeal.
>
> She owns three motorcycles.
>
> Depression is a common mood disorder.

The **subject** of a sentence is the person, thing, or idea that the sentence is about. To find a sentence's subject, ask yourself, "Who or what is this sentence about?" or "Who or what is doing something in this sentence?"

Let's look again at the sentences above.

> Who is the first one about? *Eric.* (He's the one who tripped.)
>
> What is the second one about? *Brakes.* (They are what squeal.)
>
> Who is the third one about? *She.* (She's the one who owns three motorcycles.)
>
> What is the fourth one about? *Depression.* (It's a common mood disorder.)

So, in the sentences above, the subjects are *Eric, brakes, she,* and *depression.*

Note   Each of these subjects is either a **noun** (the name of a person, place, or thing—including a quality or an idea) or a **pronoun** (a word—such as *I, you, he, she, it, we,* or *they*—that stands for a noun). The subject of a sentence will always be either a noun or a pronoun.

The Subject Is Never in a Prepositional Phrase

The subject of a sentence will never be part of a prepositional phrase. A **prepositional phrase** is a group of words that begins with a preposition, ends with a noun or pronoun (the object of the preposition), and answers a question such as "Which one?" "What kind?" "How?" "Where?" or "When?"

Here are some common prepositions:

Prepositions					
about	around	beside	for	off	under
above	at	between	from	on, onto	until
across	before	by	in, into	over	up
after	behind	down	inside	through	upon
along	below	during	like	to	with
among	beneath	except	of	toward	without

As you look for the subject of a sentence, it may help to cross out any prepositional phrases that you find.

The vase ~~on the bedside table~~ belonged ~~to my grandparents~~. (*Vase* is the subject; *on the bedside table* is a prepositional phrase telling us which vase.)

~~With smiles or frowns~~, students left the exam room. (*Students* is the subject; *with smiles or frowns* is a prepositional phrase describing how they left.)

The noise ~~during the thunderstorm~~ was frightening. (*Noise* is the subject; *during the thunderstorm* is a prepositional phrase telling when it happened.)

FINDING THE VERB

The subject of a sentence is what that sentence is about. The **verb** explains what that sentence says about the subject. Consider the four sentences on the previous page:

What does the first sentence say about Eric? He *tripped*.

What does the second sentence say about the brakes? They *squeal*.

What does the third sentence say about the woman? She *owns* (three motorcycles).

What does the last sentence say about depression? It *is* (a mood disorder).

The verbs in the sentences above are *tripped, squeal, owns,* and *is*.
Here are two other ways to identify a verb:

1   Try putting a pronoun such as *I, you, he, she, it,* or *they* in front of it. If the word is a verb, the resulting sentence will make sense. Notice that in the examples above, *he tripped, they squeal, she owns,* and *it is* all make sense.

2   Look at what the verb tells us. Most verbs show action; they are called **action verbs.** (*Tripped, owns,* and *squeal* are action verbs.) A few verbs, however, are **linking verbs.** They link (join) the subject to something that is said about the subject. In the fourth example, *is* is a linking verb. It connects the subject, *depression,* with an idea about depression (it is a *common mood disorder*). *Am, are, was, were, look, feel, sound, appear, seem,* and *become* are other common linking verbs.

Practice 1

In each of the sentences below, cross out the prepositional phrases. Then underline the subject once and the verb twice. The first one is done for you as an example.

1. <u>Nikki</u> <u><u>waited</u></u> ~~in the supermarket checkout line for nearly half an hour~~.

2. A <u>dog</u> ~~with muddy paws~~ <u><u>padded</u></u> ~~across the clean kitchen floor~~.

3. <u>One</u> ~~of my cousins~~ <u><u>is</u></u> a tightrope walker ~~in the circus~~.

4. Those <u>kittens</u> ~~at the animal shelter~~ <u><u>need</u></u> a good home.

5. ~~By the end of the month~~, <u>I</u> <u><u>have</u></u> very little money ~~in my wallet~~.

ADDITIONAL FACTS ABOUT VERBS

The hints that follow will further help you find the verb in a sentence.

1 Verbs do not always consist of just one word. Sometimes they consist of a main verb plus one or more **helping verbs,** such as *do, have, may, would, can, could,* or *should.* Here, for example, are some of the forms of the verb *love:*

love	could love	is loving	may have loved
loves	would love	was loving	might have loved
loved	will love	will be loving	must have loved
may love	do love	has loved	should have loved
must love	does love	have loved	could have loved
should love	did love	had loved	would have loved

2 Although words like *not, just, never, only,* and *always* may appear between the main verb and the helping verb, they are never part of the verb.

Ellen might not make the basketball team this year.

You should always count the change the cashier gives you.

That instructor can never end her class on time.

3 The verb of a sentence never comes after the word *to.*

Sal chose to live with his parents during college. (Although *live* is a verb, *to live* cannot be the verb of the sentence.)

4 A word ending in *-ing* cannot by itself be the verb of the sentence. It can be part of the verb, but it needs a helping verb before it.

The strikers were hoping for a quick settlement. (You could not correctly say, "The strikers hoping for a quick settlement.")

Practice 2

In each of the sentences below, cross out the prepositional phrases. Then underline the subject once and the verb twice.

1. Everyone ~~at the plant~~ is working overtime ~~during August~~.

2. The middle child ~~in a family~~ may experience neglect.

3. ~~Around midnight~~, a police siren began to wail ~~in the nearby street~~.

4. That shirt should not have been put ~~in the washing machine~~.

5. ~~On hot days~~, you must always remember to provide extra water ~~for the dog~~.

Note   Additional information about subjects and verbs appears on pages 208–209.

Name _____ Section _____ Date _____

Score: (Number right) _____ × 5 = _____ %

■   **Subjects and Verbs: Test 1**

In each sentence below, cross out the prepositional phrases. Then underline the subject once and the verb twice. Remember to underline all the parts of the verb.

Note   To help in your review of subjects and verbs, use the explanations given for half of the sentences.

1. My <u>brother</u> <u>plays</u> computer games ~~until well past midnight~~.

   Until is a preposition, so *until well past midnight* is a prepositional phrase. The sentence is about my *brother. Plays* (computer games) is what he does.

2. ~~With a satisfied grunt~~, <u>Darnell</u> <u>lifted</u> the hundred-pound barbell ~~over his head.~~

3. ~~Without a doubt~~, <u>Ramon</u> <u>will win</u> the race.

   Without is a preposition, so *without a doubt* is a prepositional phrase. The sentence is about Ramon. *Will win* (*win* plus the helping verb *will*) is what the sentence says about him.

4. Some <u>students</u> <u>have had</u> a terrible case ~~of the flu for two weeks~~.

5. The <u>stars</u> ~~in the cloudless sky~~ <u>seem</u> especially bright tonight.

   In the cloudless sky is a prepositional phrase. The verb *seem* (a linking verb) joins what the sentence is about *(stars)* to a statement describing them *(especially bright)*.

6. That freshly baked apple <u>pie</u> ~~on the kitchen counter~~ <u>smells</u> heavenly.

7. The boss's temper <u>tantrums</u> <u>are</u> impossible to ignore.

   The sentence is about the boss's temper *tantrums*. The linking verb *are* joins the subject to a statement about the subject *(impossible to ignore)*. Since *ignore* has the word *to* in front of it, it cannot be the verb of the sentence.

8. Our <u>neighbors</u> <u>have complained</u> ~~about the old car in our front yard~~.

9. Some <u>people</u> <u>can</u> never <u>forget</u> an insult.

   People are the ones doing something in the sentence. What the sentence says about people is that they *can* never *forget*. The word *never* describes the verb, but it is not part of the verb.

10. ~~During the warm weather~~, homeless <u>people</u> <u>have</u> not <u>been coming</u> ~~into the shelter~~.

To the Instructor   Additional tests on subjects and verbs can be found in the *Instructor's Manual*.

Name _____ Section _____ Date _____

Score: (Number right) _____ × 5 = _____%

■ Subjects and Verbs: Test 2

In each sentence below, cross out the prepositional phrases. Then underline the subject once and the verb twice. Remember to underline all the parts of the verb.

1. The tree ~~in our backyard~~ looks dead.

2. It always relaxes me to walk ~~along the path around the lake~~.

3. My roommate has been sending romantic e-mails ~~to her new boyfriend during computer lab~~.

4. ~~In all his career~~, Simon has never missed one day ~~of work~~.

5. Several shark attacks ~~during the summer~~ alarmed people ~~about swimming in the ocean~~.

6. The last three pages ~~of Elena's term paper~~ vanished ~~from her computer screen~~.

7. The quartz battery ~~in my watch~~ did not need to be replaced ~~for a period of three years~~.

8. Several companies ~~in the city~~ are planning to move ~~to the suburbs~~ to escape the city wage tax.

9. ~~From my bedroom window~~, I can watch all the games ~~on the high school football field~~.

10. The service agreement ~~for the copying machine~~ covers the cost ~~of any kind of breakdown~~, regardless ~~of the number of the copies~~.

Name _____ Section _____ Date _____

Score: (Number right) _____ × 5 = _____%

■ Subjects and Verbs: Test 3

Cross out the prepositional phrases. Then, on the lines provided, write the subject and verb of each of the sentences. Remember to find all the parts of the verb.

Note   To help in your review of subjects and verbs, use the explanations given for half of the sentences.

1. The manager ~~of the hospital thrift shop~~ dresses ~~in unusual outfits~~. Today she is wearing a man's tuxedo and a baseball cap.

    a. *Subject:* _____ manager _____ *Verb:* _____ dresses _____
    The sentence is about the *manager. Dresses* is what she does.

    b. *Subject:* _____ she _____ *Verb:* _____ is wearing _____

2. ~~With a shout of delight~~, the girls leaped ~~into the huge pile of dry leaves~~. They could not resist the urge to crunch the leaves ~~under their feet~~.

    a. *Subject:* _____ girls _____ *Verb:* _____ leaped _____
    The girls are the ones doing something. *Leaped* is what they did.

    b. *Subject:* _____ They _____ *Verb:* _____ could resist _____

3. An enormous oil truck was racing ~~down the highway at a dangerously high speed~~. Fortunately, a police car ~~with flashing red lights~~ soon appeared.

    a. *Subject:* _____ truck _____ *Verb:* _____ was racing _____
    The sentence is about a *truck. Was racing* is what it did.

    b. *Subject:* _____ car _____ *Verb:* _____ appeared _____

4. The young couple stood ~~in front of the jewelry store for a long time~~. The diamond rings ~~in the window~~ seemed to fascinate them.

    a. *Subject:* _____ couple _____ *Verb:* _____ stood _____
    The young *couple* are performing an action. *Stood* is what they did.

    b. *Subject:* _____ rings _____ *Verb:* _____ seemed _____

5. The icy sidewalk gleamed ~~in the morning sunshine~~. But ~~to nervous pedestrians~~, it did not look beautiful.

    a. *Subject:* _____ sidewalk _____ *Verb:* _____ gleamed _____
    The sentence is about a *sidewalk. Gleamed* is what it did.

    b. *Subject:* _____ it _____ *Verb:* _____ did look _____

Name _____   Section _____   Date _____

Score: (Number right) _____ × 5 = _____ %

■ Subjects and Verbs: Test 4

Cross out the prepositional phrases. Then, on the lines provided, write the subject and verb of each of the sentences. Remember to find all the parts of the verb.

1. Our office has not been cleaned ~~for several days~~. The wastebaskets are full ~~of discarded paper and smelly lunch leftovers~~.

    a. *Subject:* _____office_____   *Verb:* ____has been cleaned____

    b. *Subject:* ____wastebaskets____   *Verb:* _____are_____

2. The model's fingernails were extremely long. They prevented the free use ~~of her hands~~.

    a. *Subject:* ____fingernails____   *Verb:* _____were_____

    b. *Subject:* _____They_____   *Verb:* _____prevented_____

3. Walking ~~into the dusty, moldy attic room,~~ Lori began to sneeze violently. ~~After just five minutes,~~ her allergies forced her to leave.

    a. *Subject:* _____Lori_____   *Verb:* _____began_____

    b. *Subject:* _____allergies_____   *Verb:* _____forced_____

4. ~~With ice~~ encrusting their leaves, daffodils are poking ~~through the unexpected snow~~. The unusually cold springtime weather caught both flowers and people ~~off guard~~.

    a. *Subject:* _____daffodils_____   *Verb:* _____are poking_____

    b. *Subject:* _____weather_____   *Verb:* _____caught_____

5. Old-fashioned locomotives seem romantic ~~to us~~ today. But their clouds ~~of black coal smoke~~ damaged the environment.

    a. *Subject:* ____locomotives____   *Verb:* _____seem_____

    b. *Subject:* _____clouds_____   *Verb:* _____damaged_____

Name _____ Section _____ Date _____

Score: (Number right) _____ × 5 = _____ %

■ **Subjects and Verbs: Test 5**

Cross out the prepositional phrases. Then, on the lines provided, write the subject and verb of each of the sentences in the passage. Remember to find all the parts of the verb.

Note   To help in your review of subjects and verbs, use the explanations given for five of the sentences.

[1]A delicious smell can make you hungry. [2]Certain perfumes, ~~on the right people~~, turn your thoughts ~~to romance~~. [3]Now researchers have discovered even more information ~~about the subject of odors~~. [4]Pleasant smells seem to raise people's productivity. [5]The effects ~~of fragrance~~ have been studied ~~at several universities~~. [6]Researchers there rated the productivity ~~of people in boring jobs~~. [7]Then they gave the workers brief puffs ~~of pleasantly scented air~~. [8]The workers seemed to do better ~~with peppermint or floral scents in the air~~. [9]~~In other studies~~, pleasant scents helped people to get along better ~~with each other~~. [10]Maybe peace negotiations should be conducted ~~in rose-scented rooms~~.

1. *Subject:* _____ smell _____ *Verb:* _____ can make _____
   The sentence is about a delicious *smell. Can make* (you hungry) is what it does.

2. *Subject:* _____ perfumes _____ *Verb:* _____ turn _____

3. *Subject:* _____ researchers _____ *Verb:* _____ have discovered _____
   About the subject and *of odors* are prepositional phrases. *Researchers* are the ones doing something in the sentence. *Have discovered* (information) is what they have done.

4. *Subject:* _____ smells _____ *Verb:* _____ seem _____

5. *Subject:* _____ effects _____ *Verb:* _____ have been studied _____
   Of fragrance and *at several universities* are prepositional phrases. The sentence is about *effects. Have been studied* is what the sentence says about the effects.

6. *Subject:* _____ Researchers _____ *Verb:* _____ rated _____

7. *Subject:* _____ they _____ *Verb:* _____ gave _____
   Of pleasantly scented air is a prepositional phrase. The persons who did something in the sentence are *they* (that is, the researchers); *gave* is what they did.

8. *Subject:* _____ workers _____ *Verb:* _____ seemed _____

9. *Subject:* _____ scents _____ *Verb:* _____ helped _____
   In other studies and *with each other* are prepositional phrases. The sentence is about *scents; helped* (people to get along) is what they did.

10. *Subject:* _____ negotiations _____ *Verb:* _____ should be conducted _____

Name _____   Section _____ Date _____

Score: (Number right) _____ × 5 = _____ %

■ Subjects and Verbs: Test 6

Cross out the prepositional phrases. Then, on the lines provided, write the subject and verb of each of the sentences in the passage. Remember to find all the parts of the verb.

¹~~On summer evenings~~, ~~in my childhood~~, I often went ~~with my father~~ to visit his friends, the Wilsons. ²The three adults always spent the evening talking ~~about gardening~~, their favorite hobby. ³~~During their visits~~, I played ~~with the Wilsons' terrier~~, Christine. ⁴I liked to throw apples ~~down the hill for Christine~~ to retrieve. ⁵Then we would race ~~around the garden~~. ⁶Afterward, I sprawled ~~with Christine on the grass~~, watching the goldfish ~~in Mrs. Wilson's pond~~. ⁷~~After a winter of long illness~~, Mrs. Wilson suddenly died. ⁸One ~~of the strangest things imaginable~~ happened ~~on our first visit~~, ~~about three months later~~. ⁹Christine sat down ~~at my feet~~, howling sadly. ¹⁰She must have been trying to tell me ~~about Mrs. Wilson's death~~.

1. *Subject:* _____I_____   *Verb:* _____went_____

2. *Subject:* _____adults_____   *Verb:* _____spent_____

3. *Subject:* _____I_____   *Verb:* _____played_____

4. *Subject:* _____I_____   *Verb:* _____liked_____

5. *Subject:* _____we_____   *Verb:* _____would race_____

6. *Subject:* _____I_____   *Verb:* _____sprawled_____

7. *Subject:* _____Mrs. Wilson_____   *Verb:* _____died_____

8. *Subject:* _____One_____   *Verb:* _____happened_____

9. *Subject:* _____Christine_____   *Verb:* _____sat_____

10. *Subject:* _____She_____   *Verb:* ____must have been trying____

2 More about Verbs

Seeing What You Know

For each pair, circle the letter of the sentence that you believe is correct. Then read the explanations that follow.

1. a. I brang the hot dogs to the picnic, but Jerry forgot the rolls.
   b. I brought the hot dogs to the picnic, but Jerry forgot the rolls.

2. a. Many children be afraid of thunder and lightning.
   b. Many children are afraid of thunder and lightning.

3. a. Please phone me as soon as the package arrives.
   b. Please phone me as soon as the package arrive.

4. a. Reba thought her boyfriend was faithful, but then she noticed him holding hands with another woman.
   b. Reba thought her boyfriend was faithful, but then she notices him holding hands with another woman.

Understanding the Answers

1. In the first pair, *b* is correct.
   Bring is an irregular verb; its past tense is *brought,* not *brang.*

2. In the second pair, *b* is correct.
   "Many children *be* afraid" is nonstandard English.

3. In the third pair, *a* is correct.
   Package is singular. In standard English, the verb that goes with it must end in *-s.*

4. In the fourth pair, *a* is correct.
   Since the action in the first part of the sentence is in the past *(thought her boyfriend was faithful),* the other verb in the sentence should be in the past as well *(noticed,* not *notices).*

This chapter covers three areas in which verb mistakes commonly occur: regular and irregular verbs, standard and nonstandard verbs, and shifts in verb tense.

REGULAR AND IRREGULAR VERBS

Verbs have four principal parts: the **basic form** (used to form the present tense), the **past tense,** the **past participle** (used with the helping verbs *have, has, had, is, are, was,* and *were*), and the **present participle** (the basic form of the verb plus *-ing*). All of the verb tenses come from one of the four principal parts of verbs.

Most English verbs are **regular.** That is, they form their past tense and past participle by adding *-d* or *-ed* to the basic form, like this:

Basic Form	Past Tense	Past Participle	Present Participle
ask	asked	asked	asking
drop	dropped	dropped	dropping
raise	raised	raised	raising

Irregular verbs, however, do not follow this pattern. They can have many different forms for the past and past participle. (The present participles, however, are formed in the usual way, by adding *-ing.*) Here are the four principal parts of some common irregular verbs:

Basic Form	Past Tense	Past Participle	Present Participle
become	became	become	becoming
begin	began	begun	beginning
blow	blew	blown	blowing
break	broke	broken	breaking
bring	brought	brought	bringing
catch	caught	caught	catching
choose	chose	chosen	choosing
cut	cut	cut	cutting
drink	drank	drunk	drinking
drive	drove	driven	driving
eat	ate	eaten	eating
fall	fell	fallen	falling
feel	felt	felt	feeling
find	found	found	finding
freeze	froze	frozen	freezing
get	got	got, gotten	getting
go	went	gone	going
hide	hid	hidden	hiding
keep	kept	kept	keeping
know	knew	known	knowing
lay	laid	laid	laying
leave	left	left	leaving

Basic Form	Past Tense	Past Participle	Present Participle
lend	lent	lent	lending
lie	lay	lain	lying
lose	lost	lost	losing
make	made	made	making
read	read	read	reading
ride	rode	ridden	riding
rise	rose	risen	rising
run	ran	run	running
say	said	said	saying
see	saw	seen	seeing
sell	sold	sold	selling
set	set	set	setting
shake	shook	shaken	shaking
sit	sat	sat	sitting
sleep	slept	slept	sleeping
spend	spent	spent	spending
swim	swam	swum	swimming
take	took	taken	taking
teach	taught	taught	teaching
tell	told	told	telling
think	thought	thought	thinking
throw	threw	thrown	throwing
wear	wore	worn	wearing
win	won	won	winning
write	wrote	written	writing

If you think a verb is irregular, and it is not in the list above, look it up in your dictionary. If it is irregular, the principal parts will be listed.

Practice 1

Underline the correct form of the verb in parentheses.

1. We (began, begun) to argue about which route to take to the stadium.

2. The high jumper has just (broke, broken) the world record.

3. After Gino had (ate, eaten) the salty pretzels and peanuts, he (drank, drunk) several glasses of water.

4. After the campers had (drove, driven) away, they looked back and (saw, seen) their dog running after them.

5. Before the writing course ended, students had (read, readed) fifteen essays, had (wrote, written) ten short papers, and had (took, taken) a midterm and a final exam.

STANDARD AND NONSTANDARD VERBS

Some of us are accustomed to using nonstandard English with our families and friends. Like slang, expressions such as *it ain't, we has, I be,* or *he don't* may be part of the rich language of a particular community or group.

However, nonstandard English can hold us back when used outside the home community, in both college and the working world. Standard English helps ensure that we will communicate clearly with other people, especially on the job.

The Differences between Standard and Nonstandard Verb Forms

Study the chart below, which shows both standard and nonstandard forms of the regular verb *like.* Practice using the standard forms in your speech and writing.

Nonstandard Forms		Standard Forms	
Present Tense			
I ~~likes~~	we ~~likes~~	I like	we like
you likes	you likes	you like	you like
~~he, she, it like~~	they ~~likes~~	he, she, it likes	they like
Past Tense			
I ~~like~~	we ~~like~~	I liked	we liked
you like	you like	you liked	you liked
~~he, she, it like~~	they ~~like~~	he, she, it liked	they liked

Notes

1 In standard English, always add *-s* or *-es* to a verb in the present tense when the subject is *he, she, it,* or any one person or thing (other than *I* or *you*).

Nonstandard: Aunt Bessie play bingo regularly at her church.
Standard: Aunt Bessie play**s** bingo regularly at her church.

2 Always add the ending *-d* or *-ed* to a regular verb to show it is past tense.

Nonstandard: Last year, Aunt Bessie play bingo 104 times.
Standard: Last year, Aunt Bessie play**ed** bingo 104 times.

Practice 2

Underline the standard form of the verb in parentheses.

1. On April Fools' Day, the principal (dress, <u>dresses</u>) up like a clown.

2. The fans groaned when the receiver (drop, <u>dropped</u>) the pass in the end zone.

3. I (look, <u>looked</u>) all over for my keys and finally found them in my coat pocket.

4. Most people (<u>hate</u>, hates) going to the dentist.

5. Though Kia moved last year, she still (manage, <u>manages</u>) to keep in touch.

Three Problem Verbs

Three irregular verbs that often cause special problems are *be, do,* and *have*. Non-standard English often uses forms such as *I be* (instead of *I am*), *you was* (instead of *you were*), *they has* (instead of *they have*), *he do* (instead of *he does*), and *she done* (instead of *she did*). Here are the correct present- and past-tense forms of these three verbs.

Present Tense		Past Tense	
	Be		
I am	we are	I was	we were
you are	you are	you were	you were
he, she, it is	they are	he, she, it was	they were
	Do		
I do	we do	I did	we did
you do	you do	you did	you did
he, she, it does	they do	he, she, it did	they did
	Have		
I have	we have	I had	we had
you have	you have	you had	you had
he, she, it has	they have	he, she, it had	they had

Practice 3

Underline the standard form of the verb in parentheses.

1. To my surprise, my little sister (<u>did</u>, done) a terrific job of cleaning the house.

2. Jamal (have, <u>has</u>) the best handwriting in our family.

3. You (was, <u>were</u>) wrong to assume that because the instructor gave you an F, he dislikes you.

4. It (<u>doesn't</u>, don't) make sense to sign up for a course and then not go to class.

5. Fran (were, <u>was</u>) halfway to the supermarket when she realized she had no money in her wallet.

SHIFTS IN VERB TENSE

In writing and in conversation, people sometimes shift from one verb tense (the form of the verb that tells us when something happened) to another. Note the tense shifts in the following passage:

> With his oversized T-shirt, the little boy looked even smaller than he was. His skinny arms extend out of the flopping sleeves that reach to his elbows. He needed a haircut; he has to brush his bangs out of his eyes to see. His eyes fail to meet those of the people passing by as he asked them, "Could you give me fifty cents?"

Although the action is in the past, the writer continuously shifts from the past tense (*boy looked . . . he was . . . He needed . . . he asked*) to the present (*arms extend . . . that reach . . . he has . . . eyes fail*). These tense shifts will confuse a reader, who won't know when the events happened. In the above passage, the verbs should be consistently in the past tense:

> With his oversized T-shirt, the little boy looked even smaller than he was. His skinny arms extended out of the flopping sleeves that reached to his elbows. He needed a haircut; he had to brush his bangs out of his eyes to see. His eyes failed to meet those of the people passing by as he asked them, "Could you give me fifty cents?"

In your own writing, shift tenses only when the time of the action actually changes.

Practice 4

Cross out the one verb in each item that is not in the same tense as the others. Then write the correct form of that verb on the line provided.

realized   1. The mossy green log lay in the shallow water. When it began to move, I ~~realize~~ that it was an alligator.

disappears   2. Every time my mother feels like snacking, she brushes her teeth and the hunger ~~disappeared.~~

discovered   3. I came home early because I felt sick; then I ~~discover~~ I was locked out of my house.

want   4. The children love going to the school library because they can take out any book they ~~wanted,~~ even if they can't read it yet.

yelled   5. After the coach ~~yells~~ at him, Gary thought all night about quitting the team, but then he decided to give himself one more chance.

Note   Additional information about verbs appears on pages 209–212.

Name _____ Section _____ Date _____

Score: (Number right) _____ × 10 = _____%

■ More about Verbs: Test 1

For each sentence below, fill in the correct form of the verb.

Note   To help you master the different verb skills in this chapter, directions are given for half of the sentences.

fell
falled

1. The security guard broke his hip when he _____*fell*_____ at the store.
   Use the past tense of the irregular verb *fall*.

stops
stop

2. The police officers in this town _____*stop*_____ anyone who has out-of-state license plates.

don't
doesn't

3. Charles gets pretty good grades, but he _____*doesn't*_____ seem to have much common sense.
   Use the standard present tense form of the verb *do*.

ate
eaten

4. The children have already _____*eaten*_____ all the Halloween candy.

starts
started

5. A colorful hot-air balloon drifted over the meadow, and then it _____*started*_____ a slow descent to the landing area.
   The sentence begins in the past tense, so the past tense of *start* is needed.

forgets
forgot

6. The man began to introduce his boss; then, in his nervousness, he _____*forgot*_____ his boss's name.

be
is

7. My brother and I are outgoing, but our sister _____*is*_____ very shy.
   Use the standard present tense form of the verb.

has
have

8. Some people brag a lot about their money-making schemes, but they never actually _____*have*_____ very much cash.

ran
run

9. When the girls returned to the locker room run after their softball game, they were arguing about who had _____*run*_____ the bases the fastest.
   Use the past participle of the irregular verb *run*.

wore
worn

10. Martin enjoys wearing his old blue shorts so much that he has practically _____*worn*_____ them out.

To the Instructor   Additional tests on verbs can be found in the *Instructor's Manual*.

Name _____   Section _____   Date _____

Score: (Number right) _____ × 10 = _____ %

■   More about Verbs: Test 2

For each sentence below, fill in the correct form of the verb.

drove
drived

1. To get home in time for her family's Thanksgiving dinner, Eve _____*drove*_____ the whole night without stopping.

are
were

2. Two flavorings that seem to go well with just about everything _____*are*_____ garlic and lemon juice.

wrote
written

3. So many students had _____*written*_____ such poor essays that over half the class failed the exam.

was
were

4. In the original *Star Trek* series, Captain James T. Kirk's middle name _____*was*_____ Tiberius.

needs
needed

5. The manager of the auto repair shop telephoned a customer with the bad news that his car's transmission _____*needed*_____ replacing.

did
done

6. Even though I _____*did*_____ the reading for the course, I still felt lost in class.

jams
jam

7. The copying machine always _____*jams*_____ when someone tries to make more than ten copies of anything.

froze
frozen

8. Helen bought a lot of chicken when it was on sale; she has _____*frozen*_____ most of it to use later.

serve
served

9. The waiter took our order, disappeared for twenty minutes, and then _____*served*_____ us the wrong food.

took
taken

10. Delores didn't do very much work on the project, but she has _____*taken*_____ all the credit.

Name _____ Section _____ Date _____

■ **More about Verbs: Test 3**

Each of the items below contains two of the types of verb errors discussed in this chapter. Find these errors and cross them out. Then, in the spaces provided, write the correct forms of the verbs.

Note　To help you master the different verb skills in this chapter, directions are given for half of the sentences.

1. The boy ran into the house and angrily ~~throws~~ his books on the kitchen table. "I've ~~spended~~ enough time on school," he shouted. "On Monday I'm quitting and getting a job."

   a. _____threw_____　Change the one present tense verb to the

   b. _____spent_____　past tense.

2. Even though Rita ~~winned~~ her company's "Employee of the Month" award, she doesn't believe she ~~be~~ doing a good enough job. She worries all the time that she's about to be fired.

   a. _____won_____　Use the past tense of the irregular

   b. _____is_____　verb *win*.

3. I tried to stay interested in the movie, but as it ~~turn~~ more and more boring, I began to feel sleepy. Next thing I knew, my brother had ~~shook~~ me awake. "You slept through the whole second half," he said accusingly.

   a. _____turned_____　Use the standard English past tense of

   b. _____shaken_____　the regular verb *turn*.

4. The dog circled the tree and then ~~barks~~ as if he spotted something. We looked up and ~~seen~~ a raccoon hiding among the leaves.

   a. _____barked_____　Other verbs in the passage (*circled,*

   b. _____saw_____　*looked,* etc.) are in the past tense.

5. Toshio asked me to lend him twenty dollars until payday. I ~~knowed~~ he wasn't working then, so I asked, "Just when is your payday?" He ~~glares~~ at me and said, "If you don't want to help me out, just say so."

   a. _____knew_____　Use the past tense of the irregular

   b. _____glared_____　verb *know.*

■ More about Verbs: Test 4

Each of the items below contains two of the types of verb errors discussed in this chapter. Find these errors and cross them out. Then, in the spaces provided, write the correct forms of the verbs.

1. The office workers did not like their new supervisor at all. After a month, they went to the company vice president to present their complaints. The vice president said, "You should have ~~came~~ to me about this sooner." Then he ~~arranges~~ for the supervisor to be transferred.

    a. _____come_____

    b. _____arranged_____

2. Last year my nephew ~~readed~~ *Charlotte's Web,* a story about a spider who made friends with a pig. He liked the story a great deal. In fact, afterward he ~~refuse~~ to eat bacon or kill spiders.

    a. _____read_____

    b. _____refused_____

3. The housepainters didn't seem to be very well organized. First, they forgot what day they were supposed to begin work. Then once they ~~finish~~ the job, they ~~leaved~~ a ladder behind.

    a. _____finished_____

    b. _____left_____

4. When she was in her twenties, Belle ~~decide~~ to become a registered nurse. For years, she worked during the day, ~~attends~~ classes in the evening, and then came home and cared for her children.

    a. _____decided_____

    b. _____attended_____

5. Every time Megan placed her new puppy out on the porch for the night, he ~~cries~~ pitifully. After she brought his box into the living room, he ~~were~~ quiet for the rest of the night.

    a. _____cried_____

    b. _____was_____

Name _____ Section _____ Date _____

■ **More about Verbs: Test 5**

Each of the sentences in the following passage contains one of the verb problems discussed in this chapter. Underline these errors. Then, in the spaces provided, write the correct forms of the verbs.

Note To help you master the different verb skills in this chapter, directions are given for five of the sentences.

[1]My favorite day of the whole summer be the Fourth of July. [2]To begin with, since I don't have to work, I sleeps late. [3]Then my family and I pack up hot dogs, potato salad, and lots of cold drinks and headed over to my aunt's house. [4]We spent the rest of the afternoon eating and visiting with a big gang of friends and relatives, and there are usually games of volleyball, horseshoes, and softball going on as well. [5]Last year many of the children brang along wading pools and had fun splashing around together. [6]The greatest thing about my aunt's house is that it is right beside a fairground where the town fireworks is shot off after dark. [7]Instead of sitting on crowded bleachers at the fairground, we stretches out on blankets or sit in lawn chairs in the yard, enjoying the beautiful display in the sky above. [8]Every year more of my relatives come to my aunt's for the Fourth; last year I seen two cousins I hadn't seen since we were in third grade. [9]One time it rained on the Fourth, so we all go to the movies instead—about thirty of us. [10]When we sitted down, we took up two complete rows.

1. _____ is _____   Use the standard English form of the verb.

2. _____ sleep _____

3. _____ head _____   The second verb should match the present tense form of the first verb.

4. _____ spend _____

5. _____ brought _____   Here the passage switches briefly to the past tense. Use the correct past tense of the irregular verb *bring*.

6. _____ are _____

7. _____ stretch _____   Use the standard English form of the regular verb *stretch*.

8. _____ saw _____

9. _____ went _____   Here the passage switches again to the past tense. Use the correct past tense form of the irregular verb *go*.

10. _____ sat _____

Name _____   Section _____   Date _____

Score: (Number right) _____ × 10 = _____%

■ More about Verbs: Test 6

Each of the sentences in the following passage contains one of the verb problems discussed in this chapter. Underline these errors. Then, in the spaces provided, write the correct forms of the verbs.

[1]Vincent Van Gogh were one of the greatest painters of all time. [2]But during his own lifetime, people consider Van Gogh a failure, even a madman. [3]Only one Van Gogh painting selled while he was alive. [4]Van Gogh was an odd, passionate man with whom few people feeled comfortable. [5]An illness that causes him to behave in violent, self-destructive ways made his life difficult. [6]During one attack of this illness, he remove part of his ear with a razor. [7]Lonely and isolated, Van Gogh throwed himself into his work. [8]He often produce a wonderful painting in just one day. [9]His intense, colorful paintings of sunflowers and wheat fields have became world-famous since his death, and collectors now pay millions of dollars for them. [10]Sadly, Van Gogh ends his own unhappy life when he was only thirty-seven.

1. _____ was _____

2. _____ considered _____

3. _____ sold _____

4. _____ felt _____

5. _____ caused _____

6. _____ removed _____

7. _____ threw _____

8. _____ produced _____

9. _____ become _____

10. _____ ended _____

3 Subject-Verb Agreement

Seeing What You Know

Underline the verb that you think should be used in each of the following sentences. Then read the explanations below.

1. The two gray cats sitting by the trash can (belongs, <u>belong</u>) to a neighbor.

2. Which one of the bikes (<u>is</u>, are) Enrique going to buy?

3. Nobody in my family (<u>carries</u>, carry) a gun.

4. Chicago and Atlanta (has, <u>have</u>) the busiest airports in the United States.

Understanding the Answers

1. The two gray cats sitting by the trash can **belong** to a neighbor.
   The subject, *cats,* is plural, so the verb must be plural as well.

2. Which one of the bikes **is** Enrique **going** to buy?
   The subject, *Enrique,* and the verb, *is going,* are both singular.

3. Nobody in my family **carries** a gun.
   The subject, *nobody,* is a singular indefinite pronoun, so it requires a singular verb.

4. Chicago and Atlanta **have** the busiest airports in the United States.
   Chicago and Atlanta is a compound subject and requires a plural verb.

41

In a correctly written sentence, the subject and verb **agree** (match) **in number.** Singular subjects have singular verbs; plural subjects have plural verbs.

In a simple sentence of few words, it's not difficult to make the subject (*s*) and verb (*v*) agree:

s   v (plural)   s   v (singular)

My **parents work** at two jobs. My **grandmother takes** care of the children.

However, not all sentences are this straightforward. This chapter will present four types of situations that can pose problems in subject-verb agreement: (1) subject and verb separated by a prepositional phrase, (2) verb coming before the subject, (3) indefinite pronoun subject, and (4) compound subjects.

1 SUBJECT AND VERB SEPARATED BY A PREPOSITIONAL PHRASE

In many sentences, the subject is close to the verb, with the subject coming first. But in some sentences, the subject and verb do not appear side by side:

s   v

Most **stores** in the mall **are having** sales this weekend.

Who or what is the sentence about? The answer is *stores* (not *mall*). What are the stores doing? They *are having* (sales). Since the subject *(stores)* is plural, the verb *(are having)* must be plural as well.

In the sentence above, a prepositional phrase, *in the mall,* separates the subject and the verb. (A **prepositional phrase** is a group of words that begins with a preposition and ends with a noun or pronoun. *In, on, for, from, of, to,* and *by* are prepositions; a longer list of prepositions is on page 20.) Remember that the subject of the sentence is never part of a prepositional phrase. To find the subject, cross out prepositional phrases. Then make the verb agree with the subject—not with a word in the prepositional phrase.

Practice 1

Cross out the prepositional phrases in the sentences below. Then underline the subject of each sentence. Finally, double-underline the verb in parentheses that agrees with the subject.

1. The guys ~~behind the counter~~ (likes, <u>like</u>) to joke ~~with their customers~~.

2. Two women ~~on my bowling team~~ always (scores, <u>score</u>) over 250.

3. The noise ~~in the city streets~~ sometimes (<u>hurts</u>, hurt) my ears.

4. A bag ~~of nonfat potato chips~~ (<u>contains</u>, contain) 440 calories.

5. The instructions ~~for downloading software from the Internet~~ (is, <u>are</u>) confusing ~~for many people~~.

2 VERB COMING BEFORE THE SUBJECT

In most English sentences, the verb follows the subject. (*I saw an eagle. The knife fell to the floor. A train crashed.*) But in some sentences, the verb comes *before* the subject. These sentences often are questions, or they may begin with prepositional phrases or word groups like *there is* and *here are*. The verb must agree with the subject—even when the verb comes before the subject.

There **are** many starving **actors** in Hollywood. *(plural verb, plural subject)*

Here **is** the computer **disk** for that project. *(singular verb, singular subject)*

In that box **are** other **supplies.** *(plural verb, plural subject)*

What **was** the **purpose** of that assignment? *(singular verb, singular subject)*

If you are not sure of the subject in a sentence, find the verb and then ask "Who?" or "What?" In the first sentence above, for example, you would ask, "What are there in Hollywood?" The answer, "starving *actors*," is the subject. For the second sentence, the question would be, "What is here?" The answer: "The computer *disk.*"

Practice 2

Cross out the prepositional phrases in the sentences below. Then underline the subject of each sentence. Finally, double-underline the verb in parentheses that agrees with the subject.

1. Where (is, are) the keys ~~to the minivan~~?
2. ~~Underneath that big rock~~ (lives, live) hundreds ~~of bugs~~.
3. There (was, were) seventeen people ~~ahead of me in the bank line~~ today.
4. Why (does, do) geese always fly ~~in a V-shaped group~~?
5. ~~Inside each cardboard carton~~ (is, are) a dozen boxes ~~of Girl Scout cookies~~.

3 INDEFINITE PRONOUN SUBJECTS

The following **indefinite pronouns** always take singular verbs.

Singular Indefinite Pronouns			
each	anyone	anybody	anything
either	everyone	everybody	everything
neither	someone	somebody	something
one	no one	nobody	nothing

Note the subject-verb relationships in the following sentences with indefinite pronouns:

> **One** of those writing courses **is** still open. *(singular subject, singular verb)*
>
> **Neither** of my parents **has** called. *(singular subject, singular verb)*
>
> **Somebody was** reading my mail. *(singular subject, singular verb)*
>
> **Everyone loves** to get something for nothing. *(singular subject, singular verb)*

Practice 3

Underline the subject of each sentence. Then double-underline the verb in parentheses that agrees with the subject.

1. <u>Everything</u> on those shelves (<u>is</u>, are) on sale at 50 percent off.
2. <u>Neither</u> of the lights in the basement (<u>works</u>, work).
3. <u>No one</u> in my family (<u>is</u>, are) right-handed.
4. <u>Each</u> of the fires (<u>appears</u>, appear) to have been set by the same person.
5. <u>Everybody</u> in my apartment building (<u>knows</u>, know) when someone is having a party.

4 COMPOUND SUBJECTS

A **compound subject**—usually two or more subjects joined by *and*—requires a plural verb.

> Rent and car insurance **were** my biggest expenses each month.
>
> There **are** canoes and sailboats for rent.
>
> **Do** the TV and DVD player **provide** stereo sound?

Practice 4

Underline the compound subject of each sentence. Then double-underline the verb in parentheses that agrees with the compound subject.

1. Our <u>cats</u> and <u>dog</u> (stays, <u>stay</u>) at a neighbor's house when we go on vacation.
2. (Is, <u>Are</u>) all the <u>CDs</u> and <u>DVDs</u> in the store included in the sale?
3. <u>Staples</u> and <u>Scotch tape</u> (holds, <u>hold</u>) all the old record album covers together.
4. The <u>scratches</u> and <u>dents</u> on our new car (was, <u>were</u>) definitely our son's fault.
5. My accounting <u>course</u> and my statistics <u>course</u> (requires, <u>require</u>) long written reports.

Note   Additional information about subject-verb agreement appears on pages 212–213.

Name _____   Section _____   Date _____

■ Subject-Verb Agreement: Test 1

In each sentence, fill in the correct form of the missing verb.

Note   To help you learn subject-verb agreement, explanations are given for five of the sentences.

likes
like

1. Nobody ____likes____ to be laughed at.
    Nobody is an indefinite pronoun that always requires a singular verb.

smells
smell

2. Everything in our attic ____smells____ of mothballs.

is
are

3. Black and white ____are____ the only colors Jermaine wears.
    Black and white is a compound subject requiring a plural verb.

makes
make

4. Bright yellow daisies and blue morning glories ____make____ the tiny yard beautiful.

gives
give

5. The lamps on either side of the couch ____give____ very little light.
    Lamps, the subject, is a plural noun and so needs a plural verb. *On either side* and *of the couch* are prepositional phrases. The subject is never in—or affected by—a prepositional phrase.

plans
plan

6. All the teachers except one ____plan____ to give final exams.

is
are

7. There ____is____ no doubt that the witnesses are telling the truth.
    When a sentence begins with *here* or *there,* the subject will come after the verb. *Doubt,* the subject, is singular and requires a singular verb.

is
are

8. Here ____are____ the names of three doctors you can call.

is
are

9. When ____is____ the deadline for dropping a course?
    In a question, the subject often follows the verb. The subject, *deadline,* is singular, so it requires a singular verb form.

Does
Do

10. ____Do____ your aunt and uncle know that you wrote an essay about them?

To the Instructor   Additional tests on subject-verb agreement can be found in the *Instructor's Manual.*

Name _____   Section _____   Date _____

Score: (Number right) _____ × 10 = _____%

■ Subject-Verb Agreement: Test 2

In each sentence, fill in the correct form of the missing verb.

stands
stand

1. Across the avenue _____*stands*_____ the post office.

belongs
belong

2. The leather jacket beside the books _____*belongs*_____ to our teacher.

is
are

3. Rags and spray cleaner _____*are*_____ needed to wash the windows.

annoys
annoy

4. Junk e-mail and chain letters _____*annoy*_____ many Internet users.

Is
Are

5. _____*Are*_____ those parking spaces in front of the administration building reserved for the faculty?

attracts
attract

6. The flowers in my neighbor's garden _____*attract*_____ many butterflies.

is
are

7. Magnolia trees and Spanish moss _____*are*_____ common in many parts of the South.

was
were

8. Running down the back alley toward the fire _____*were*_____ several police officers.

seems
seem

9. Tom and Caroline's marriage _____*seems*_____ like a happy one.

is
are

10. Every one of my roommates _____*is*_____ depressed over getting poor grades on the psychology exam.

Name _____ Section _____ Date _____

Score: (Number right) _____ × 10 = _____ %

■ Subject-Verb Agreement: Test 3

Each of the following passages contains **two** mistakes in subject-verb agreement. Find and underline the two verbs that do not agree with their subjects. Then write the correct form of each verb in the spaces provided.

Note   To help you learn subject-verb agreement, explanations are given for the first mistake in each passage.

1. Construction of the apartment buildings <u>have</u> been going on for months. The noise from the bulldozers, cranes, and backhoes <u>are</u> deafening. Everyone in the neighborhood wants it to end.

   a. _____has_____   *Of the apartment buildings* is a prepositional phrase. The
   b. _____is_____   subject of the first sentence, *construction,* is singular.

2. It is not true that the skin of snakes <u>are</u> slimy. Also, warts are not caused by touching a toad. Why <u>does</u> reptiles and amphibians have so many false stories told about them?

   a. _____is_____   The subject of the first sentence is *skin; of snakes* is a
   b. _____do_____   prepositional phrase.

3. Nothing about my restaurant job <u>bother</u> me as much as the way the chef makes fun of the mentally challenged man who runs the dishwasher. The chef simply doesn't realize that people with a disability also <u>has</u> feelings.

   a. _____bothers_____   The subject *nothing* is an indefinite pronoun. It takes a
   b. _____have_____   singular verb.

4. The new employee's quick wit and willingness to work hard <u>pleases</u> her boss very much. She is the kind of person whom everyone in the office <u>enjoy</u> having as a coworker.

   a. _____please_____   The compound subject, *wit and willingness,* requires
   b. _____enjoys_____   a plural verb.

5. "Having a successful marriage is not easy," admitted Neal. "There <u>has</u> been many times I've thought about leaving. However, my commitment to my marriage and my love for my family <u>stops</u> me. Later, I'm always glad that I stayed."

   a. _____have_____   The subject of the second sentence, *times,* is plural.
   b. _____stop_____

■ Subject-Verb Agreement: Test 4

Each of the following passages contains **two** mistakes in subject-verb agreement. Find and underline the two verbs that do not agree with their subjects. Then write the correct form of each verb in the spaces provided.

1. The students and the teacher <u>is</u> having a disagreement about the upcoming test. The teacher says it is scheduled for Friday, but every one of the students <u>believe</u> she announced it for the following Monday.

   a. _____*are*_____

   b. ____*believes*____

2. There are a lot of young women in my office. It seems as if everyone <u>have</u> had a baby recently. All the baby presents <u>costs</u> me a fortune.

   a. _____*has*_____

   b. _____*cost*_____

3. High on the closet shelf <u>is</u> several brightly wrapped packages—the little girl's birthday presents. The girl knows that they are there. Every day, she and her sister <u>tries</u> for hours to guess what might be inside those mysterious boxes.

   a. _____*are*_____

   b. _____*try*_____

4. Cara invited her two sisters to the party, but neither of them <u>are</u> coming. Each sister is busy, one with a work deadline and the other with a school reunion. "Why," Cara complained, "<u>does</u> the only important events in their lives this month have to happen at the same time?"

   a. _____*is*_____

   b. _____*do*_____

5. The computers in the office <u>gives</u> me heartburn. Everybody, it seems, <u>have</u> success with them except me. I'd rather work with a pen and paper than deal with a computer.

   a. _____*give*_____

   b. _____*has*_____

Name _____   Section _____   Date _____

Score: (Number right) _____ × 10 = _____ %

■ Subject-Verb Agreement: Test 5

Each sentence in the following passage contains one mistake in subject-verb agreement. Find and underline the ten verbs that do not agree with their subjects. Then write the correct form of each verb on the lines below.

Note   To help you learn subject-verb agreement, explanations are given for five of the mistakes.

¹I used to think there was few tasks more difficult than picking out birthday presents for my friends. ²Since my husband and I don't have much extra money, big luxuries are out, and the household goods on sale at K-Mart is not the kinds of presents they'd enjoy getting. ³But birthday shopping has become simpler since I decided that what everybody really like is toys. ⁴Forget the big, expensive department stores; children's catalogs and novelty shops is where I do my buying. ⁵My favorites of the whole toy collection has been the rubber stamp sets. ⁶One of them contain funny pictures of parts of faces: eyes, ears, noses, and so on. ⁷With it, anyone become a cartoonist, creating silly faces to decorate all kinds of things. ⁸To another friend was sent flying saucers that soar into the air when you pull their strings. ⁹There is now saucers all over the roof of her apartment building, and she tells me her neighbors and the building superintendent have no idea where the saucers came from. ¹⁰I'm actually looking forward to shopping for another friend's birthday—I think a couple of trick hand buzzers and a glow-in-the-dark yo-yo is what we'll buy next.

1. _____ *were* _____   The subject is *tasks. Was,* a singular verb, needs to be replaced by a plural verb.

2. _____ *are* _____

3. _____ *likes* _____   *Everybody,* an indefinite pronoun, is singular and thus needs a singular verb.

4. _____ *are* _____

5. _____ *have* _____   The subject is *favorites. Of the whole collection* is a prepositional phrase that does not affect the number of the subject.

6. _____ *contains* _____

7. _____ *becomes* _____   *Anyone* is an indefinite pronoun and needs a singular verb.

8. _____ *were* _____

9. _____ *are* _____   When a sentence begins with *here* or *there,* the subject will follow the verb. The subject is *saucers,* which requires a plural verb.

10. _____ *are* _____

Name _____ Section _____ Date _____

Score: (Number right) _____ × 10 = _____ %

■ Subject-Verb Agreement: Test 6

Each sentence in the following passage contains one mistake in subject-verb agreement. Find and underline the ten verbs that do not agree with their subjects. Then write the correct form of each verb on the lines below.

¹The aroma from skillets of Southern fried chicken fill the air. ²In the warm breezes wave the Confederate flag, symbol of the old South. ³Here in Americana, Brazil, lives the descendants of about 3,500 Southerners who left the United States after the Civil War. ⁴Almost every one of these people get together with the others once a year to picnic, hear a band play "Dixie," and remember their American ancestors. ⁵The American settlers in Brazil was attracted by reports sent back by American missionaries. ⁶"If anyone really want to work, he can make a living raising cotton here," the missionaries said. ⁷Today there are little of the old South left in Americana. ⁸Only 300 of the 160,000 people living in this place is directly descended from those American settlers. ⁹Both Portuguese and English is spoken in Americana, with fewer people remembering English every year. ¹⁰Intermarriage with Brazilians has become common, and the language, names, and customs of Brazil has been adopted by these grandchildren and great-grandchildren of Confederates.

1. _____ fills _____

2. _____ waves _____

3. _____ live _____

4. _____ gets _____

5. _____ were _____

6. _____ wants _____

7. _____ is _____

8. _____ are _____

9. _____ are _____

10. _____ have _____

4 Sentence Types

Seeing What You Know

A. In each blank, add a word that fits the sentence.
Answers will vary.

1. The noisy _____ woke the baby.

2. The forest ranger _____ at the campers.

B. In each sentence that follows, insert *and, but,* or *so.* Use each word once.

3. My pencil is broken, _____*and*_____ my pen is out of ink.

4. The pool is closed, _____*so*_____ we can't go swimming.

5. I have an envelope, _____*but*_____ I can't find a stamp.

C. In each sentence that follows, insert *after, although,* or *because.* Use each word once.

6. We called an exterminator _____*because*_____ we have termites.

7. _____*After*_____ their big fight, Jessica sent her boyfriend flowers.

8. _____*Although*_____ my closet is full of clothes, I have nothing to wear.

Understanding the Answers

A. Sentence 1 could be completed with a subject such as *party;* the verb is *woke.* Sentence 2 could be completed with a verb such as *waved;* the subject is *ranger.*

Some sentences in English are **simple,** made up of one subject-verb combination expressing a complete thought. Sentences 1 and 2 are examples of simple sentences.

B. You should have inserted *and* in sentence 3, *so* in 4, and *but* in 5.

Other sentences are **compound,** made up of two or more complete thoughts connected by a joining word such as *and, so,* or *but.* Sentences 3–5 are all compound sentences.

C. You should have inserted *because* in sentence 6, *after* in 7, and *although* in 8.

Yet other sentences are **complex,** made up of one complete thought and at least one dependent thought. Dependent thoughts begin with a dependent word such as *because, although,* or *after.* Sentences 6–8 are all complex sentences.

The three most basic kinds of sentences in English are simple, compound, and complex sentences. This chapter explains and provides practice in all three sentence types. It also discusses two types of words you can use to combine ideas into one sentence: (1) joining words (for compound sentences) and (2) dependent words (for complex sentences).

THE SIMPLE SENTENCE

A **simple sentence** has only one subject-verb combination and expresses a complete thought.

> An owl hooted.
>
> The winning contestant could have chosen money or a car.

A simple sentence may have more than one subject:

> Lemons and limes taste sharp and tangy.
>
> (In this sentence, *lemons* and *limes* are the subjects.)

A simple sentence may have more than one verb:

> The puppies nipped and nuzzled one another playfully.
>
> (In this sentence, *nipped* and *nuzzled* are the verbs.)

A simple sentence may even have several subjects and verbs:

> Every New Year's Eve, my parents, aunts, and uncles eat, dance, and welcome the new year together.
>
> (There are three subjects in this sentence: *parents, aunts,* and *uncles.* There are also three verbs: *eat, dance,* and *welcome.*)

Practice 1

Complete the simple sentences below by filling in one or more subjects, one or more verbs, or both. Answers will vary. Some possibilities are given.

1. The _____library_____ is unusually crowded today.

2. A thoughtless driver _____threw_____ an empty soda can onto the highway.

3. _____Roast beef_____ and _____Swiss cheese_____ make a delicious sandwich combination.

4. Mike and _____Sylvia_____ often _____jog_____ together in the park.

5. _____My aunt_____ and _____uncle_____ looked at old family photographs and then _____ate_____ dinner on the porch.

THE COMPOUND SENTENCE

A **compound sentence** is made up of two or more complete thoughts. For instance, look at the following simple sentences:

Supper is ready.

The guests have not arrived.

These two simple sentences can be combined to form one compound sentence:

Supper is ready, **but** the guests have not arrived.

The process of joining two ideas of equal importance is known as **coordination.** Put a comma plus a joining word (also known as a coordinating conjunction), such as *and, but,* or *so,* between the two complete thoughts. (Additional joining words appear on page 75.)

The cover is torn off this book, **and** the last few pages are missing. (**And** means *in addition:* The cover is torn off this book; *in addition,* the last few pages are missing.)

The kittens are darling, **but** we can't have another pet. (**But** means *however:* The kittens are darling; *however,* we can't have another pet.)

Kendra has to get up early tomorrow, **so** she isn't going to the party tonight. (**So** means *as a result:* Kendra has to get up early tomorrow; *as a result,* she isn't going to the party tonight.)

Practice 2

Use a comma and a suitable joining word to combine each pair of simple sentences into a compound sentence. Use each of the following joining words once.

and   **but**   **so**

1. Rodrigo is usually cheerful.
   He seems quiet and troubled today.

   Rodrigo is usually cheerful, but he seems quiet and troubled today.

   _____

2. All my clothes were dirty this morning.
   I'm wearing my husband's shirt.

   All my clothes were dirty this morning, so I'm wearing my husband's shirt.

   _____

3. Virginia has learned karate.
   She carries a can of self-defense spray.

   Virginia has learned karate, and she carries a can of self-defense spray.

   _____

THE COMPLEX SENTENCE

As you have learned, a compound sentence is made up of two or more complete thoughts. Each thought could stand alone as an independent statement. A **complex sentence,** on the other hand, includes one independent statement and at least one dependent statement, which *cannot* stand alone. Look at the following example:

> If it thunders, our dog hides under the bed.

The second statement in this sentence is **independent.** It can stand alone as a simple sentence: *Our dog hides under the bed.* The first statement, however, cannot stand alone. It is **dependent**—it depends on the rest of the sentence to finish the thought *If it thunders.* Dependent statements begin with dependent words (also known as subordinating conjunctions), such as *after, although, as, because, when,* and *while.* (A full list is on page 62.) A dependent statement also includes a subject and a verb. (The subject of the dependent statement above is *it;* the verb is *thunders.*)

Punctuation note   Put a comma at the end of a dependent statement that begins a sentence, as in the example above.

Practice 3

Combine each pair of simple sentences into a complex sentence. To change a simple sentence into a dependent statement, add a dependent word to it, as shown in the example. Choose a suitable dependent word from the following:

after   **although**   **as**

Use each word once. Put a comma after a dependent statement that starts a sentence.

Example   We ate the pork chops with our hands.
　　　　　　We were out of clean silverware.

We ate the pork chops with our hands because we were out of clean silverware.

1. The family members were enjoying the wedding.
   Burglars stole the wedding gifts from their home.

   As the family members were enjoying the wedding, burglars stole the wedding gifts from their home.

2. Jeff broke out in red blotches.
   He walked through a bank of poison ivy.

   Jeff broke out in red blotches after he walked through a bank of poison ivy.

3. Mei Lin scrubbed for an hour.
   She could not get the crayon marks off the wall.

   Although Mei Lin scrubbed for an hour, she could not get the crayon marks off the wall.

Name _____   Section _____   Date _____

Score: (Number right) _____ × 20 = _____ %

■ **Sentence Types: Test 1**

Part A   Use a comma and a suitable joining word to combine the following pairs of simple sentences into compound sentences. Choose from *and, but,* and *so.*
Answers may vary.

1. Alvin could not stop yawning.
   He decided to take a nap until dinnertime.

   Alvin could not stop yawning, so he decided to take a nap until dinnertime.

   _____

2. My niece is an excellent basketball player.
   She does not plan to try out for the team.

   My niece is an excellent basketball player, but she does not plan to try out for

   the team.

Part B   Use a suitable dependent word to combine the following pairs of simple sentences into complex sentences. Choose from *although, because,* and *when.* Use each word once. Place a comma after a dependent statement when it starts a sentence.

3. Sandra never rides the Ferris wheel.
   She is afraid of heights.

   Sandra never rides the Ferris wheel because she is afraid of heights.

   _____

4. I get home after work.
   I'll give you a call.

   When I get home after work, I'll give you a call.

   _____

5. I had promised never to tell the secret.
   I couldn't resist telling my wife.

   Although I had promised never to tell the secret, I couldn't resist telling

   my wife.

To the Instructor   Additional tests on sentence types can be found in the *Instructor's Manual.*

■ Sentence Types: Test 2

Part A   Use a comma and a suitable joining word to combine the following pairs of simple sentences into compound sentences. Choose from *and, but,* and *so.*

Answers may vary.

1. The bookstore is out of history textbooks.
    I will have to borrow my roommate's book.

    The bookstore is out of history textbooks, so I will have to borrow my

    roommate's book.

2. The workers dripped paint on the carpet.
    They stomped through the flower bed.

    The workers dripped paint on the carpet, and they stomped through the

    flower bed.

Part B   Use a suitable dependent word to combine the following pairs of simple sentences into complex sentences. Choose from *although, because,* and *when.* Use each word once. Place a comma after a dependent statement when it starts a sentence.

3. Strawberries become ripe.
    They must be picked quickly.

    When strawberries become ripe, they must be picked quickly.

4. Gingko trees are very pretty.
    Their fruit smells dreadful.

    Although gingko trees are very pretty, their fruit smells dreadful.

5. I was nervous all morning.
    I had to get a tooth extracted in the afternoon.

    I was nervous all morning because I had to get a tooth extracted in the

    afternoon.

Name _____   Section _____   Date _____

Score: (Number right) _____ × 20 = _____ %

■ Sentence Types: Test 3

Combine each group of simple sentences into compound sentences, complex sentences, or both. Write two sentences for item 1 and three sentences for item 2. Use any of the following joining words and dependent words.

Joining words:	**and**	**but**	**so**	
Dependent words:	**after**	**although**	**because**	**when**

Here are two hints about commas: (1) Use a comma between two thoughts joined by *and, but,* or *so.* (2) Place a comma after a dependent statement when it starts a sentence.

Answers may vary.

1. My company is very conservative.
   I have to wear a suit every day.
   I get home from work.
   I immediately slip into a sweatshirt and jeans.

   My company is very conservative, so I have to wear a suit every day. When I get home from work, I immediately slip into a sweatshirt and jeans.

2. Grandpa never graduated from high school.
   He strongly believes in education.
   He was the first one to take me to a library.
   He has always encouraged me to study hard.
   Grandpa retired from his job at the factory.
   He began studying to get a high school diploma.

   Grandpa never graduated from high school, but he strongly believes in education. He was the first one to take me to a library, and he has always encouraged me to study hard. After Grandpa retired from his job at the factory, he began studying to get a high school diploma.

Name _____   Section _____ Date _____

Score: (Number right) _____ × 20 = _____ %

■ ## Sentence Types: Test 4

Combine each group of simple sentences into compound and/or complex sentences. Write two sentences for item 1 and three sentences for item 2. Use any of the following joining words and dependent words.

Joining words:	**and**	**but**	**so**	
Dependent words:	**after**	**although**	**because**	**when**

Here are two hints about commas: (1) Use a comma between two thoughts joined by *and, but,* or *so.* (2) Place a comma after a dependent statement when it starts a sentence.

Answers may vary.

1. Robert Louis Stevenson wrote about Dr. Jekyll and Mr. Hyde.
   He heard about a man named William Brodie.
   Brodie was a respected businessman during the day.
   At night he led a gang of robbers.

   Robert Louis Stevenson wrote about Dr. Jekyll and Mr. Hyde after he heard

   about a man named William Brodie. Brodie was a respected businessman

   during the day, but at night he led a gang of robbers.

   _____

   _____

   _____

2. You want to save money in the supermarket.
   You should learn where the bargains are and are not.
   Managers want to sell high-cost items like imported mustard.
   They place those items on eye-level shelves.
   Shoppers are less likely to look on lower shelves.
   Managers put less profitable items there.

   Because you want to save money in the supermarket, you should learn

   where the bargains are and are not. When managers want to sell high-cost

   items like imported mustard, they place those items on eye-level shelves.

   Shoppers are less likely to look on lower shelves, so managers put less

   profitable items there.

   _____

Name _____   Section _____ Date _____
Score: (Number right) _____ × 20 = _____ %

■ Sentence Types: Test 5

Combine the five pairs of italicized simple sentences into compound or complex sentences. Write the new sentences on the lines provided, adding commas as needed. Use any of the following joining words and dependent words. (Remember that there is more than one way of revising these sentences.)

Joining words: **and**   **but**   **so**
Dependent words: **although**   **as**   **because**   **while**

Here are two hints about commas: (1) Use a comma between two thoughts joined by *and, but,* or *so.* (2) Place a comma after a dependent statement when it starts a sentence. Answers may vary.

Jay's fishing trip with his buddies was not exactly a success. *They drove to the cabin in the mountains. They had a flat tire.* As they drove to the cabin in the mountains, they had a flat tire.

Once they arrived at the cabin, they found the last renters had left the place in terrible condition. *The cabin was full of dirty dishes, empty food containers, food scraps, and newspapers. Jay and his friends had to spend a long time cleaning.* The cabin was full of dirty dishes, empty food containers, food scraps, and newspapers, so Jay and his friends had to spend a long time cleaning.

They did manage to catch a few trout before suppertime. Bad luck soon struck again. Although they did manage to catch a few trout before suppertime, bad luck soon struck again.

Jay was frying fish over the campfire. His flannel shirt burst into flames. While Jay was frying fish over the campfire, his flannel shirt burst into flames.

Thinking quickly, Jay jumped into the nearby lake and put the fire out. The guys went to bed early after their unlucky first day. *"Surely tomorrow will be better," thought Jay, climbing into his bunk. He was wrong.* "Surely tomorrow will be better," thought Jay, climbing into his bunk, but he was wrong.

As Jay ran down the stairs the next morning, a step broke under his weight. He spent the rest of the day in a nearby emergency room, having a cast put on his broken ankle.

Name _____   Section _____   Date _____

Score: (Number right) _____ × 20 = _____%

■ Sentence Types: Test 6

Combine the five pairs of italicized simple sentences into compound or complex sentences. Write the new sentences on the lines provided, adding commas as needed. Use any of the following joining words and dependent words. (Remember that there is more than one way of revising these sentences.)

Joining words:	**and**	**but**	**so**	
Dependent words:	**although**	**as**	**because**	**where**

Answers may vary.

Mental illness has always frightened people. It is so little understood.

Mental illness has always frightened people because it is so little understood.

_____ .

As a result, some past attempts to treat mental illness were very strange and even cruel. *In the Middle Ages, for instance, some mentally ill people were thought to be witches. They were burned alive at the stake.* In the Middle Ages, for instance, some mentally ill people were thought to be witches, so they were burned alive at the stake.

Later, communities established asylums for the mentally ill. *Offering disturbed people a place to live was better than treating them as witches. These places were not run humanely.* Although offering disturbed people a place to live was better than treating them as witches, these places were not run humanely.

_____ .

In colonial Philadelphia, for instance, insane people were kept in unheated basement cells. They were chained to the wall and displayed like zoo animals.

In colonial Philadelphia, for instance, insane people were kept in unheated basement cells where they were chained to the wall and displayed like zoo animals.

The doctors then believed mentally ill people to be unaware of their surroundings. The patients were quite aware of pain—and embarrassment. The doctors then believed mentally ill people to be unaware of their surroundings, but the patients were quite aware of pain—and embarrassment.

5 Fragments

Seeing What You Know

Underline the statement in each item that you think is *not* a complete sentence. Then read the explanations below.

1. <u>After the shopping mall opened.</u> Several local stores went out of business.

2. The nursing student poked my arm four times. <u>Trying to take a blood sample.</u> I was beginning to feel like a pincushion.

3. Some young people are learning old-fashioned dances. <u>Such as the waltz, polka, and lindy.</u>

4. The manager always wears a suit and tie to the office. <u>Then takes off his jacket and tie by ten o'clock.</u>

Understanding the Answers

1. *After the shopping mall opened* is not a complete sentence.
   The writer does not follow through and complete the thought by telling us what happened after the shopping mall opened. Correct the fragment by adding it to the sentence that follows it.

2. *Trying to take a blood sample* is not a complete sentence.
   The word group lacks both a subject and a verb, and it does not express a complete thought. Correct the fragment by adding it to the sentence that precedes it.

3. *Such as the waltz, polka, and lindy* is not a complete sentence.
   Again, the word group lacks a subject and a verb, and it does not express a complete thought. Correct the fragment by adding it to the sentence that precedes it.

4. *Then takes off his jacket and tie by ten o'clock* is not a complete sentence.
   The word group lacks a subject. Correct the fragment by adding the subject *he*.

To be a complete sentence, a group of words must contain a subject and a verb. It must also express a complete thought—in other words, it must make sense by itself. A **fragment** is *less than a sentence* because it lacks a subject, lacks a verb, or does not express a complete thought.

This chapter describes the most common types of fragments: dependent-word fragments, *-ing* and *to* fragments, added-detail fragments, and missing-subject fragments.

DEPENDENT-WORD FRAGMENTS

Although dependent-word fragments contain a subject and a verb, they do not express a complete thought. To complete the thought, they depend on another statement, usually one that comes after the fragment. For instance, below is a word group that starts with the dependent word *because.* The incomplete thought it expresses is completed in the statement that follows it.

Because there was a mosquito in the room. I could not fall asleep.

The dependent-word group is a fragment because it does not express a complete thought. It leaves the reader expecting something more. The writer must follow through *in the same sentence* and tell what happened because there was a mosquito in the room. In the sentence below, the writer has corrected the fragment by completing the thought in one sentence:

Because there was a mosquito in the room, I could not fall asleep.

Here is a list of some common dependent words:

Dependent Words				
after	even if	since	until	wherever
although	even though	so that	what	whether
as	how	that	when	which
because	if	though	whenever	while
before	in order that	unless	where	who

Whenever you begin a statement with a dependent word, make sure that you complete your thought. Look at the following examples:

Although we had eaten a full meal. We still ordered dessert. The rum cake was irresistible.

Some people are victims of migraine headaches. That force them to lie motionless in bed for many hours. Medications do not offer much relief.

The word groups that begin with the dependent words *although* and *that* are fragments. Neither word group expresses a complete thought. The reader wants to know *what happened* although a full meal had been eaten and *what* forces people to lie motionless in bed for many hours.

A common way to correct a dependent-word fragment is to connect it to the sentence that comes before or after it. For example,

Although we had eaten a full **meal, we** still ordered dessert. The rum cake was irresistible.

Some people are victims of migraine **headaches that** force them to lie motionless in bed for many hours. Medications do not offer much relief.

Punctuation note   Put a comma at the end of a dependent-word group that starts a sentence. (See the first example above.)

Practice 1

Underline the dependent-word fragment in each of the following. Then correct it on the lines provided. *Corrections may vary.*

1. When the Wal-Mart discount store opened outside town. Stores on Main Street lost a lot of business.

   When the Wal-Mart discount store opened outside town, stores on Main

   Street lost a lot of business.

2. Because smoke detectors are so important to a family's safety. Their batteries should be checked often.

   Because smoke detectors are so important to a family's safety, their

   batteries should be checked often.

3. After the children washed the family car. They had a water fight with the wet sponges.

   After the children washed the family car, they had a water fight with the wet

   sponges.

4. Please hang up the damp towel. That you just threw on the floor.

   Please hang up the damp towel that you just threw on the floor.

-ING AND TO FRAGMENTS

When -*ing* or *to* appears at or near the beginning of a word group, a fragment may result. Consider this example:

Cliff sat by the telephone for hours. Hoping that Lisa would call.

The first statement is a complete sentence. However, the second word group is not a complete thought, so it cannot stand on its own as a sentence.

Consider the following example as well:

To balance their checkbooks without making mistakes. Many people use pocket calculators.

The second statement is a complete sentence. But the first word group lacks a subject and verb *and* fails to express a complete thought.

There are two ways to correct *-ing* and *to* fragments:

a Connect an *-ing* or a *to* fragment to the sentence it explains.

Cliff sat by the telephone for **hours hoping** that Lisa would call.

To balance their checkbooks without making **mistakes, many** people use pocket calculators.

b Create a complete sentence by adding a subject and a verb to the fragment. To do so, revise the material as necessary.

Cliff sat by the telephone for hours. **He hoped** that Lisa would call.

Many people use pocket calculators. **They want** to balance their checkbooks without making mistakes.

Practice 2

Underline the *-ing* or *to* fragment in each of the following. Then correct it on the lines provided, using one of the two methods given above. *Corrections may vary.*

1. Police officers stood near the corner. Directing people around the accident.

   Police officers stood near the corner. They were directing people around

   the accident.

2. The magician ran a sword through the box. To prove no one was hiding inside.

   The magician ran a sword through the box to prove no one was hiding inside.

3. Sitting quietly on the couch. The dog didn't look as if he'd eaten my sandwich.

   Sitting quietly on the couch, the dog didn't look as if he'd eaten my

   sandwich.

4. The restaurant has introduced a new vegetarian menu. To attract diners who prefer not to eat meat.

   The restaurant has introduced a new vegetarian menu. Its purpose is to

   attract diners who prefer not to eat meat.

ADDED-DETAIL FRAGMENTS

Another common kind of fragment often begins with one of the following words: *like, including, especially, also, for example, for instance, except, without,* or *such as.*

Almost everyone loves ice cream. Especially vanilla.

Many college students experience a great deal of stress. For instance, about money, grades, and personal relationships.

In the above examples, the second word group lacks both a subject and a verb. There are two ways to correct an added-detail fragment:

a Simply add the fragment to the sentence it explains. In most cases, use a comma to set off the fragment from the rest of the sentence.

Almost everyone loves ice **cream, especially** vanilla.

b Create a new sentence by adding a subject and verb to the fragment.

Many college students experience a great deal of stress. For instance, **they worry** about money, grades, and personal relationships.

Practice 3

Underline the added-detail fragment in each of the following. Then correct it on the lines provided, using one of the two methods given above.

Corrections may vary.

1. Television censors watch out for material that viewers might find offensive. Such as sexual or racial jokes.

   Television censors watch out for material that viewers might find

   offensive, such as sexual or racial jokes.

2. The children's toys were everywhere. Except in the toy chest.

   The children's toys were everywhere except in the toy chest.

3. All applicants at that company must take a skills assessment test. Also a personality profile test.

   All applicants at that company must take a skills assessment test.

   They must also take a personality profile test.

4. The film class saw every Dustin Hoffman film. Including his first one, *The Graduate.*

   The film class saw every Dustin Hoffman film, including his first one,

   The Graduate.

MISSING-SUBJECT FRAGMENTS

Some word groups are fragments because, while they do have a verb, they lack a subject. Here are examples:

> The telephone caller kept asking questions. But did not identify herself.
>
> The children dug a large hole in the grass. And then tried to fill it with water.

There are two ways to correct a missing-subject fragment:

a Connect the missing-subject fragment to the sentence it follows.

> The telephone caller kept asking **questions but** did not identify herself.
>
> The children dug a large hole in the **grass and** then tried to fill it with water.

b Create a new sentence by adding a subject to the fragment. Normally, you will add a pronoun standing for the subject of the previous sentence.

> The telephone caller kept asking questions. **She** did not identify herself.
>
> The children dug a large hole in the grass. Then **they** tried to fill it with water.

Practice 4

Underline the missing-subject fragment in each of the following items. Then correct it on the lines below, using one of the two methods given above.

Corrections may vary.

1. Greta is friendly to people's faces. But criticizes them behind their backs.

   Greta is friendly to people's faces but criticizes them behind their backs.

2. A mouse's face popped out of a hole near the sink. Then disappeared quickly.

   A mouse's face popped out of a hole near the sink. Then it disappeared quickly.

3. The nurse brought the patient an extra pillow and a glass of water. But forgot his pain medication.

   The nurse brought the patient an extra pillow and a glass of water. But she forgot his pain medication.

4. The pot of coffee sat on the burner for hours. And became too strong and bitter to drink.

   The pot of coffee sat on the burner for hours and became too strong and bitter to drink.

Note   Not all word groups beginning with *and, but, so,* or another joining word are fragments. A sentence beginning with a joining word is grammatically complete—and correct—if both a subject and a verb follow the joining word.

Name _____ Section _____ Date _____

Score: (Number right) _____ × 12.5 = _____%

■ **Fragments: Test 1**

Underline the fragment in each item that follows. Then correct the fragment, using one of the methods described in the chapter.

Note   To help you recognize and correct these fragments, directions are given for half of the items.

Corrections may vary.

1. <u>Before the tornado appeared.</u> The air became perfectly still.

   Before the tornado appeared, the air became perfectly still.

   The first word group begins with the dependent word *Before*. Correct the fragment by adding it to the second word group.

2. <u>Until an American reaches the age of eighteen.</u> He or she cannot vote in a presidential election.

   Until an American reaches the age of eighteen, he or she cannot vote in a presidential election.

3. <u>To let students get home before the storm.</u> The school dismissed classes early.

   To let students get home before the storm, the school dismissed classes early.

   The first word group lacks a subject and verb. Connect it to the complete statement that follows it.

4. <u>To make a long story short.</u> I lost my job.

   To make a long story short, I lost my job.

5. Every surface in the apartment was cluttered. <u>Including the top of the stove.</u>

   Every surface in the apartment was cluttered, including the top of the stove.

   The second word group lacks a subject and verb. Connect it to the complete statement that comes before it.

6. The six-year-old girl already loves to read. <u>Especially books about animals.</u>

   The six-year-old girl already loves to read, especially books about animals.

7. Near the end of the race, the runner felt a cramp developing in her leg. <u>But gritted her teeth and continued running.</u>

   Near the end of the race, the runner felt a cramp developing in her leg. But she gritted her teeth and continued running.

   Add a subject to the second word group to make it a complete thought.

8. The party had barely gotten started. <u>And was already so noisy that the neighbors were complaining.</u>

   The party had barely gotten started. It was already so noisy that the neighbors were complaining.

To the Instructor   Additional tests on fragments can be found in the *Instructor's Manual.*

Name _____   Section _____   Date _____

Score: (Number right) _____ × 12.5 = _____ %

■ **Fragments: Test 2**

Underline the fragment in each item that follows. Then correct the fragment, using one of the methods described in the chapter.

Corrections may vary.

1. <u>Often barking all night.</u> The neighbor's dog has become a serious nuisance.

   Often barking all night, the neighbor's dog has become a serious nuisance.

2. <u>After last week's heat and humidity.</u> Today's cold and rainy weather is actually a relief.

   After last week's heat and humidity, today's cold and rainy weather is

   actually a relief.

3. The restaurant specializes in Mexican food. <u>Including burritos, tacos, and refried beans.</u>

   The restaurant specializes in Mexican food. Its menu includes burritos, tacos,

   and refried beans.

4. The moon rose, full and silvery. <u>And cast its magical light over the countryside.</u>

   The moon rose, full and silvery, and cast its magical light over the countryside.

5. Hundreds of people called the radio station. <u>Hoping to win the concert tickets.</u>

   Hundreds of people called the radio station. They were hoping to win the

   concert tickets.

6. All the food in the refrigerator will certainly spoil. <u>Unless the power comes back on soon.</u>

   All the food in the refrigerator will certainly spoil unless the power comes

   back on soon.

7. No one could believe the honor student had committed the crime. <u>Especially his family.</u>

   No one could believe the honor student had committed the crime, especially

   his family.

8. The luscious-looking cake was covered with a cherry glaze. <u>And decorated with sugar swans.</u>

   The luscious-looking cake was covered with a cherry glaze and decorated with

   sugar swans.

Name _____ Section _____ Date _____

Score: (Number right) _____ × 12.5 = _____%

■ Fragments: Test 3

Underline the two fragments in each short passage that follows. Then correct the fragments, using one of the methods described in the chapter.

Note To help you recognize and correct fragments, explanations are given for two of the passages.

Corrections may vary.

1. Many people have poor telephone manners. <u>Such as beginning all of their conversations by saying, "Who's this?"</u> Some people don't ask if their call has come at a convenient time. <u>Or identify themselves when calling.</u>

   Many people have poor telephone manners, such as beginning all of their

   conversations by saying, "Who's this?" Some people don't ask if their call has

   come at a convenient time or identify themselves when calling.

   The word group beginning with *Such as* needs a subject and verb. It can be added to the previous sentence. The word group beginning with *Or* needs a subject.

2. <u>Although hot dogs, french fries, and rich ice cream are not healthy foods.</u> They're still favorites for many Americans. People are determined to enjoy themselves. <u>And don't want to hear about fat and cholesterol.</u>

   Although hot dogs, french fries, and rich ice cream are not healthy foods,

   they're still favorites for many Americans. People are determined to enjoy

   themselves. They don't want to hear about fat and cholesterol.

3. Sarita boasts that she can read a book in one evening. But she doesn't read the whole book. <u>For example, a chapter here and a page there.</u> She misses a lot of the book's detail. <u>Because she skips parts that she thinks won't interest her.</u>

   Sarita boasts that she can read a book in one evening. But she doesn't read the

   whole book. For example, she reads a chapter here and a page there. She misses a lot

   of the book's detail because she skips parts that she thinks won't interest her.

   The word group starting with *For example* needs a subject and verb. The word group starting with *Because,* a dependent word, needs to be added to the sentence it explains.

4. <u>Unless the teachers' strike ends tonight.</u> School will not open on schedule this year. Parents and their lawyers have called for a special meeting. <u>To pressure the school board into reaching a settlement.</u>

   Unless the teachers' strike ends tonight, school will not open on schedule this

   year. Parents and their lawyers have called for a special meeting. They want to

   pressure the school board into reaching a settlement.

Name _____   Section _____   Date _____
                                                           Score: (Number right) _____ × 12.5 = _____ %

■ Fragments: Test 4

Underline the two fragments in each short passage that follows. Then correct the fragments, using one of the methods described in the chapter.

Corrections
may vary.

1. <u>Because members of a youth group in Finland once felt that Donald Duck was immoral.</u> They tried to have Donald Duck cartoons banned from their town. They objected to the fact that Donald had been keeping company with Daisy Duck for more than fifty years. <u>Without ever getting married.</u>

   Because members of a youth group in Finland once felt that Donald Duck was

   immoral, they tried to have Donald Duck cartoons banned from their town.

   They objected to the fact that Donald had been keeping company with Daisy

   Duck for more than fifty years without ever getting married.

2. <u>Itching for several days.</u> Mosquito bites are one of the little miseries of summer. The itch is the result of the mosquito's saliva. <u>Which produces a mild allergic reaction in most people.</u>

   Itching for several days, mosquito bites are one of the little miseries of

   summer. The itch is the result of the mosquito's saliva, which produces a mild

   allergic reaction in most people.

3. <u>Although Western movies show cowboys as being mainly white and American-born.</u> The facts about America's cowboys are otherwise. Many of the cowboys were black or Mexican. <u>Also Native Americans.</u>

   Although Western movies show cowboys as being mainly white and American-

   born, the facts about America's cowboys are otherwise. Many of the cowboys

   were black or Mexican. Also, some were Native Americans.

4. In 1891, an English sailor was swallowed by a whale. <u>And lived to tell the story.</u> James Bartley survived for most of a day in the belly of a whale that his ship had been chasing. <u>When the animal was butchered.</u> Bartley was found unconscious but unharmed.

   In 1891, an English sailor was swallowed by a whale and lived to tell the

   story. . . . When the animal was butchered, Bartley was found unconscious

   but unharmed.

Name _____   Section _____   Date _____

Score: (Number right) _____ × 12.5 = _____ %

■ Fragments: Test 5

The following passage contains eight fragments. Underline each fragment and then rewrite it correctly on the lines below.

Note   To help you recognize and correct fragments, explanations are given for half of the items.

Corrections may vary.

Some people drink in secret. Others binge on chocolate. I, too, have a secret passion. Not drinking, smoking, or gambling. Instead, loving to visit office-supply stores. I feel a thrill of excitement as I walk into one of these stores. And stroll down the aisles. The smooth blank pages of notebooks make me itch. To write a masterpiece. I'm inspired by the packs of new pens and pencils. That wait on the shelves. The colorful file folders and sleek drawer dividers make me believe that I'm going to become incredibly organized. Even though that will never happen. Recently I came home from a buying spree with a bagful of treasures. Including a load of bright new paper clips, a pad of clean white paper, and markers in assorted colors. I felt a sense of pleasure. Which lasted for days.

1. It is not drinking, smoking, or gambling.

   The words *Not drinking, smoking, or gambling* need a subject and verb.

2. Instead, I love visiting office-supply stores.

3. I feel a thrill of excitement as I walk into one of these stores and stroll down the aisles.

   And stroll down the aisles needs a subject. It can be added to the previous sentence.

4. The smooth blank pages of notebooks make me itch to write a masterpiece.

5. I'm inspired by the packs of new pens and pencils that wait on the shelves.

   That wait on the shelves is a dependent-word fragment. Adding it to the sentence it explains will complete its meaning.

6. The colorful file folders and sleek drawer dividers make me believe that I'm going to become incredibly organized, even though that will never happen.

7. They included a load of bright new paper clips, a pad of clean white paper, and markers in assorted colors.

   The word group beginning with *Including* is a fragment. It needs a subject and a verb.

8. I felt a sense of pleasure which lasted for days.

Name _____   Section _____   Date _____

Score: (Number right) _____ × 12.5 = _____%

■ Fragments: Test 6

The following passage contains eight fragments. Underline each fragment and then rewrite it correctly on the lines below.

Corrections may vary.

<u>To have fun and raise some money.</u> The children in our neighborhood have a circus every summer. For weeks before the event, they post signs on every telephone pole announcing the date and time of the show. Everyone in the neighborhood looks forward to the big day. <u>Since it is one of the top social events of the summer.</u> On the day of the show, everybody crowds into the Nelsons' big garage. <u>Which has been transformed into a "big top."</u> Small people in clown suits pass out snacks. <u>Like Kool-Aid and pretzels.</u> The circus always includes a fortune-teller. <u>Who sits at a covered table and kicks her hidden assistant, telling him how many times to flash a light into her "crystal ball."</u> "Wild animals," of course, are part of any circus. The local cats and dogs patiently sit in cages, wearing signs saying they are "Rare Siberian Tigers" and "Fierce Wolves." Somebody's dad usually volunteers to be the "hairy wild man." <u>Jumping around in a wig and pounding his chest.</u> The comedy show is always hilarious. Imagine a bunch of five- and six-year-old comedians. <u>Forgetting punch lines and sometimes entire jokes.</u> After the show everyone applauds and hugs and kisses the performers. <u>And looks forward to next year's circus.</u>

1. To have fun and raise some money, the children in our neighborhood have a circus every summer.

2. Everyone in the neighborhood looks forward to the big day since it is one of the top social events of the summer.

3. On the day of the show, everybody crowds into the Nelsons' big garage, which has been transformed into a "big top."

4. Small people in clown suits pass out snacks like Kool-Aid and pretzels.

5. The circus always includes a fortune-teller who sits at a covered table and kicks her hidden assistant, telling him how many times to flash a light into her "crystal ball."

6. Somebody's dad usually volunteers to be the "hairy wild man," jumping around in a wig and pounding his chest.

7. They forget punch lines and sometimes entire jokes.

8. After the show everyone applauds and hugs and kisses the performers and looks forward to next year's circus.

6 Run-Ons

Seeing What You Know

Read the following pairs of items and, for each pair, check the item that is punctuated correctly. Then read the explanations below.

1. ___ a. Our math professor has the flu, half the class is sick as well.

   _✓_ b. Our math professor has the flu, and half the class is sick as well.

2. _✓_ a. Sue seldom got to play in an actual game. She was tempted to quit the team.

   ___ b. Sue seldom got to play in an actual game she was tempted to quit the team.

3. ___ a. My father had no brothers or sisters, he never learned to share.

   _✓_ b. Because my father had no brothers or sisters, he never learned to share.

Understanding the Answers

1. **Item *b* is punctuated correctly.**
   Item *a* is a comma splice. It is made up of two complete statements that are incorrectly connected by only a comma. In item *b,* the two statements are correctly connected—by a comma and a joining word, *and.*

2. **Item *a* is punctuated correctly.**
   Item *b* is a run-on sentence. It is made up of two complete statements: (1) *Sue seldom got to play in an actual game.* (2) *She was tempted to quit the team.* In item *a,* each of these two complete thoughts is stated in a separate sentence.

3. **Item *b* is punctuated correctly.**
   Item *a* is a comma splice. It is made up of two complete statements: (1) *My father had no brothers or sisters.* (2) *He never learned to share.* In item *b,* the first statement is subordinated to the second statement with the addition of the dependent word *because.*

A **run-on** is two complete thoughts that are run together with no adequate sign given to mark the break between them. This chapter will show you how to recognize and how to correct run-ons.

FUSED SENTENCES

When there is *no* punctuation at all separating two complete statements, the run-on sentence is called a **fused sentence.** The two statements are simply fused, or stuck together, into one sentence.

Complete statement 1: Test anxiety is a very real condition.

Complete statement 2: Some symptoms are stomach cramps and headaches.

Fused sentence: Test anxiety is a very real condition some symptoms are stomach cramps and headaches.

Complete statement 1: Computer skills are useful in college.

Complete statement 2: They will help you in the job market as well.

Fused sentence: Computer skills are useful in college they will help you in the job market as well.

A good way to prevent fused sentences is to read your work aloud. You will naturally tend to pause between complete thoughts. Also look within the sentence for words like *I, you, he, she, it, we, they, there, this, that, now, then,* and *next.* Such words often signal the beginning of a second complete thought.

Correcting Fused Sentences

Here are three methods of correcting a fused sentence:

1   Divide the fused sentence into two sentences.

Fused: Test anxiety is a very real condition some symptoms are stomach cramps and headaches.

Corrected: Test anxiety is a very real condition**. S**ome symptoms are stomach cramps and headaches.

2   Put a comma plus a joining word (such as *and, but,* or *so*) between the two complete thoughts.

Fused: Computer skills are useful in college they will help you in the job market as well.

Corrected: Computer skills are useful in college**, and** they will help you in the job market as well.

Fused: I'd love to go out to eat tonight I'm short of money right now.

Corrected: I'd love to go out to eat tonight**, but** I'm short of money right now.

Fused: Carmen has a broken foot she won't do any hiking this fall.

Corrected: Carmen has a broken foot, **so** she won't do any hiking this fall.

Note 1   Be sure to use a logical joining word. In the first example, *and* is appropriate because it means *in addition.* (Computer skills are useful in college; *in addition,* they will help you in the job market as well.) In the second example, *but* is appropriate because it means *however.* (I'd love to go out to eat tonight; *however,* I'm short of money right now.) In the third example, *so* means *as a result.* (The third example tells us that Carmen has a broken foot; *as a result,* she won't do any hiking this fall.)

Note 2   The comma always goes *before* the joining word—not after it.

Note 3   Other joining words are *for* (which means *because*), *or, nor,* and *yet.*

3   Use subordination to make one of the complete thoughts dependent on the other one.

To subordinate a complete thought, change it from a statement that can stand alone as a sentence to one that cannot stand by itself. To do so, begin the thought with an appropriate dependent word, such as *because, when, if, before, since, until, unless, while, as, although,* and *after.* (Additional dependent words appear on page 62.)

Fused: Carmen has a broken foot she won't do any hiking this fall.

Corrected: **Because** Carmen has a broken foot, she won't do any hiking this fall.

Punctuation note   Put a comma at the end of a dependent-word group that begins a sentence.

Practice 1

Draw a slash (/) between the two complete thoughts in each of the fused sentences that follow. Then correct each fused sentence, using one of the methods described above. Use a different method for each sentence.

Corrections may vary.

1. It's easy to begin smoking/it's much harder to quit.

   It's easy to begin smoking, but it's much harder to quit.

   _____

2. Some people at the office have been laid off/the other workers are nervous.

   Because some people at the office have been laid off, the other workers

   are nervous.

3. The patient's blood pressure was low/his temperature was low as well.

   The patient's blood pressure was low. His temperature was low as well.

   _____

COMMA SPLICES

When a comma alone separates two complete thoughts, the result is called a **comma splice.** A comma alone is not enough to mark the break between complete statements. Something stronger is needed.

Complete statement 1: Kevin was always nervous about tests.

Complete statement 2: His grades were usually the highest in the class.

Comma splice: Kevin was always nervous about tests, his grades were usually the highest in the class.

Correcting Comma Splices

A comma splice can be corrected by using one of the same three methods suggested for correcting a fused sentence:

1   Divide the comma splice into two sentences: Kevin was always nervous about tests. **H**is grades were usually the highest in the class.

2   Connect the two complete thoughts by placing a joining word (such as *and, but,* or *so*) after the comma: Kevin was always nervous about tests, **but** his grades were usually the highest in the class.

3   Use subordination (add a dependent word to one of the complete thoughts): Kevin was always nervous about tests **although** his grades were usually the highest in the class.

Practice 2

Correct each of the comma splices that follow, using one of the methods described above. Use a different method for each sentence.

Answers may vary.

1. Hakim was talking on the phone, he was switching TV channels with his remote control at the same time.

   Hakim was talking on the phone, and he was switching TV channels with his remote control at the same time.

2. I chose the shortest checkout line at the supermarket, then the one customer in front of me pulled out dozens of coupons.

   I chose the shortest checkout line at the supermarket. Then the one customer in front of me pulled out dozens of coupons.

3. The electricity at Jasmin's house went out, she had to write her paper by candlelight.

   Since the electricity at Jasmin's house went out, she had to write her paper by candlelight.

Note   Additional information about run-ons appears on pages 213–215.

Name _____   Section _____   Date _____

■ ## Run-Ons: Test 1

Put a slash (/) between the two complete thoughts in each of the following fused sentences or comma splices. Then rewrite the sentences, using, variously, (1) a period and capital letter, (2) a comma and a joining word, or (3) a dependent word.

Note   To help you correct run-ons, explanations are given for half of the sentences.

Corrections
may vary.

1. My alarm clock rang like a fire bell./I slowly rolled out of bed.

   When my alarm clock rang like a fire bell, I slowly rolled out of bed.

   My alarm clock rang like a fire bell is a complete thought. *I slowly rolled out of bed* is also a complete thought. Use the subordinating word *when* before the first thought.

2. Rosa got a parking ticket/she decided to go to traffic court.

   After Rosa got a parking ticket, she decided to go to traffic court.

3. One student made a lasting impression at his interview/he arrived an hour late.

   One student made a lasting impression at his interview. He arrived an hour late.

   The word group *he arrived an hour late* is a second complete thought. Put each complete thought into its own sentence.

4. Tyrone got lost driving to the wedding/he refused to stop to ask for directions.

   Tyrone got lost driving to the wedding, but he refused to stop to ask for directions.

5. The salad included shredded carrots/chopped peanuts were sprinkled on top.

   The salad included shredded carrots, and chopped peanuts were sprinkled on top.

   Use a comma and the joining word *and* to connect the two complete thoughts.

6. Prices were high at the concession stand,/the lines were long as well.

   Prices were high at the concession stand, and the lines were long as well.

7. Sharon drove halfway home,/then she noticed her pocketbook was missing.

   Sharon drove halfway home. Then she noticed her pocketbook was missing.

   Put each complete thought into its own sentence.

8. Bicycles may be the world's best method of transportation,/they require little maintanance and don't pollute.

   Bicycles may be the world's best method of transportation. They require little maintenance and don't pollute.

To the Instructor   Additional tests on run-ons can be found in the *Instructor's Manual.*

Score: (Number right) _____ × 12.5 = _____ %

■ Run-Ons: Test 2

Put a slash (/) between the two complete thoughts in each of the following fused sentences or comma splices. Then rewrite the sentences, using, variously, (1) a period and capital letter, (2) a comma and a joining word, or (3) a dependent word.

Corrections may vary.

1. David tried to appear calm/his trembling hands gave him away.

   David tried to appear calm, but his trembling hands gave him away.

2. The couple both came down with measles/they had to postpone their wedding.

   The couple both came down with measles, so they had to postpone their

   wedding.

3. The customer waited impatiently/the clerk seemed to be filling his grocery bags in slow motion.

   The customer waited impatiently. The clerk seemed to be filling his grocery

   bags in slow motion.

4. My doctor can seem cold and distant/he cares deeply for his patients.

   Although my doctor can seem cold and distant, he cares deeply for his

   patients.

5. The boy in "The Boy Who Cried Wolf" was finally telling the truth/nobody believed him.

   The boy in "The Boy Who Cried Wolf" was finally telling the truth, but nobody

   believed him.

6. The substitute teacher was ready to quit by ten o'clock/he had no idea eighth-graders could be such savages.

   The substitute teacher was ready to quit by ten o'clock. He had no idea

   eighth-graders could be such savages.

7. The flashlight was very bright/even its beams could not reach the back of the deep cave.

   The flashlight was very bright, but even its beams could not reach the back of

   the deep cave.

8. Many people never buy hardcover books/they prefer to wait for the paperback versions.

   Many people never buy hardcover books because they prefer to wait for the

   paperback versions.

Name _____ Section _____ Date _____

■ **Run-Ons: Test 3**

Correct the two run-ons in each passage by using (1) a period and capital letter, (2) a comma and a joining word, or (3) a dependent word. Be sure to use all three methods.

Note   To help you correct run-ons, explanations are given for two of the passages.

Corrections may vary.

1. The female panda was thought to be pregnant the zookeepers watched her closely for signs of the coming birth. However, many months went by with no baby panda, the keepers finally gave up hope.

   Because the female panda was thought to be pregnant, the zookeepers

   watched her closely for signs of the coming birth. However, many months

   went by with no baby panda, so the keepers finally gave up hope.

   Correct the first run-on by adding the dependent word *Because* before the first complete thought. Correct the second run-on by adding the joining word *so* between the two complete thoughts.

2. My nephew goes to the fairgrounds every night, he doesn't go to see the sights. Instead, he goes to pick up extra money. He searches the ground for coins that people have dropped one night he collected almost five dollars.

   My nephew goes to the fairgrounds every night, but he doesn't go to see the

   sights. . . . He searches the ground for coins that people have dropped. One

   night he collected almost five dollars.

3. Many of us have heard warnings about swimming on a full stomach the truth is that we are better off swimming when full. Muscles are starved for energy in a hungry body, they cannot work efficiently and may cramp.

   Many of us have heard warnings about swimming on a full stomach. The truth

   is that we are better off swimming when full. Because muscles are starved for

   energy in a hungry body, they cannot work efficiently and may cramp.

   Correct the first run-on by using a period and a capital letter. Correct the second run-on by adding *Because* before the first complete thought.

4. The most popular song in the world was composed in 1893, it was written by two sisters in Kentucky. Mildred and Patty Hill's song was first titled "Good Morning to You" later the sisters changed the words to "Happy Birthday to You."

   The most popular song in the world was composed in 1893. It was written by two

   sisters in Kentucky. Mildred and Patty Hill's song was first titled "Good Morning

   to You," but later the sisters changed the words to "Happy Birthday to You."

■ Run-Ons: Test 4

Correct the two run-ons in each passage by using (1) a period and capital letter, (2) a comma and a joining word, or (3) a dependent word. Be sure to use all three methods.

Corrections may vary.

1. June is a month of nice weather that doesn't explain why it is the most popular month for weddings. The month is named after Juno, the Roman goddess of marriage. People believed that Juno would bless couples married during her month, we've now forgotten about Juno but still prefer June weddings.

   June is a month of nice weather, but that doesn't explain why it is the most popular

   month for weddings. . . . People believed that Juno would bless couples married during

   her month. We've now forgotten about Juno but still prefer June weddings.

2. Teenagers often have a strong need to show their independence this desire often brings them into conflict with their parents. Some teens rebel in harmless ways, others show their independence in more dangerous fashion, such as by drinking and driving.

   Teenagers often have a strong need to show their independence, and this desire often

   brings them into conflict with their parents. Some teens rebel in harmless ways. Others

   show their independence in more dangerous fashion, such as by drinking and driving.

3. On their first date, Alicia and Mark went to a movie. The story was very sad Alicia tried to keep from crying. She glanced over at Mark she was surprised to see a tear running down his cheek. Alicia was glad that she didn't have to hide her feelings from Mark.

   . . . The story was very sad, but Alicia tried to keep from crying. When she

   glanced over at Mark, she was surprised to see a tear running down his

   cheek. . . .

4. Everyone has a cure for hiccups, there's holding your breath, breathing into a paper bag, or having someone scare you. These methods do not work for me, the only home remedy that really helps is sugar. Swallowing a teaspoon of white granulated sugar always stops my hiccups.

   Everyone has a cure for hiccups. There's holding your breath, breathing into a

   paper bag, or having someone scare you. These methods do not work for me.

   The only home remedy that really helps is sugar. . . .

Name _____ Section _____ Date _____

Score: (Number right) _____ × 10 = _____%

■ Run-Ons: Test 5

The following passage contains ten run-ons. Correct each run-on in the space provided by using (1) a period and capital letter, (2) a comma and a joining word, or (3) a dependent word. Be sure to use all three methods.

Note   To help you correct the run-ons, explanations are given for half of the sentences.

[1]Terry is a lively talker, her listening skills are underdeveloped. [2]She calls herself a caring person the truth is, however, that she never really listens to anyone. [3]Terry is thinking about what to say next, she only *seems* to be listening. [4]Her friends know she doesn't listen to them, they don't discuss important things with her. [5]One friend learned the hard way he told Terry that his mother had cancer. [6]Terry was full of sympathy, she kept saying, "I'm so glad you told me." [7]She sounded very supportive, the friend felt better. [8]His mother died, Terry asked, "Why didn't you tell me your mother wasn't well?" [9]Terry thinks she is a kind and loyal friend she doesn't realize the truth. [10]She isn't a real friend at all, her only real friend is herself.

Corrections may vary.

1. Terry is a lively talker, but her listening skills are underdeveloped.
Correct the run-on by inserting *but* between the two complete thoughts.

2. She calls herself a caring person. The truth is, however, that she never really listens to anyone.

3. Since Terry is thinking about what to say next, she only <u>seems</u> to be listening.
Correct the run-on by inserting *since* before the first complete thought.

4. Her friends know she doesn't listen to them, so they don't discuss important things with her.

5. One friend learned the hard way when he told Terry that his mother had cancer.
Correct the run-on by inserting *when* before *he told Terry that his mother had cancer.*

6. Terry was full of sympathy. She kept saying, "I'm so glad you told me."

7. She sounded very supportive, so the friend felt better.
Correct the run-on by inserting so before *the friend felt better.*

8. After his mother died, Terry asked, "Why didn't you tell me your mother wasn't well?"

9. Terry thinks she is a kind and loyal friend. She doesn't realize the truth.
Correct the run-on by putting a period and capital after *kind and loyal friend.*

10. She isn't a real friend at all, and her only real friend is herself.

Name _____ Section _____ Date _____

Score: (Number right) _____ × 10 = _____%

■ Run-Ons: Test 6

The following passage contains ten run-ons. Correct each run-on in the space provided by using (1) a period and capital letter, (2) a comma and a joining word, or (3) a dependent word. Be sure to use all three methods.

In-Ho-Oh, a young man living in Korea, was a bright student he was accepted at the University of Pennsylvania. His parents were not wealthy, they did everything they could to make his trip possible. In-Ho-Oh worked very hard at the university he wrote to his parents frequently. One day his parents received a message with tragic news. In-Ho-Oh had been mailing a letter, a group of boys ganged up on him. They beat him, then they took his wallet. He was taken to the hospital, he was too badly hurt to live. In-Ho-Oh's parents mourned for their son, they were sad as well that the boys could receive the death penalty. The boys were poor and had no education the parents felt sorry for them. They wrote to the judge hearing the boys' case. Their letter said, "We cannot help our son any more, but we would like to help someone else." In-Ho-Oh's parents asked that the boys be given the lightest sentence possible. They wanted the boys to have a second chance they even set up a fund to help them get training and jobs. In-Ho-Oh's parents had lost their son, they did not want his life to go to waste.

Corrections may vary.

1. In-Ho-Oh, a young man living in Korea, was a bright student. He was accepted at the University of Pennsylvania.

2. Although his parents were not wealthy, they did everything they could to make his trip possible.

3. In-Ho-Oh worked very hard at the university, and he wrote to his parents frequently.

4. In-Ho-Oh had been mailing a letter when a group of boys ganged up on him.

5. They beat him, and then they took his wallet.

6. He was taken to the hospital, but he was too badly hurt to live.

7. While In-Ho-Oh's parents mourned for their son, they were sad as well that the boys could receive the death penalty.

8. The boys were poor and had no education, so the parents felt sorry for them.

9. They wanted the boys to have a second chance. They even set up a fund to help them get training and jobs.

10. Although In-Ho-Oh's parents had lost their son, they did not want his life to go to waste.

7 Pronouns

Seeing What You Know

Cross out the pronoun mistake in each of the following sentences, and write the corrections above the mistakes. Then read the explanations below.

Some answers may vary.

1. Each of my sons required two chances to pass ~~their~~ *his* driver's test.

2. If there are stains on any hotel towels, ~~they~~ *the towels* should be removed immediately.

3. I don't shop at that supermarket because ~~they~~ *the clerks* are so slow at the checkout counters.

4. People go to the local diner because ~~you~~ *they* can get low-priced meals there all day.

Understanding the Answers

1. Each of my sons required two chances to pass **his** driver's test.
   Each is singular. It needs a singular pronoun, *his,* to refer to it.

2. If there are stains on any hotel towels, **the towels** should be removed immediately.
   Which does the writer want us to remove—the stains or the towels? The pronoun *they* could refer to either one. Replacing *they* with *the towels* makes the meaning of the sentence clear.

3. I don't shop at that supermarket because **the clerks** are so slow at the checkout counters.
   Who are *they*? The word *they* doesn't refer to anything specific. The sentence should be clarified by replacing *they* with what it is meant to represent.

4. People go to the local diner because **they** can get low-priced meals there all day.
   People requires a third-person pronoun, *they.* Sentences that begin in the third person should not suddenly shift their point of view to the second person, *you.*

To the Instructor   Students unfamiliar with pronouns should first study the material in Chapter 19, "Parts of Speech: A Review," pages 190–198. More detailed information appears in Chapter 20, "Pronoun Types," pages 198–202.

Pronouns are words that stand for nouns (names of persons, places, or things). Personal pronouns are *I, me, my, mine, you, your, yours, he, him, his, she, her, hers, it, its, we, us, our, ours, they, them, their,* and *theirs.*

Freddy is a wrestler. **He** weighs 270 pounds. (*He* stands for *Freddy.*)

Rita always writes **her** letters in purple ink. (*Her* stands for *Rita's.*)

"If **my** kids talk back, **I** let **them** know **they** are asking for trouble," Jeff said. (*My* stands for *Jeff's; I* stands for *Jeff. Them* and *they* stand for *kids.*)

This chapter shows you how to avoid the three most frequent kinds of pronoun mistakes: in pronoun agreement, in pronoun reference, and in pronoun point of view. Additional information about pronouns appears on pages 198–202.

PRONOUN AGREEMENT

A pronoun must agree in number with the word it refers to (sometimes called the pronoun's *antecedent*). Singular words require singular pronouns; plural words require plural pronouns.

The book Henry lent me is missing **its** cover. (*Its,* a singular pronoun, refers to *book,* a singular noun.)

If your cousins don't get here soon, **they** will miss the movie. (*They,* a plural pronoun, refers to *cousins,* a plural noun.)

The indefinite pronouns listed below are always singular. (See also page 43.)

Singular Indefinite Pronouns			
each	anyone	anybody	anything
either	everyone	everybody	everything
neither	someone	somebody	something
one	no one	nobody	nothing

Each of the wild horses raced for **its** freedom.

Neither of my sisters ever feels like cleaning **her** room.

No one in the class wanted to read **his** (or **her**) paper out loud.

Note   In the last example, choose a pronoun that fits the situation. If all the members of the class are male, use *his.* If they all are female, use *her.* If the class includes both men and women, use *his or her:*

No one in the class wanted to read **his or her** paper out loud.

Or avoid the extra words by rewriting the sentence in the plural:

No **students** in the class wanted to read **their papers** out loud.

Practice 1

Underline the correct word or words in the parentheses in the sentences below.

1. Each of the actresses who auditioned believes (she / they) should be chosen for the starring role.

2. Many high schools now require (its / their) students to take a computer course.

3. If anybody here has a cell phone, (they / he or she) should turn it off now so that it doesn't ring during the performance.

4. Either exercise is fine, but (it / they) must be done regularly to do any good.

5. Somebody in the men's locker room stole Paco's wristwatch, and Paco would love to get back at (him / them).

PRONOUN REFERENCE

A pronoun must also refer *clearly* to the word it stands for. If the meaning of a pronoun is uncertain, the sentence will be confusing. For example,

> Gloria told Renée that she had gotten an A on her paper. (Who got the A—Gloria or Renée? The words *she* and *her* could refer to either one.)

> I wanted a ham and cheese sandwich, but they were all out of cheese. (Who was all out of cheese? The word *they* has no one to refer to.)

> There were no questions after the lecture, which was regrettable. (What was regrettable—the lecture or the lack of questions? Be careful how you use the pronouns *which* and *this*. They must clearly refer to *one* thing or situation.)

> Both of Ben's parents are accountants, but this doesn't interest Ben. (What doesn't interest Ben? The pronoun *this* doesn't refer to anything in the sentence.)

To avoid mistakes like these, simply write what you mean by the pronoun.

> Gloria told Renee, "**You** got an A on **your** paper."
>
> *Or:* Gloria told Renee, "**I** got an A on **my** paper."
>
> I wanted a ham and cheese sandwich, but **the deli** was all out of cheese.
>
> There were no questions after the lecture. **Not having questions** was regrettable.
>
> Both of Ben's parents are accountants, but **accounting** doesn't interest Ben.

Practice 2

Underline the correct word or words in the parentheses in the sentences below.

1. As Rudy told his father about being arrested, (Rudy / he) began to cry.

2. Students complain that (they / the maintenance people) keep the library too hot.

3. While Eric was adding sugar to his coffee, he spilled (it / the sugar) all over the table.

4. Someone offered to show me a copy of next week's history test, but I said that I didn't believe in (this / <u>cheating</u>).

5. Many older people shop at the mall because (they / <u>the stores</u>) give a 15 percent discount to senior citizens.

PRONOUN POINT OF VIEW

Pronouns are either **first person** (referring to the speaker), **second person** (referring to the one spoken to), or **third person** (referring to everyone else):

	First person	*Second person*	*Third person*
Singular	I, me, my, mine	you, your, yours	he, him, his; she, her, hers; it, its
Plural	we, us, our, ours	you, your, yours	they, them, their, theirs

When you write, your pronoun point of view must stay the same. Do not shift unnecessarily from one point of view to another, as in the following sentences:

What **I** like best about vacations is that **you** don't have to set an alarm.

The **workers** here have to take a break at 10:30 whether **we** want to or not.

Instead, write the entire sentence in the same person:

What **I** like best about vacations is that **I** don't have to set an alarm.

The **workers** here have to take a break at 10:30 whether **they** want to or not.

Practice 3

Underline the correct pronoun in the parentheses in the sentences below.

1. First-year students at this school are required to take a math course. (You / <u>They</u>) must also take a computer course.

2. My father says he prefers to drive at night because then the sun won't get in (<u>his</u> / your) eyes.

3. I know spring is really here when (<u>I</u> / you) see neighborhood kids playing softball.

4. Although Sharon and I were good friends, (<u>we</u> / you) could tell that we would not be good roommates.

5. If you want to advance in this company, (we / <u>you</u>) must be willing to work overtime and to move to a new location every couple of years.

Note   Additional information about pronouns appears on pages 191–192 and 198–202.

Name _____ Section _____ Date _____

Score: (Number right) _____ × 10 = _____ %

■ Pronouns: Test 1

Underline the correct word or words in the parentheses in the sentences below.

Note   To help you recognize and correct pronoun mistakes, explanations are given for half of the items.

1. Neither of the friends wants to work in (<u>his</u> / their) family business.

    Neither, an indefinite pronoun, is singular. The second pronoun must agree with it in number.

2. If anyone doesn't want (<u>his or her</u> / their) dessert, I'll eat it.

3. My mother told my girlfriend (she looked marvelous. / , <u>"You look marvelous."</u>)

    The pronoun *she* could refer to either *my mother* or *my girlfriend.*

4. Mrs. Owen told her daughter (that she couldn't baby-sit Friday night. / , <u>"I can't baby-sit Friday night."</u>)

5. When you drive from New York to South Carolina, (<u>you</u> / one) should plan to stay overnight at a motel on the way.

    The sentence begins in the second person (*you*). Do not shift the pronoun point of view.

6. We don't want the local clinic to close because then (you / <u>we</u>) would have to drive all the way to the city for medical treatment.

7. Both travel agents thought that (she / <u>they</u>) had won the free trip to Hawaii.

    Agents is plural. The second pronoun must agree in number.

8. For Halloween, Dave and Scott both dressed up in (his / <u>their</u>) sisters' cheer-leading uniforms.

9. When Lian learned that her new sister-in-law was a Navy pilot, she became interested in (it / <u>a Navy career</u>) too.

    For the sentence to be clear, the writer must state what Lian is interested in.

10. Many people enjoy hiking and camping, but I'm not interested in (them / <u>those activities</u>).

To the Instructor   Additional tests on pronouns can be found in the *Instructor's Manual.*

Name _____ Section _____ Date _____

Score: (Number right) _____ × 12.5 = _____ %

■ Pronouns: Test 2

Underline the pronoun mistake in each of the sentences that follow. Then correct the mistake by rewriting the sentence in the space provided.

Corrections
may vary.

1. Mario told the manager that he needed to hire more help.

   Mario told the manager, "You need to hire more help." Or: Mario told the

   manager, "I need to hire more help."

2. Each of the sisters is a successful artist in their own field.

   Each of the sisters is a successful artist in her own field.

3. I won't go to the concert tonight because there's no way you could get a ticket.

   I won't go to the concert tonight because there's no way I could get a ticket.

4. Maria enjoys reading to her little girl even though she sometimes gets sleepy during the stories.

   Maria enjoys reading to her little girl even though the little girl (or: her

   daughter) sometimes gets sleepy during the stories.

5. Any basketball player who fails a course will lose their scholarship.

   Any basketball player who fails a course will lose his or her scholarship.

6. Every time Barb paints her nails, I have to leave the room because the smell of it makes me sick.

   Every time Barb paints her nails, I have to leave the room because the smell of

   the nail polish makes me sick.

7. Many people love trying foreign restaurants where you can experience a whole new way of cooking.

   Many people love trying foreign restaurants where they can experience a

   whole new way of cooking.

8. When I was stopped for speeding, he said I'd been going fifteen miles over the limit.

   When I was stopped for speeding, the police officer said I'd been going fifteen

   miles over the limit.

Name _____ Section _____ Date _____

■ Pronouns: Test 3

Each of the following passages contains **two** pronoun mistakes. Find and underline these two mistakes. Then write the corrections in the spaces provided.

Note   To help you recognize and correct pronoun mistakes, explanations are given for the first error in each passage.

Corrections may vary.

1. The bookstore clerks don't go to the deli next door any more, even though the food is pretty good. They complain that you get bad service there. For instance, it's not unusual to wait twenty minutes for them to make a simple sandwich.

   a. ____they_____   *You* is a shift in pronoun point

   b. __the people at the deli counter__   of view.

2. A sad, angry man stood outside of the bank, shouting that they had stolen his money. Passersby walked around him quickly because you did not know what he might do.

   a. __the bank employees_____   *They* has nothing in the sentence

   b. ____they_____   to refer to.

3. In the department store, women often block the aisles and spray perfume samples on the shoppers. This annoys many people, so you have to avoid that part of the store.

   a. __Being sprayed with perfume__   *This* could refer to either blocking

   b. ____they_____   the aisles or spraying the perfume.

4. Although every person has the right to their own opinion, heckling a speaker is not the way to express a view. Instead, one should picket a speech or write a letter to their local newspaper.

   a. __his or her_____   *Every person* is singular and

   b. __his or her_____   requires a singular pronoun.

5. Bob told Luis that he needed a new car. Bob went on to say, "I still like my old Corvette, but the car spends more time in the garage than on the road." Luis agreed that anybody who had to pay for so many repairs to their car should buy a new one.

   a. __Luis, "I need a new car."__   *He* could refer to either Bob

   b. __his_____   or Luis.

Name _____   Section _____   Date _____

Score: (Number right) _____ × 10 = _____%

■ Pronouns: Test 4

Each of the following passages contains **two** pronoun mistakes. Find and underline
these two mistakes. Then write the corrections in the spaces provided.

Corrections
may vary.

1. The thing that customers like about shopping at McRay's Hardware is that
   you get a great deal of assistance from the clerks there. He must spend a lot
   of time training people after he hires them.

   a. _____they_____

   b. _____Mr. McRay_____

2. Everyone in my family was late to their job on Tuesday. A storm had knocked
   down power lines during the night. The utility plant got all of their workers to
   restore power, but most people's alarm clocks fell behind by two hours during
   the outage.

   a. _____his or her_____

   b. _____its_____

3. The town diner isn't making a profit these days, and there's a good reason
   why. During an inspection last month, they found rats and mice in the kitchen.
   The diner was closed for a week for cleanup, and the owners promised to be
   more careful about this in the future.

   a. _____health officials_____

   b. _____cleanliness_____

4. A well-known columnist advises us not to respond to e-mail messages from
   strangers. Somebody who tries to start a relationship by e-mail could be lying
   about their age, marital status, or even gender. Or the writer could be tempting us
   to go to a Web site where your password or credit card number will be stolen.

   a. _____his or her_____

   b. _____our_____

5. As we watched, two movers carried the piano out to their double-parked van,
   then left it in the middle of the street while they went for coffee. Fifteen
   minutes later, the movers had still not come back, and you could see cars
   backed up for several blocks.

   a. _____the van_____

   b. _____we_____

Name _____ Section _____ Date _____

Score: (Number right) _____ × 10 = _____ %

■ **Pronouns: Test 5**

Each sentence in the following passage contains one pronoun mistake. Find and underline these ten mistakes. Then write the corrections on the lines below.

Note   To help you recognize and correct pronoun mistakes, explanations are given for five of the errors.

¹When Aunt Rose and Uncle Morris finally arrived, we all jumped up from the dinner table and rushed to the door, shouting their greetings. ²"I'm sorry we're late," said Morris, "but Rose insists on driving forty-five miles an hour, no matter how late you are." ³"But don't forget we were late in coming home from shopping and also in leaving the house, and it's your fault," Rose teased. ⁴"The worst thing for me about living with Morris is you always have to wait for him to finish selecting his wardrobe, trimming his beard, and combing his hair just right." ⁵Then everyone sat back down to eat, and Rose told her sister Nancy that her red dress fit better than ever. ⁶Both Morris and his brother-in-law ate more than his share of the roast beef. ⁷The dinner was interrupted when Mr. Nichols came to the door and said, "Sorry to bother you, folks, but someone parked their car partly in front of my driveway. ⁸This could lead to a scratched and dented car—unless the car gets moved." ⁹Rose had stepped out of the room for a minute, and Morris responded, "I told Rose that nobody would be able to get their car around ours if she parked there—I'll go park the car somewhere else." ¹⁰When Uncle Morris went to move the car, the rest of us immediately sprang into action—quickly clearing the table, hanging up streamers, bringing out their presents, and opening the back door to let in the other guests for Morris's surprise birthday party.

Corrections
may vary.

1. *our*
   We is a first-person pronoun. *Their* is a shift to the third-person point of view.

2. *we*

3. *the lateness is*
   It does not refer to anything in the sentence.

4. *I*

5. *Nancy, "Your red dress fits better than ever."*
   The pronoun *her* could refer to either Rose or Nancy.

6. *their*

7. *his or her*
   Someone is an indefinite pronoun. Indefinite pronouns are singular and need another singular pronoun to keep the point of view consistent.

8. *Parking there*

9. *his or her*
   Nobody is an indefinite pronoun, so it is singular. *Their* is plural.

10. *our*

Name _____ Section _____ Date _____
Score: (Number right) _____ × 10 = _____%

■ Pronouns: Test 6

Each sentence in the following passage contains one pronoun mistake. Find and underline these ten mistakes. Then write the corrections on the lines below.

[1]I work in a twenty-four-hour coffee and doughnut shop in New York, and in my job, I think <u>you</u> see every type of person in the city. [2]Early morning brings in the sleepy, grumpy commuters; it's a time of day when everybody seems at <u>their</u> worst. [3]Most early-morning customers don't even say hello—they just grunt out <u>his or her</u> orders. [4]Little kids and their parents come in later in the morning, and some of <u>them</u> are absolutely adorable. [5]Yesterday in the store a lady told her little girl <u>she</u> had to wash her hands before eating. [6]The little girl said, "I don't understand why I have to wash my hands—I'm going to eat a chocolate doughnut, and <u>they're</u> the same color as the dirt." [7]Late at night, when we're surprisingly busy, anyone might come in for <u>their</u> nightly cup of coffee. [8]The door is always opening, and <u>they</u> could be cops, homeless people, or night-shift factory workers. [9]Part of the reason I like my job is <u>you</u> never know who will drop by. [10]One night the door opened and I said, "What'll you have?" before I realized <u>he</u> was Nick Nolte, one of my favorite actors.

Corrections
may vary.

1. I
2. his or her
3. their
4. the kids
5. , "You have to wash your hands before eating."
6. it's
7. his or her
8. the patrons
9. I
10. the customer

8 Comma

Seeing What You Know

Insert commas where needed in the following sentences. Then read the explanations below.

1. The restaurant dessert tray featured carrot cake,coconut cream pie,and something called death-by-chocolate.

2. Because I was three hours short of graduation requirements,I had to take a course during the summer.

3. The weather,according to last night's forecast,will improve by Saturday.

4. Students hurried to the campus store to buy their fall textbooks,but several of the books were already out of stock.

5. My sister asked,"Are you going to be on the phone much longer?"

Understanding the Answers

1. The restaurant dessert tray featured carrot cake, coconut cream pie, and something called death-by-chocolate.
   Commas are needed to separate the items in a series.

2. Because I was three hours short of graduation requirements, I had to take a course during the summer.
   The comma separates the introductory words from the rest of the sentence.

3. The weather, according to last night's forecast, will improve by Saturday.
   The words *according to last night's forecast* interrupt the flow of the rest of the sentence, so they are set off by commas.

4. Students hurried to the campus store to buy their fall textbooks, but several of the books were already out of stock.
   The comma separates two complete thoughts connected by the joining word *but*.

5. My sister asked, "Are you going to be on the phone much longer?"
   The comma separates a direct quotation from the rest of the sentence.

93

This chapter explains five main uses of the comma.

1 BETWEEN ITEMS IN A SERIES

Commas are used to separate three or more items in a series.

> Bears, chipmunks, raccoons, and groundhogs all hibernate during the winter.
>
> Felipe groaned when he learned that his exams in biology, economics, and sociology were scheduled for the same day.
>
> The mechanic started the engine, fiddled with the fan belt, and announced that the problem was solved.

But   Do not use a comma when the series contains only two items.
The mechanic started the engine and fiddled with the fan belt.

Practice 1

In the following sentences, insert commas between items in a series.

1. Most communities now recycle newspapers,aluminum,and plastic.
2. Walking,bicycling,and swimming are all good aerobic exercises.
3. We collected the kids,loaded the van,and set off for the amusement park.
4. Signs of burnout include insomnia,inability to concentrate,and depression.

2 AFTER INTRODUCTORY MATERIAL

A comma is used to separate introductory material from the rest of the sentence. (If you were reading the sentence aloud, you would probably pause slightly at the end of the introductory material, where the comma belongs.)

> Although the county issues a large number of jury-duty notices, many people find reasons not to serve.
>
> Pushing and laughing, the second-graders spilled onto the playground.
>
> In the middle of the thunderstorm, all the lights on our street went out.

Practice 2

Insert a comma after the introductory material in each of the following sentences.

1. During the first-aid course,one student accidentally broke her finger.
2. When the power went back on,all the digital clocks in the house began to blink.
3. Pausing in the doorway,the actress smiled warmly at the photographers.
4. After waiting in line for two hours,the students were told that the registrar's office was closing for lunch.

3 AROUND WORDS THAT INTERRUPT THE FLOW OF A SENTENCE

Sentences sometimes contain material that interrupts the flow of thought. Such words and word groups should be set off from the rest of the sentence by commas. For example,

My brother, who is very neat, complains that I am too messy.

If you read this sentence out loud, you can hear that the words *who is very neat* interrupt the flow of thought. Such interrupters often contain information that is less important to the sentence.

Here are some other examples of sentences with interrupters:

The owner of the blue Ford, *grumbling angrily,* came out to move his car.

Our house, *which was built in 1975,* needs a new roof and extra insulation.

The house's storm windows, *though,* are in fairly good shape.

Note   Some interrupters, however, are needed to make the sentence clear. Information about punctuating these word groups appears on pages 215–216.

Practice 3

Insert commas around the interrupting words in each of the following sentences.

1. The Beatles,who originally called themselves the Quarrymen,released twenty-nine single records in their first year.

2. Frozen yogurt,which is relatively low in calories,is as delicious to many people as ice cream.

3. Some dieters,on the other hand,would rather give up desserts completely.

4. The new office building,forty stories high,provides a fine view of the parkway.

4 BETWEEN COMPLETE THOUGHTS CONNECTED BY A JOINING WORD

When two complete thoughts are combined into one sentence by a joining word like *and, but,* or *so,* a comma is used before the joining word.

They were five strangers stuck in an elevator, **so** they told each other jokes to ease the tension.

Each part of the sentence is a complete thought: *They were five strangers stuck in an elevator. They told each other jokes to ease the tension.* The parts are combined into one sentence by the joining word *so.*

Here are more sentences with complete thoughts connected by joining words:

Money may not buy happiness, **but** it makes misery a lot more comfortable.

Ved has a restaurant job this summer, **and** his sister has an office position.

Punctuation note   Don't add a comma just because a sentence contains the word *and, but,* or *so.* Use a comma only when the joining word comes between two complete thoughts. Each of those thoughts must have its own subject and verb.

> *Comma:* Lois spent two hours in the *gym,* **and then she went** to class. (Each complete thought has a subject and a verb: *Lois spent* and *she went.*)

> *No comma:* Lois spent two hours in the **gym and then went** to class. (The second thought isn't complete because it doesn't have its own subject.)

Practice 4

Insert a comma before the joining words in the following sentences.

1. Someone had broken into the house, but nothing had been taken.

2. Melba wasn't wearing her glasses, so she couldn't read the fine print in the ad.

3. I used to be able to type very quickly, but now I'm out of practice.

4. Frequent TV watchers spend less time interacting with friends and family, and their reading is often limited to magazines such as *TV Guide.*

5 WITH DIRECT QUOTATIONS

A comma is used to separate directly quoted material from the rest of the sentence.

> Someone shouted, "Look out below!"

> The customer grumbled to the waiter, "This coffee tastes like mud."

> "To learn more about lions," the zookeeper told the visiting children, "you should read the book *Born Free.*"

Punctuation note   When the comma is placed at the end of a quotation, it is included within the quotation marks.

Practice 5

Insert commas to set off quoted material in the following sentences.

1. When the bank robber Willie Sutton was asked why he robbed banks, he replied, "Because that's where the money is."

2. "Only fifteen more minutes until this class ends," Sharon whispered.

3. "We have everything for tall women," the mall store owner bragged, "except tall men."

4. "When you hear the beep, you know what to do," says the message on my friend's answering machine.

Note   Additional information about the comma appears on pages 215–218.

Name _____   Section _____   Date _____

■ Comma: Test 1

On the lines provided, write the word or words in each sentence that need to be followed by a comma. Be sure to include each comma.

Note   To help you master the comma, explanations are given for five of the sentences.

1. The kids' Halloween bags were full of quarters peanuts gum and candy bars.

   <u>quarters, peanuts, gum,</u>   Commas separate items in a series.

2. Opal has evening classes on Mondays Wednesdays and Thursdays.

   <u>Mondays, Wednesdays,</u>

3. Carrying her popcorn Sylvia looked for an empty seat in the theater.

   <u>popcorn,</u>   Use a comma after introductory material.

4. After she read the Harry Potter books Yoko began calling her younger brothers and sisters "Muggles."

   <u>books,</u>

5. That pizza the one with broccoli and mushrooms is the best I've ever eaten.

   <u>pizza, mushrooms,</u>   Place commas around interrupting words in a sentence.

6. Mata Hari a famous spy and exotic dancer reportedly charged her lovers at least $7,500 to spend a night with her.

   <u>Hari, dancer,</u>

7. My father wanted to attend college but his family didn't have the money.

   <u>college,</u>   A comma is needed before the word that joins two complete thoughts.

8. Bad weather destroyed much of last season's orange crop so the price of orange juice is high this year.

   <u>crop,</u>

9. "You look as if you've seen a ghost" my brother remarked when he saw the scared expression on my face.

   <u>ghost,"</u>   The comma separates a direct quotation from the rest of the sentence.

10. "All I want" said Jeff wearily "is to crawl into bed and stay there for a week."

    <u>want," wearily,</u>

To the Instructor   Additional tests on the comma can be found in the *Instructor's Manual*.

Name _____ Section _____ Date _____

Score: (Number right) _____ × 10 = _____%

■ Comma: Test 2

In the space provided, write the letter of the one comma rule that applies to each of the following sentences. Then insert one or more commas where they belong in each sentence.

a	Between items in a series
b	After introductory material
c	Around interrupting words
d	Before a word that joins two complete thoughts
e	With direct quotations

_____c_____   1. The caged panther, which kept striding from one side of its enclosure to the other, looked both magnificent and pitiful.

_____b_____   2. When I first picked up the telephone, I didn't recognize Roger's voice.

_____a_____   3. You'll know my uncle immediately—he has a walrus mustache, an eye patch, and a wooden leg.

_____d_____   4. The roast should have been ready, but I had forgotten to turn on the oven.

_____e_____   5. "I'll go to the party," said Vicky, "if you promise to be there."

_____c_____   6. Many parents, although they dearly love their children, sometimes dream about being young and free again.

_____d_____   7. Being educated doesn't mean having a head full of facts, but it does mean knowing how and where to find the facts.

_____e_____   8. The insensitive TV reporter shouted to his camera crew, "Make sure you get some close-ups of the accident victims!"

_____a_____   9. The supermarket is having specials this week on ground beef, coffee, and cereal.

_____b_____   10. On the other hand, the store has raised its prices on fish and milk.

Name _____ Section _____ Date _____

Score: (Number right) _____ × 10 = _____ %

■ **Comma: Test 3**

On the lines provided, write out the parts of each passage that need commas. Be sure to include the commas.

Note   To help you master the comma, explanations are given for half of the items.

1. The principal announced in a loud voice "Please welcome our graduates!" The graduating class wearing royal blue caps and gowns then marched into the auditorium.

   a. ___*voice,"*_____

   A comma is needed to separate quoted words from the rest of the sentence.

   b. ___*class, wearing royal blue caps and gowns,*___

2. My psychology class is very practical. We've learned about causes of stress everyday defense mechanisms and coping skills. In addition I now understand a good deal about the anger I have toward my parents.

   a. ___*stress, everyday defense mechanisms,*_____

   Commas are needed to separate the items in a series.

   b. ___*addition,*_____

3. A fire siren outside woke Kim at 5:30 so she got dressed and went for an early morning run. "You're up bright and early" a neighbor called to her.

   a. ___*5:30,*_____

   Put a comma before the word that joins two complete thoughts.

   b. ___*early,"*_____

4. Alvin who weighs 260 pounds works as a bouncer in a nightclub. When he tells people it's time to leave few of them argue with Alvin.

   a. ___*Alvin, who weighs 260 pounds,*_____

   Commas are needed around the words that interrupt the first sentence.

   b. ___*leave,*_____

5. Home from his first day at kindergarten the little boy stumbled into the house. He dropped his brightly colored book bag on the floor collapsed on the couch and promptly fell asleep.

   a. ___*kindergarten,*_____

   Put a comma after the introductory words.

   b. ___*floor, collapsed on the couch,*_____

Name _____   Section _____   Date _____

Score: (Number right) _____ × 10 = _____ %

■ Comma: Test 4

On the lines provided, write out the parts of each passage that need commas. Be sure to include the commas.

1. The trees especially the newly planted maples were badly damaged by the construction trucks. Broken branches oozing bark and wilted leaves were all signs that the trees might die.

   a. _trees, especially the newly planted maples,_____

   b. _branches, oozing bark,_____

2. After Gerald smashed the front end of the family car he called his parents. "I wasn't driving carelessly" he said. "The other driver was entirely at fault. Even he admits he caused the accident."

   a. _car,_____

   b. _carelessly,"_____

3. The cable company despite its claim of providing superior service has not been welcomed in our town. High prices power outages and limited channel coverage are all reasons why the company is unpopular.

   a. _company, despite its claim of providing superior service,_____

   b. _prices, power outages,_____

4. P. T. Barnum the master showman once hitched an elephant to a plow in order to promote his circus. As a result it is still a crime in North Carolina to plow a field with an elephant.

   a. _Barnum, the master showman,_____

   b. _result,_____

5. Early in the twentieth century women did not have the right to vote. That was not the only injustice experienced by women. Many people thought that higher education was wasted on women so very few women had the opportunity to attend college.

   a. _century,_____

   b. _on women,_____

Name _____   Section _____   Date _____

Score: (Number right) _____ × 10 = _____ %

■ **Comma: Test 5**

On the lines provided, write the word or words in each sentence that need to be followed by a comma. Be sure to include the commas. One comma rule applies in each sentence.

Note   To help you maste   the comma, explanations are given for half of the items.

¹Edgar Allan Poe the famous American short-story writer died in 1849. ²He was drunk alone and friendless at his death. ³His family purchased a tombstone for him but it was smashed on its way to the cemetery by a runaway freight train. ⁴Because his family could not afford another one Poe was buried in an unmarked grave. ⁵A group of Baltimore teachers admirers of Poe's work began to raise money for a tombstone. ⁶They held fund-raisers asked for donations invested what they earned and waited. ⁷After ten long years they raised the $1,000 they needed. ⁸The newspaperman H. L. Mencken wrote angrily "During all this time not a single American author of position gave the project any aid." ⁹The Baltimore group made it possible for teachers students or anyone who admires Poe's work to visit his grave. ¹⁰Twenty-six years after his death Edgar Allan Poe finally had a tombstone bearing his name.

1. _Poe, the famous American short-story writer,_ _____
   Use commas around interrupting words in a sentence.

2. _drunk, alone,_ _____

3. _him,_ _____
   Use a comma before a word that joins two complete thoughts.

4. _one,_ _____

5. _teachers, admirers of Poe's work,_ _____
   Use commas around interrupting words in a sentence.

6. _fund-raisers, asked for donations, invested what they earned,_ _____

7. _years,_ _____
   Use a comma after introductory material.

8. _angrily,_ _____

9. _teachers, students,_ _____
   Use commas to separate items in a series.

10. _death,_ _____

Name _____   Section _____   Date _____
                                                   Score: (Number right) _____ × 10 = _____ %

■ Comma: Test 6

On the lines provided, write the word or words in each sentence that need to be followed by a comma. Be sure to include the commas. One comma rule applies in each sentence.

[1] I love old-fashioned horror films that feature vampires werewolves mummies and zombies. [2] The monster movie I love best of all is *Frankenstein* but it was only recently that I read the original book by that name. [3] I was surprised to learn that its author Mary Shelley was very young. [4] The daughter of scholars Mary was an intelligent and talented young woman. [5] She eloped at seventeen with Percy Shelley a well-known poet and traveled to Switzerland. [6] In Switzerland, their party included Mary her husband another poet (Lord Byron) and Byron's physician. [7] Someone in the group said "Let's each write a story about the supernatural." [8] Mary's contribution a story about a living creature made from dead bodies was *Frankenstein*. [9] The story published when Mary was twenty-one years old became an instant classic. [10] Because of its wide appeal it has been the subject of many movies—and nightmares.

1. vampires, werewolves, mummies, _____

2. Frankenstein, _____

3. author, Mary Shelley, _____

4. scholars, _____

5. Shelley, a well-known poet, _____

6. Mary, her husband, another poet (Lord Byron), _____

7. said, _____

8. contribution, a story about a living creature made from dead bodies, ___

9. story, published when Mary was twenty-one years old, _____

10. appeal, _____

9 Apostrophe

Seeing What You Know

Insert apostrophes where needed in the four sentences below. Then read the explanations that follow.

1. Its impossible for water to run uphill.

2. The prosecutor cant try the date-rape case until next month.

3. No one likes the registrars new procedures for dropping a course.

4. The omelets at the Greens diner are the best in town. Mrs. Green is the chef, and her husband is the host.

Understanding the Answers

1. **It's** impossible for water to run uphill.
   It's is the contraction of the words *it is.* The apostrophe takes the place of the letter *i,* which has been left out.

2. The prosecutor **can't** try the date-rape case until next month.
   Can't is the contraction of the words *can not.* The apostrophe shows that two letters, *n* and *o,* have been left out.

3. No one likes the **registrar's** new procedures for dropping a course.
   The apostrophe plus *s* shows that the new procedures belong to the registrar. The apostrophe goes after the last letter of *registrar. Likes* does not get an apostrophe; it is a verb. *Procedures* also does not get an apostrophe, because it is not possessive. It is a plural word meaning "more than one procedure."

4. The omelets at the **Greens'** diner are the best in town. Mrs. Green is the chef, and her husband is the host.
   The apostrophe after the *s* shows that the Greens own the diner. With possessive plural words ending in *s,* the apostrophe alone shows possession. *Omelets* does not need an apostrophe, because it is simply a plural word meaning "more than one omelet."

The apostrophe is a punctuation mark with two main purposes. It is used in a **contraction** to show that one or more letters have been left out of a word. The apostrophe is also used to show **possession**—that is, to show that something belongs to someone or something.

APOSTROPHE IN CONTRACTIONS

A contraction is formed when two words are combined to make a new word. The apostrophe takes the place of the letter or letters omitted in forming the contraction. It goes where the missing letters used to be.

Here are a few common contractions:

I + am = **I'm** (the letter *a* in *am* has been left out)

it + is = **it's** (the *i* in *is* has been left out)

does + not = **doesn't** (the *o* in *not* has been left out)

do + not = **don't** (the *o* in *not* has been left out)

she + will = **she'll** (the *wi* in *will* has been left out)

you + would = **you'd** (the *woul* in *would* has been left out)

will + not = **won't** (*o* takes the place of *ill;* the *o* in *not* has been left out)

Contractions are commonly used in everyday speech and writing, as seen in this passage:

Let's go to the movies tonight. *There's* a film *I've* been wanting to see, but it *hasn't* been in town until now. *Didn't* you say *you've* been wanting to see it too? *Shouldn't* we ask Michael and Ana to go with us? *They're* always ready to see a good film. And they *don't* have anything to do this evening.

Practice 1

In the spaces provided, write the contractions of the words in parentheses.

1. When the timer goes off, *(you will)* ____you'll____ know *(it is)* ____it's____ time to take the potatoes out of the microwave.

2. *(I would)* ____I'd____ like to speak to the person *(who is)* ____who's____ in charge of the shoe department.

3. *(What is)* ____What's____ the answer to the question *(that is)* ____that's____ at the bottom of the page?

4. It *(is not)* ____isn't____ fair that some companies *(are not)* ____aren't____ hiring older workers.

5. The game show contestants *(did not)* ____didn't____ win the trip to Hawaii, but *(they are)* ____they're____ getting a box of pineapples as a consolation prize.

Four Confusing Pairs

Four contractions that can cause problems are ***they're*** (meaning *they are*), ***it's*** (meaning *it is* or *it has*), ***you're*** (meaning *you are*), and ***who's*** (meaning *who is*). They are easily confused with the possessive forms ***their*** (meaning *belonging to them*), ***its*** (meaning *belonging to it*), ***your*** (meaning *belonging to you*), and ***whose*** (meaning *belonging to whom*). Notice how each of these words is used in the sentences below:

> **They're** *(they are)* very angry about the damage done to **their** new mailbox *(the new mailbox belonging to them)*.
>
> **It's** *(it is)* a shame that your car has blown **its** engine *(the engine belonging to it)*.
>
> **Your** parents *(the parents belonging to you)* said that **you're** *(you are)* supposed to be home by midnight.
>
> **Who's** *(who is)* the person **whose** car *(the car belonging to whom)* is taking up two parking spaces?

Practice 2

Underline the correct word in each set of parentheses.

1. (It's, <u>Its</u>) too late now to give the dog (it's, <u>its</u>) bath.

2. Have Matt and Sara told (they're, <u>their</u>) parents that (<u>they're</u>, their) planning to start their own business?

3. (<u>Who's</u>, Whose) going to tell me (who's, <u>whose</u>) drink this is?

4. I think that (you're, <u>your</u>) best quality is (you're, <u>your</u>) sense of humor.

5. (<u>It's</u>, Its) revealing that only four pieces of United States currency have had women's pictures on (they're, <u>their</u>) front or back sides. The women (who's, <u>whose</u>) faces have been on U.S. money are Martha Washington, Pocahontas, Susan B. Anthony, and Sacajawea. What's (<u>your</u>, you're) guess as to why this has happened?

THE APOSTROPHE TO SHOW POSSESSION

To show that something belongs to someone or something, we could say, for example, *the truck owned by Sally, the radial tires belonging to the car,* or *the Great Dane of the neighbor.* But it's much simpler to say the following:

> *Sally's* truck
>
> *the car's* radial tires
>
> *the neighbor's* Great Dane

To make a singular word (or a plural word not ending in *s*) possessive, add an apostrophe plus an *s.* To decide *what* to make possessive, ask yourself the following:

1   Who or what is owned?

2   Who or what owns something?

Then put the apostrophe plus an *s* after the name of the owner.
    For example, look at the following word group:

the truck owned by Sally

First ask yourself, "What is owned?" The answer is *the truck*. Then ask, "Who is the owner?" The answer is *Sally*. So add an apostrophe plus *s* after the name of the owner: *Sally's truck*. The apostrophe plus *s* shows that the truck belongs to Sally.
    Here is another example:

the toys belonging to the children

Again, ask yourself, "What is owned?" The answer is *toys*. Then ask, "Who is the owner?" The answer is *the children*. So add an apostrophe plus *s* after the name of the owner: *the children's toys*. The apostrophe plus *s* shows that the toys belong to the children.

Notes

1   An apostrophe plus *s* is used to show possession, even with a singular word that already ends in *s:*

Tess**'s** purse (the purse belonging to Tess)

the boss**'s** car (the car owned by the boss)

2   But an apostrophe alone is used to show possession with a plural word that ends in *s:*

several students**'** complaints (the complaints of several students)

the two teams**'** agreement (the agreement of the two teams)

Practice 3

Two apostrophes are needed to show possession in each sentence below. In each space provided, write the word or words that need the apostrophe (the owner) as well as what is owned. The first sentence is done for you as an example.

1. The spiders web glistened with moisture from last nights rain.

    spider's web   *last night's rain*

2. The mail carriers job is not made any easier by that mans vicious dog.

    mail carrier's job   *that man's vicious dog*

3. Everyones assignment is to prepare a two-minute speech for Mondays class.

    Everyone's assignment   *Monday's class*

4. Ben Franklins inventions were often a combination of other peoples ideas.

Ben Franklin's inventions   _people's ideas_

5. Doriss grades are better than both of her brothers grades ever were.

Doris's grades   _her brothers' grades_

When Not to Use an Apostrophe: In Plurals and Verbs

People sometimes confuse possessive and plural forms of words. Remember that a plural is formed simply by adding an *s* to a word; no apostrophe is used. Look at the sentence below to see which words are plural and which are possessive:

Tina's new boots have silver buckles.

The words *boots* and *buckles* are plurals—there is more than one boot, and there is more than one buckle. But *Tina's,* the word with the apostrophe plus *s,* is possessive. Tina owns the boots.

Also, many verbs end with just an *s*—for example, the word *owns* in the sentence "Tina owns the boots." Do not put an apostrophe in a verb.

Practice 4

In the spaces provided under each sentence, add the one apostrophe needed and explain why the other words ending in *s* do not get apostrophes.

Example   The little boys daily temper tantrum seems to last for hours.

boys: _boy's, meaning "belonging to the little boy"_

seems: _verb_

hours: _plural meaning "more than one hour"_

1. One of the police officers asked to see my owners card.

officers: _plural meaning "more than one officer"_

owners: _owner's, meaning "belonging to the owner"_

2. That old storefronts grimy window has not been cleaned in many years.

storefronts: _storefront's, meaning "belonging to the storefront"_

years: _plural meaning "more than one year"_

3. The managers mood is much better after she gives out the assignments for the day.

managers: _manager's, meaning "belonging to the manager"_

gives: _verb_

assignments: _plural meaning "more than one assignment"_

4. This years new television shows are much worse than the programs of past seasons.

years: _year's, meaning "belonging to this year"_

shows: _plural meaning "more than one show"_

programs: _plural meaning "more than one program"_

seasons: _plural meaning "more than one season"_

5. The motor of our sons old car coughs and wheezes whenever it starts.

sons: _son's, meaning "belonging to our son"_

coughs: _verb_

wheezes: _verb_

starts: _verb_

6. One of Theos failings is jumping to conclusions.

Theos: _Theo's, meaning "belonging to Theo"_

failings: _plural meaning "more than one failing"_

conclusions: _plural meaning "more than one conclusion"_

7. Dieters should drink eight glasses of water a day because of waters ability to make the stomach feel more full.

Dieters: _plural meaning "more than one dieter"_

glasses: _plural meaning "more than one glass"_

waters: _water's, meaning "belonging to water"_

8. On the game reserve, dozens of elephants crowded around the two water holes edges.

dozens: _plural meaning "more than one dozen"_

elephants: _plural meaning "more than one elephant"_

water holes: _water holes', meaning "belonging to the two water holes"_

edges: _plural meaning "more than one edge"_

Note   Additional information about the apostrophe appears on page 218.

Name _____   Section _____   Date _____

■   Apostrophe: Test 1

Each of the sentences below contains one word that needs an apostrophe. Write each word, with its apostrophe, in the space provided.

Note   To help you master the apostrophe, explanations are given for half of the sentences.

1. The teachers broken leg kept her out of class for two weeks.

   _____ *teacher's* _____   The broken leg belongs to the teacher. *Weeks* is plural.

2. That insurance companys best customers are construction workers.

   _____ *company's* _____

3. Im planning to take a night school course next semester.

   _____ *I'm* _____   An apostrophe should take the place of the missing *a* in the contraction.

4. The students know that they cant fool Mrs. Striker with phony excuses.

   _____ *can't* _____

5. The huge green frogs sticky tongue soon captured several flies.

   _____ *frog's* _____   The frog owns the sticky tongue. *Flies* is a simple plural.

6. Endorphins, the bodys natural painkillers, are released when people exercise.

   _____ *body's* _____

7. A sign in front of the store entrance says, "Dont even *think* of parking here!"

   _____ *Don't* _____   *Don't* is a contraction of *do not,* with the *o* in *not* left out. *Says* is a verb.

8. Its supposed to rain for the next three days, so we can skip watering the lawn.

   _____ *It's* _____

9. A tornado destroyed the barns roof, but no animals were killed.

   _____ *barn's* _____   The roof belongs to the barn. *Animals* is a simple plural.

10. Even though they live a thousand miles apart, the two brothers relationship has remained strong through the years.

   _____ *brothers'* _____

To the Instructor   Additional tests on the apostrophe can be found in the *Instructor's Manual.*

Name _____   Section _____   Date _____

Score: (Number right) _____ × 10 = _____%

■ Apostrophe: Test 2

Each of the sentences below contains one word that needs an apostrophe. Write each word, with its apostrophe, in the space provided.

1. The shrinking of Earths ozone layer will result in rising temperatures.

   _____Earth's_____

2. When the ballparks gates opened, hundreds of fans were already waiting outside.

   _____ballpark's_____

3. Why should Leroy forgive your insult when you havent even apologized?

   _____haven't_____

4. Many of the streets residents have lived there for at least twenty years.

   _____street's_____

5. If the canary hasnt eaten its food by morning, you should take the canary to the veterinarian.

   _____hasn't_____

6. Baby-sitters dont usually agree to take care of those twins a second time.

   _____don't_____

7. More than one-fourth of the librarys books are missing from the shelves.

   _____library's_____

8. My grandmothers hairdo looks the same today as it did when she was twenty.

   _____grandmother's_____

9. I went to the post office, but its open only until noon on Saturdays.

   _____it's_____

10. Ramona couldnt start either of her cars, so she had to call a tow truck.

    _____couldn't_____

Name _____   Section _____   Date _____

■ Apostrophe: Test 3

Each of the short passages below contains two words that need apostrophes. Underline the words that need apostrophes. Then write each word, with its apostrophe, in the space provided.

Note   To help you master the apostrophe, explanations are given for the first sentence in each passage.

1. <u>Gregs</u> jeans should go into the ragbag. <u>Theyve</u> got to be at least fifteen years old.

   a. _____Greg's_____   The jeans belong to Greg.

   b. _____They've_____

2. <u>Whos</u> the person in charge of repairs around here? The copy <u>machines</u> red light is flashing again.

   a. _____Who's_____   An apostrophe should take the place of the

   b. _____machine's_____   missing *i* in the contraction.

3. "<u>Im</u> surprised that you take my grades so seriously," said Ned to his father. "Grades are no measure of a <u>persons</u> true worth."

   a. _____I'm_____   An apostrophe should take the place of the

   b. _____person's_____   missing *a* in the contraction.

4. <u>Kates</u> tights began to slip down to her knees as she walked back from the school stage. She <u>couldnt</u> do anything about it, so she kept her head down and hoped nobody would notice.

   a. _____Kate's_____   The tights belong to Kate.

   b. _____couldn't_____

5. A tiny crack appeared in the fish <u>tanks</u> corner. The goldfish looked unconcerned, but their owner <u>didnt</u> feel as calm.

   a. _____tank's_____   The corner belongs to the fish tank.

   b. _____didn't_____

■ Apostrophe: Test 4

Each of the short passages below contains two words that need apostrophes. Underline the words that need apostrophes. Then write each word, with its apostrophe, in the space provided.

1. The <u>janitors</u> job is made more difficult by thoughtless students. They hide his brooms and dump wastebaskets in the school <u>buildings</u> corridors.

    a. _____janitor's_____

    b. _____building's_____

2. The <u>books</u> cover shows a beautiful woman and a handsome man in each <u>others</u> arms. That is odd, because the book is not a love story at all.

    a. _____book's_____

    b. _____other's_____

3. "<u>Ricks</u> sneakers are in the middle of the kitchen floor," his father said. "So <u>hes</u> sure to be around here somewhere."

    a. _____Rick's_____

    b. _____he's_____

4. Some <u>peoples</u> lack of consideration is beyond belief. Our neighbors, for example, have parties every Saturday night where they sing and play loud music until dawn. And they <u>havent</u> invited us to a single one.

    a. _____people's_____

    b. _____haven't_____

5. "<u>Youre</u> not thinking of asking me for my car keys again, are you?" Ivan said to his sixteen-year-old daughter. "Getting a <u>drivers</u> license does not mean you automatically get a car to go with it."

    a. _____You're_____

    b. _____driver's_____

Name _____ Section _____ Date _____

Score: (Number right) _____ × 10 = _____ %

■ Apostrophe: Test 5

Each sentence in the following passage contains a word that requires an apostrophe. Underline the ten words. Then, on the lines following the passage, write the corrected form of each word.

Note   To help you master the apostrophe, explanations are given for five of the sentences.

¹When I was in high school, my family lived near Chicago, and my sister and I enjoyed the citys museums, parks, and zoos. ²Ive got many happy memories of time spent there; however, one visit was a different story. ³We were walking down the sidewalk eating hot dogs, enjoying the suns warmth on a beautiful May day. ⁴My sister said, "Lets feed the pigeons." ⁵I knelt on the sidewalk and began throwing bits of bread to the hungry birds, and then I felt someones hands closing around my neck from behind. ⁶I wasnt scared because I thought it was just my sister goofing around. ⁷Suddenly I heard her scream, "Whos that?" ⁸I realized a strangers hands were beginning to choke me. ⁹I jumped up, ran as fast as I could, and looked back to see an unshaven man in a ragged raincoat laughing at me and calling, "Im going to catch you!" ¹⁰He didnt follow us, and I never saw him again, but I had nightmares about him for weeks.

1. ____city's____   The museums, parks, and zoos belong to the city.
2. ____I've____
3. ____sun's____   The writer means "the warmth of the sun."
4. ____Let's____
5. ____someone's____   Someone owns the hands.
6. ____wasn't____
7. ____Who's____   The contraction of *who is* needs an apostrophe.
8. ____stranger's____
9. ____I'm____   The contraction of *I am* needs an apostrophe.
10. ____didn't____

Name _____   Section _____   Date _____

Score: (Number right) _____ × 10 = _____%

■ Apostrophe: Test 6

Each sentence in the following passage contains a word that requires an apostrophe. Underline the ten words. Then, on the lines following the passage, write the corrected form of each word.

[1]One of <u>historys</u> most fascinating figures is Cleopatra, a queen of ancient Egypt. [2]She was born in the year 69 B.C., and in keeping with one of the ancient Egyptian traditions, she became her <u>brothers</u> wife when she was made queen. [3]Her brother soon drove her from <u>Egypts</u> throne, however, and she began making plans to go to war against him. [4]When <u>Cleopatras</u> beauty and charm caught the eye of the Roman general Julius Caesar, they became lovers. [5]<u>Caesars</u> feelings for Cleopatra were so strong that he went to war for her, killing her brother. [6]She became queen again, marrying a younger brother, but it <u>wasnt</u> long before she poisoned her new husband. [7]Later on, Caesar was murdered, and Cleopatra became the mistress of one of <u>Romes</u> most powerful military figures, Mark Antony. [8]But when <u>Antonys</u> soldiers were defeated in battle, Cleopatra agreed to join the plot of an enemy, Octavian, by pretending to commit suicide. [9]Antony <u>didnt</u> want to live without her, so he killed himself. [10]When she <u>couldnt</u> persuade Octavian to become her lover and ally, Cleopatra put an end to her own violent life.

1. _____history's_____
2. _____brother's_____
3. _____Egypt's_____
4. _____Cleopatra's_____
5. _____Caesar's_____
6. _____wasn't_____
7. _____Rome's_____
8. _____Antony's_____
9. _____didn't_____
10. _____couldn't_____

10 Quotation Marks

Seeing What You Know

Insert quotation marks or underlines as needed in the following sentences. One sentence does not need quotation marks. Then read the explanations below.

1. The mechanic said,"Your car needs more than a tune-up."

2. "To tell you the truth,"said my husband,"I'm thinking of quitting my job."

3. My sister called to say that she needed heart surgery.

4. According to <u>The Book of Answers</u>, the most widely sung song in the English-speaking world is"Happy Birthday to You."

Understanding the Answers

1. The mechanic said, "Your car needs more than a tune-up."
   The words *Your car needs more than a tune-up* need quotation marks. These are the exact words that the mechanic said. Since *Your* is the first word of a quoted sentence, it is capitalized.

2. "To tell you the truth," said my husband, "I'm thinking of quitting my job."
   Each of the two word groups spoken by the husband, since they are his exact words, needs a set of quotation marks.

3. My sister called to say that she needed heart surgery.
   The words *that she needed heart surgery* are not the speaker's exact words. (Her exact words would have been "I need heart surgery.") In such an indirect quotation, no quotation marks are used.

4. According to <u>The Book of Answers</u>, the most widely sung song in the English-speaking world is "Happy Birthday to You."
   Titles of short works, such as songs, are put in quotation marks. Titles of longer works, such as books, are either italicized or underlined.

Quotation marks enclose the exact words of a speaker or writer. Quotation marks also set off the title of a short work.

QUOTATION MARKS TO SET OFF THE WORDS OF A SPEAKER OR WRITER

Use quotation marks to set off the exact words of a speaker or writer.

> After the bombing of Pearl Harbor, President Franklin Roosevelt described the day as "a date which will live in infamy."
> (President Roosevelt's exact words are enclosed between quotation marks.)

> "When we're done with the dishes," said Terry, "we'll be ready to go."
> (Terry's exact words are set off by two sets of quotation marks. The words *said Terry* are not included in the quotation marks since they were not spoken by him.)

> Opal told her uncle, "We'll serve dinner at seven o'clock. If you can't make it then, stop in later for dessert."
> (Because the two sentences give Opal's words without interruption, they require just one set of quotation marks.)

> "Experience," wrote Vernon Law, "is a hard teacher because she gives the test first, the lesson afterward."
> (The exact words that Law wrote are enclosed in quotation marks.)

Punctuation note   Quoted material is usually set off from the rest of the sentence by a comma. When the comma comes at the end of quoted material, it is included inside the quotation marks. The same is true for a period, exclamation point, or question mark that ends quoted material:

Incorrect:	"If it rains", said Connie, "the ball game will be canceled".
Correct:	"If it rains," said Connie, "the ball game will be canceled."

Notice, too, that a quoted sentence begins with a capital letter, even when it is preceded by other words.

Incorrect:	Marco said, "let's go to the fair tonight."
Correct:	Marco said, "Let's go to the fair tonight."

Practice 1

Insert quotation marks where needed.

1. "My throat is so sore I can't talk," Larry whispered.

2. Wilson Mizner once said, "Life's a tough proposition, and the first hundred years are the hardest."

3. "Don't go in that door!" the audience shouted to the actor on the movie screen.

4. Louise was just about to park in back of the administration building when she saw a sign reading, "Parking By Permit Only—Violators Will Be Towed."

5. "After all the trouble the customers at that table have caused," grumbled the waitress, "they'd better leave a decent tip."

Direct and Indirect Quotations

Often we communicate someone's spoken or written thoughts without repeating the exact words used. We quote indirectly by putting the message into our own words. Such **indirect quotations** do not require quotation marks. The word *that* often signals an indirect quotation.

The following example shows how the same material could be handled as either a direct or an indirect quotation.

Direct Quotation

Keshia said, "If I pass all my exams, I will graduate this June."
(These are Keshia's exact words, so they are put in quotation marks.)

Indirect Quotation

Keshia said that if she passes all her exams, she will graduate this June.
(These are *not* Keshia's exact words. No quotation marks are used.)

Practice 2

Turn each of the following indirect quotations into a direct quotation. You will have to change some of the words as well as add quotation marks. The first one is done for you as an example.

1. Emmet asked if he could borrow my dictionary.
   Emmet asked, "Could I borrow your dictionary?"

2. Coach Hodges told Lori that she had played an outstanding game.
   Coach Hodges told Lori, "You played an outstanding game."

3. Manuel insisted that his new glasses haven't improved his vision one bit.
   Manuel insisted, "My new glasses haven't improved my vision one bit."

4. The detective exclaimed that he knew the murderer's identity.
   The detective exclaimed, "I know the murderer's identity!"

5. I told Dr. Patton that I hadn't been to a dentist since high school.
   I told Dr. Patton, "I haven't been to a dentist since high school."

QUOTATION MARKS TO SET OFF THE TITLES OF SHORT WORKS

The titles of short works are set off in quotation marks. Short works include short stories, newspaper and magazine articles, song titles, poems, episodes of television shows, and chapters of books.

Note   The titles of longer works, such as books, newspapers, magazines, plays, movies, television series, and albums, should be underlined when written. (When longer works are mentioned in printed material, their titles are usually set in *italic type.*)

"The Body," a short story by Stephen King, was later made into the movie Stand By Me.

I remember memorizing Robert Frost's poem "Stopping by Woods on a Snowy Evening" when I was in eighth grade.

"Jimmy's World," an article in the Washington Times about a drug-addicted child, won a Pulitzer Prize, but the story was later proved to be a fake.

Bing Crosby's recording of the song "White Christmas" is still one of the biggest sellers of all time.

Practice 3

Insert quotation marks or underlines where needed in the sentences below.

1. I bought a copy of the cookbook titled The Good Food Book because I wanted to read the chapter called "How to Eat More and Weigh Less."

2. Professor Porter told the class that the next exam would be on the short story "The Garden Party."

3. Whenever Gina sees the movie The Sound of Music, the song near the end, "Climb Every Mountain," makes her cry.

4. Randy couldn't remember whether he had read the article "All Gamblers Lose" in Newsweek or in Time.

5. An article called "Will the Circle Be Unbroken?" in The Atlantic Monthly includes interviews with four people about death and dying.

Note   Additional information about quotation marks appears on pages 219–220.

Name _____   Section _____   Date _____

Score: (Number right) _____ × 12.5 = _____ %

■ **Quotation Marks: Test 1**

On the lines provided, rewrite the following sentences, adding quotation marks as needed. Two of the sentences do not need quotation marks.

Note   To help you master quotation marks, explanations are given for half of the sentences.

1. Beverly said, I'm not doing your share of the work.

    Beverly said, "I'm not doing your share of the work."

    Beverly's words and the period at the end of the sentence should be included within quotation marks.

2. Stop shouting or you'll wake the children, Chris whispered.

    "Stop shouting or you'll wake the children," Chris whispered.

3. I'm furious, shouted Kareem, about your constant lies!

    "I'm furious," shouted Kareem, "about your constant lies!"

    Each of the two parts of Kareem's statement requires a set of quotation marks. The words *shouted Kareem* do not get quotation marks because they are not part of his statement.

4. You are fortunate, Vera said, to have a job you enjoy.

    "You are fortunate," Vera said, "to have a job you enjoy."

5. Carole said that she was staying home for the weekend.

    No quotation marks are needed.

    Carole's message is communicated indirectly.

6. The student explained that he'd fallen asleep during class.

    No quotation marks are needed.

7. Is that a wig? Can I touch it? the little girl asked her uncle.

    "Is that a wig? Can I touch it?" the little girl asked her uncle.

    The little girl's two questions are uninterrupted, so they are included within one set of quotation marks.

8. You're right! It is snowing! exclaimed Raymond.

    "You're right! It is snowing!" exclaimed Raymond.

To the Instructor   Additional tests on quotation marks can be found in the *Instructor's Manual.*

Name _____   Section _____   Date _____

Score: (Number right) _____ × 10 = _____ %

■ Quotation Marks: Test 2

On the lines provided, rewrite the part or parts of each sentence that need quotation marks. One of the ten items does not need quotation marks.

1. The waitress asked, Aren't you leaving me a tip?

   "Aren't you leaving me a tip?"

2. The food machines in the lunchroom should offer healthier choices, suggested Tran.

   "The food machines in the lunchroom should offer healthier choices,"

3. Those shoes, the salesclerk assured me, will never go out of style.

   "Those shoes," ..., "will never go out of style."

4. The bookstore manager told us that he couldn't buy back books with writing in them.

   No quotation marks are needed.

5. I told Ava that she was a cheat. It takes one to know one, she responded.

   "It takes one to know one,"

6. Can't you work any faster than that? the supervisor barked at the new stock boy.

   "Can't you work any faster than that?"

7. Did you read the funny article called What People Really Want for Christmas in today's newspaper?

   "What People Really Want for Christmas"

8. I'm afraid of only one thing, the Scarecrow told Dorothy. That's a lighted match.

   "I'm afraid of only one thing," ... "That's a lighted match."

9. The Black Cat and The Tell-Tale Heart are two of Edgar Allan Poe's most chilling stories.

   "The Black Cat" and "The Tell-Tale Heart"

10. Yogi Berra, who was famous for his odd remarks, once said, You can observe a lot just by watching.

    "You can observe a lot just by watching."

■ Quotation Marks: Test 3

Place quotation marks where needed in the short passages that follow. Each passage needs two sets of quotation marks.

Note   To help you master quotation marks, explanations are given for one set of quotation marks in each passage.

1. "May I ask you a personal question?"asked my nosy neighbor, as if she needed my permission."You may ask it, but I don't promise to answer it,"I replied.
   The neighbor's question should be set off with one set of quotation marks.

2. Benjamin Franklin is famous for his witty sayings. Many of them give advice on how to behave; others are comments on human nature. For instance, he once wrote,"To lengthen thy life, lessen thy meals."He also commented,"Three may keep a secret, if two of them are dead."
   Franklin's advice on behavior should be set off with one set of quotation marks.

3. When Mr. Benton asked to withdraw some money from his account, the bank teller said,"I'm sorry, but your account is overdrawn."Mr. Benton answered, "Nonsense, I must still have money in my account. See, I have lots of checks left."
   The teller's words should be set off with quotation marks.

4. I asked James how, if he couldn't find his shoes, he expected to get dressed for the wedding."I could always wear my sneakers,"he answered."We'll have to sit in back where nobody sees us, then,"I told him.
   James's exact words should be set off with one set of quotation marks.

5. This article titled"How to Find Your Perfect Mate"in *Cosmopolitan* is the dumbest thing I've ever read. It actually suggests that before you go on a first date, you ask your date,"Please fill out this questionnaire on your likes and dislikes."
   The title of an article is put in quotation marks.

Name _____   Section _____   Date _____

Score: (Number right) _____ × 10 = _____%

■ Quotation Marks: Test 4

Place quotation marks where needed in the short passages that follow. Each passage needs two sets of quotation marks.

1. "Lights out right now!" my mother shouted up the stairs. The lights were turned off, but a great deal of noise and giggling ensued. Mother waited patiently for things to quiet a bit and then called up, "You'll be too tired for school tomorrow if you don't get to sleep."

2. An angry-looking woman marched up to the customer service desk and slammed a large box on the counter. "You sold me this juicer, and now I want my money back," she told the clerk. "Every time I turn it on, it spits carrot pieces all over my kitchen table."

3. My father, never very excited about having visitors, once said, "I never try to make people feel at home. If they wanted to feel at home, they would have stayed there." He then quoted the famous saying, "Fish and visitors begin to smell after three days."

4. "Hey, you," called the homeless man sitting on the sidewalk. A well-dressed young man paused. "Are you talking to me?" he asked.

5. "You bet I am. How would you like to trade places with me?" said the homeless man. The young man smiled nervously and then said that he would prefer not to. The older man nodded. "I don't blame you," he said and lay back down on the pavement.

Name _____   Section _____   Date _____

Score: (Number right) _____ × 10 = _____ %

■ Quotation Marks: Test 5

Ten of the sentences in the passage below require a set of quotation marks. Insert the quotation marks where needed. On the lines provided at the bottom, write the numbers of the sentences to which you have added quotation marks.

Note   To help you master quotation marks, five of the sentences that need quotation marks are identified for you.

[1]Last summer I went with my husband Lenny to his ten-year high school reunion. [2]He kept telling me,"Oh, boy, are you going to love my old gang." [3]I'd heard a lot about the old gang, and I wondered about that."[4]Not only are we going to have a great time, but I'm going to be master of ceremonies," he announced.

[5]On the big night, we'd barely driven into the parking lot when we were surrounded by a crowd of apparently grown men shouting,"Li-zard! Li-zard! Lenny the Lizard has arrived!"[6]I turned and looked at my husband."[7]Lenny the Lizard?"I asked. [8]He didn't have time to answer."[9]Party time!"he roared, leaping out of the car and disappearing into the building.

[10]When I caught up with him, he was being hugged and kissed by a good-looking redhead."[11]Ooooohhhh," she said, looking me over."[12]You sure don't look like the type that Lenny would have married!"

[13]After a year or so we sat down to dinner. [14]There, people kept saying things like"Do you remember the time Jock dissected the frog and gave its heart to Diane on Valentine's Day?"[15]Everybody at the table would break up laughing at that point, while I was still waiting to hear what had happened.

[16]Finally it was time for Lenny to get up and speak. [17]He actually did a pretty good job, and he finished his remarks by asking the class members to introduce their spouses. [18]To get things started, he had me stand as he said,"And this is my wonderful wife, Betty."[19]Unfortunately, my name is Linda.

[20]When it's time for Lenny's twentieth, I'm going to stay home and write an article called"Surviving Your Spouse's Reunion."

1. Sentence __2__   6. Sentence __11__
2. Sentence __4__   7. Sentence __12__
3. Sentence __5__   8. Sentence __14__
4. Sentence __7__   9. Sentence __18__
5. Sentence __9__   10. Sentence __20__

Name _____   Section _____   Date _____

Score: (Number right) _____ × 10 = _____%

■ Quotation Marks: Test 6

Ten of the sentences in the passage below require a set of quotation marks. Insert the quotation marks where needed. On the lines provided at the bottom, write the numbers of the sentences to which you have added quotation marks.

[1]Our family recently hosted another family visiting from South America. [2]We soon learned from Mr. and Mrs. Rojas that the image people receive of American life in other countries is not always accurate.

[3]Soon after we picked the family up at the airport, Mrs. Rojas asked, "How many servants do you have?"[4]She was surprised to hear we didn't even know anyone who had servants. "[5]On American TV shows, everyone has cooks and maids!" she exclaimed.

[6]We stopped for a bite to eat on our way home. [7]As we walked toward the restaurant, a homeless man asked us for some change. "[8]You have beggars here?" Mr. Rojas said in astonishment. "[9]But on American TV shows, everyone is rich."

[10]During our meal, a couple of police officers came in to eat. [11]Mr. and Mrs. Rojas eyed them nervously. "[12]Maybe we should leave," Mr. Rojas said. "[13]Why?" my father asked in surprise. "[14]They have guns," replied Mr. Rojas. "[15]We know from American TV shows how often there is shooting."

[16]That night we had some neighbors in to meet the Rojas family. [17]We had a great time talking and laughing together while the children played hide-and-seek throughout the house. [18]One neighbor asked, "Well, what do you think about the United States now that you've spent a whole day in it?"[19]Mrs. Rojas laughed. "[20]I think I shouldn't believe everything I see on American TV shows!" she replied.

1. Sentence __3__   6. Sentence __13__

2. Sentence __5__   7. Sentence __14__

3. Sentence __8__   8. Sentence __15__

4. Sentence __9__   9. Sentence __18__

5. Sentence __12__   10. Sentence __20__

11 Other Punctuation Marks

Seeing What You Know

Add a period, a question mark, or an exclamation mark to each sentence that follows. Use a different end mark in each sentence. Then read the explanations below.

1. Half of all the people in America live in just eight of the fifty states.

2. Are you going to the high school reunion?

3. Stop that noise before I go crazy!

Insert a colon, a semicolon, and parentheses where needed in the following sentences.

4. Rocky Road(my favorite ice cream flavor)contains marshmallows and nuts.

5. The bearded man looked around the quiet bank;then he passed the teller a folded note. Two emotions showed on the teller's face:surprise and terror.

Insert a hyphen and dashes where needed in the following sentence.

6. Nobody not even her attorney believed the woman's odd-sounding alibi.

Understanding the Answers

1. states.   2. reunion?   3. crazy!

Sentence 1 makes a statement, so a period is needed. Sentence 2 asks a question and so must end with a question mark. Sentence 3 expresses strong feeling, so an exclamation point is appropriate.

4. (my favorite ice cream flavor)

The parentheses set off information that is not essential to the rest of the sentence.

5. bank; then . . . face: surprise

The semicolon connects two complete thoughts, each with its own subject and verb. The colon introduces an explanation of the idea stated just before the colon.

6. Nobody—not even her attorney—believed . . . odd-sounding alibi.

Dashes emphasize the words *not even her attorney*. A hyphen joins the two words that act together to describe the noun *alibi*.

This chapter first describes three marks of punctuation that are used to end a sentence: the period (.), the question mark (?), and the exclamation point (!). The chapter then describes five additional marks of punctuation: the colon (:), semicolon (;), hyphen (-), dash (—), and parentheses ( ).

PERIOD (.)

Use a period at the end of a statement, a mild command, or an indirect question.

> Only the female mosquito drinks blood.
>
> Go let the dog out.
>
> I wonder if it's going to rain.

The period is also used at the end of most abbreviations.

> Dr. Breslin   Mr. and Mrs. Liu   Ms. Barsky   M. A. degree

QUESTION MARK (?)

The question mark follows a direct question, as in the following examples.

> What's that green stuff in your hair?
>
> Have you seen the new Mel Gibson movie?
>
> "What did you put in this stew?" Grandpa asked.

Indirect questions, those that tell the reader about a question rather than ask it directly, do not require question marks. They end with periods.

> Please ask the bus driver if we can get off at Spruce Street.
>
> I wonder if I'll ever see Ali again.
>
> Gina asked Stan to jump-start her car.

EXCLAMATION POINT (!)

The exclamation point shows that a word or statement expresses excitement or another strong feeling.

> Look out for that car!
>
> I've won the lottery!
>
> If you insult my dog again, I'll let go of the leash!

Note   Exclamation points lose their power if they are used too frequently. When they are used occasionally and for good reason, they add drama to a paragraph.

Practice 1

Place a period, question mark, or exclamation point at the end of each of the following sentences.

1. When does the library close?
2. Many rush-hour drivers are impatient and aggressive.
3. Hurry up if you want to see the cat giving birth!
4. Although I followed the directions closely, the computer program didn't run.
5. Please put all cans and glass bottles in the recycling bins.

COLON (:)

The colon says, in essence, "Keep reading. Here comes something important." It has three uses:

To introduce a list. The bag lady's possessions were few: a shopping cart, a sleeping bag, and two or three ragged garments.

To introduce a long or literary quotation. Charles Dickens begins his classic novel *A Tale of Two Cities* with these well-known words: "It was the best of times, it was the worst of times, it was the age of wisdom, it was the age of foolishness. . . ."

To introduce a final fact or explanation. There's only one explanation for Maude's behavior: she's jealous.

SEMICOLON (;)

Unlike the colon, which indicates "Go on," the semicolon says "Pause here." Semicolons are used between two complete thoughts in two ways:

To join two complete thoughts not connected by a joining word. Barry cleans the house and cooks; Lana does the laundry and the grocery shopping.

To join two complete statements with a transitional word. I've never liked my father-in-law; furthermore, he knows it.

Note   Other transitional words that may come after a semicolon include *however, moreover, therefore, thus, also, consequently, otherwise, nevertheless, then, now, in addition, in fact,* and *as a result.* (A longer list appears on page 214.)

Punctuation note   Put a comma after such transitional words.

HYPHEN (-)

The hyphen is used in two ways:

To join two or more words that act together to describe a noun. We found an excuse to walk away from the fast-talking salesman. (The hyphen shows that *fast* and *talking,* combined, describe the salesman; he talks fast.)

To divide a word at the end of a line of writing. If you ever visit California, I hope you'll come see me.

Note   Always divide a word between syllables, and never divide a word of only one syllable. Your dictionary will show you where syllable divisions occur.

DASH (—)

The dash indicates a dramatic pause. By using it, the writer is giving special emphasis to the words that the dash separates from the rest of the sentence.

> CPR sometimes—but not always—succeeds in reviving heart attack victims.
>
> Randy spotted his blind date sitting in the restaurant. He straightened his tie, waved confidently to her, swaggered into the room—and tripped and fell full-length on the carpet.

Note   To type a dash, type two hyphens. Do not add space before or after a dash.

PARENTHESES ( )

Parentheses show that the information inside them is less important than the other material presented.

> Professor Rodriguez (one of my favorite teachers) is going to retire this year.
>
> The assignments that follow (Exercises 1, 2, and 3) will help sharpen your understanding of everyday defense mechanisms.

Practice 2

Insert a colon, semicolon, hyphen, a dash or dashes, or parentheses where needed in each of the sentences below. Use only one kind of mark in each sentence.

1. A black-hatted man stood in the doorway.

2. My mother's college roommate(I think I've mentioned her to you before)has invited us to visit her in Florida.

3. As Snow White learned, apples aren't so good for you after all if they're poisoned.

4. The Swiss army knife came with many attachments:a screwdriver, tweezers, magnifying glass, toothpick, and four knife blades.

5. Many people find it very hard to stay on a diet;ads tempt them constantly with images of forbidden foods.

Note   Additional information about punctuation marks appears on pages 220–221.

Name _____ Section _____ Date _____

Score: (Number right) _____ × 12.5 = _____%

■ **Other Punctuation Marks: Test 1**

Each of the following sentences needs one of the kinds of punctuation marks in the box. In the space provided, write the letter of the mark needed. Then add that mark to the sentence. Each sentence requires a different punctuation mark.

Note   To help you master these punctuation marks, explanations are given for half of the sentences.

a	Period .	**e**	Semicolon ;
b	Question mark ?	**f**	Hyphen -
c	Exclamation point !	**g**	Dash or dashes —
d	Colon :	**h**	Parentheses ( )

_____*d*_____ 1. Three languages are spoken in Switzerland:German, French, and Italian.
German, French, and Italian is a list of items.

_____*b*_____ 2. Which of these offices is the one that processes student loans?

_____*f*_____ 3. My usually soft-spoken father began to shout angrily.
The words *soft* and *spoken* need to be joined into one descriptive unit.

_____*e*_____ 4. Monica barely needed to study in high school;however, she's finding college more difficult.

_____*g*_____ 5. If you ever and I mean ever leave the store unlocked again, you'll be fired immediately.
The phrase *and I mean ever* needs to be set off. It is being emphasized dramatically.

_____*h*_____ 6. Paula's suede shoes(the ones she'd bought in Florida)were chewed up by the puppy.

_____*c*_____ 7. Don't pick up that hot plate!
The statement is a strong one, which would probably be shouted.

_____*a*_____ 8. Warren spoke to the restaurant manager and asked if the air conditioning couldn't be turned down just a little.

To the Instructor   Additional tests on other punctuation marks can be found in the *Instructor's Manual.*

Name _____   Section _____   Date _____

Score: (Number right) _____ × 10 = _____%

■ Other Punctuation Marks: Test 2

Each of the following sentences needs one of the kinds of punctuation marks shown in the box below. In the space provided, write the letter of the mark needed. Then insert the punctuation into the sentence. Each punctuation mark is used at least once.

a	Period .	**e**	Semicolon ;
b	Question mark ?	**f**	Hyphen -
c	Exclamation point !	**g**	Dash or dashes —
d	Colon :	**h**	Parentheses ( )

_f_ 1. Motorists were angered by the slow-moving car in the fast lane.

_e_ 2. Dozens of birds flocked around the birdfeeder;a gray cat crept quietly toward them in the bushes below.

_c_ 3. "If you ever take money out of my purse again, I'm throwing you out of this house!' Michiko screamed at her teenage son.

_e_ 4. Sheila said she was going to visit her sick aunt;instead, she went to the track.

_g_ 5. The little girl looked very sad as she pulled her test out of her notebook then burst out laughing when her mother saw the A+ on it.

_h_ 6. The novel *Beloved* by Toni Morrison(who also wrote *The Bluest Eye*)is a powerful story about the painful legacy of slavery.

_d_ 7. There are two kinds of moviegoers I hate to sit near:those who talk constantly and those who blurt out what is going to happen next.

_a_ 8. "Hating people," wrote Harry Emerson Fosdick, "is like burning down your own house to get rid of a rat."

_b_ 9. The supervisor wondered out loud, "Does Sam ever admit that he made a mistake?"

_g_ 10. Henry Thompson was a respected businessman, Sunday school teacher, Scout leader and occasional bank robber.

Name _____   Section _____   Date _____

Score: (Number right) _____ × 10 = _____ %

■ **Other Punctuation Marks: Test 3**

Each of the following passages requires **two** of the punctuation marks shown in the box below. In the spaces provided, write the letters of the **two** marks needed in each passage. Then insert the correct punctuation. Each punctuation mark is used at least once.

Note   To help you master these punctuation marks, hints are provided for half of the corrections.

a	Period .	**e**	Semicolon ;
b	Question mark ?	**f**	Hyphen -
c	Exclamation point !	**g**	Dash or dashes —
d	Colon :	**h**	Parentheses ( )

a *b*   1. I watched my sister searching through the drawers. Finally I asked her what she was looking for. "Why do you have to know? she asked angrily.
I asked her what she was looking for is an indirect question.

d *h*   2. Jerry's mother once worked for the Peace Corps. She traveled to several countries:Thailand, India, Nepal, and Malaysia. She often told me(I visited their home many times)that Nepal was the most beautiful country in the world.
Thailand, India, Nepal, and Malaysia is a list of items.

g *a*   3. The door-to-door salesman seemed like such a shy, kind person that we invited him in for coffee. It was several hours later—when he was probably in the next state that we discovered he had robbed us.
The words *when he was probably in the next state* should be emphasized.

f *g*   4. When I came downstairs, the kitchen was deserted. A single half-eaten doughnut was all that remained in the box. I stared at the box I couldn't believe my eyes and shouted, "Who ate all the doughnuts?"
Half and *eaten* are acting together to describe a noun, *doughnut.*

e *c*   5. Ron glanced out the diner window onto the parking lot;then he jumped to his feet. "They're towing away my truck! he exclaimed as he ran out the door.
The word group beginning with *Ron glanced* is actually two complete thoughts that have been run together with no mark of punctuation between them.

Name _____   Section _____   Date _____

Score: (Number right) _____ × 10 = _____ %

■ Other Punctuation Marks: Test 4

Each of the following passages requires **two** of the punctuation marks shown in the box below. In the spaces provided, write the letters of the **two** marks needed in each passage. Then insert the correct punctuation. Each punctuation mark is used at least once.

a Period .	**e** Semicolon ;
b Question mark ?	**f** Hyphen -
c Exclamation point !	**g** Dash or dashes —
d Colon :	**h** Parentheses ( )

<u>f</u> <u>d</u> 1. The hard-working clerks in the billing office use humorous messages to remind people to pay their bills. Their current favorite is this one:"Dear Customer, You have been on our books for a year. We have carried you longer than your mother did."

<u>e</u> <u>h</u> 2. I helped my brother clean the house;otherwise, he never would have gotten it done in time. I swept under the radiators(a job he usually forgets)and dusted the furniture.

<u>a</u> <u>g</u> 3. Raoul dressed carefully for his big date.He wore his gray suit, new shoes, and a handsome shirt and tie. Just before he went out the door, he glanced in the mirror to admire himself and noticed he had forgotten to shave.

<u>h</u> <u>f</u> 4. During the tourist season(June through August)the population of the seaside town nearly doubles. Tourists come to enjoy cool sea breezes, fresh-caught seafood, and, best of all, splashing in the Atlantic.

<u>c</u> <u>b</u> 5. "I'd like to kill whoever keeps taking my pencils!" Sandy screamed. "Don't people realize I occasionally need to write something down?"

Name _____ Section _____ Date _____

Score: (Number right) _____ × 10 = _____ %

■ Other Punctuation Marks: Test 5

Each of the ten sentences in the passage below requires punctuation: a colon, semicolon, hyphen, dash or dashes, or parentheses. In each sentence, underline the place where punctuation is needed. Then write the corrections on the lines provided. When you write each correction, include the words before and after the punctuation mark.

Note   To help you master these punctuation marks, directions are given for half of the corrections.

¹Everyone has a bad dream at times moreover, people often have the same nightmare repeatedly. ²My friend Carla I've known her since kindergarten frequently dreams she is falling off a cliff. ³"It's always a slow motion fall," she says, adding, "I have lots of time to be terrified, but I never hit bottom." ⁴My roommate Cassie's nightmare is of a huge red boulder always exactly the same size and color rolling down a hill toward her. ⁵My father's dream has been the same for years a black cat is sitting on his chest, suffocating him. ⁶In my most frequent nightmare, I'm trying to walk somewhere my shoes are terribly slippery. ⁷I can see my destination often an exam room on campus, but I just can't get there. ⁸My sense of ever increasing frustration stays with me long after I wake up. ⁹Psychologists say that nightmares especially the recurring kind tell us a great deal about our inner fears. ¹⁰My particular fear seems obvious it's the fear that I'm incapable of reaching my goals.

1. _times; moreover_ _____ Add a semicolon.

2. _Carla (I've known her since kindergarten) frequently_ _____

3. _slow-motion_ _____ Add a hyphen.

4. _boulder—always exactly the same size and color—rolling_ _____

5. _years: a_ _____ Add a colon.

6. _somewhere; my_ _____

7. _destination (often an exam room on campus), but_ _____ Add parentheses.

8. _ever-increasing_ _____

9. _nightmares—especially the recurring kind—tell_ _____ Add two dashes.

10. _obvious: it's_ _____

Name _____ Section _____ Date _____
Score: (Number right) _____ × 10 = _____ %

■ Other Punctuation Marks: Test 6

Each of the ten sentences in the passage below requires punctuation: a colon, semicolon, hyphen, dash or dashes, or parentheses. In each sentence, underline the place where punctuation is needed. Then write the corrections on the lines provided. When you write each correction, include the words before and after the punctuation mark.

¹When Patti met Scott, she thought he was a nice looking guy with pleasant manners. ²She didn't know many people in town where she'd moved only recently so was pleased when he asked her out. ³They found they liked many of the same activities playing miniature golf, going on hikes, and watching basketball on TV. ⁴Patti enjoyed Scott's company however, Scott's feelings were more intense. ⁵Soon after they met only four weeks after their first date Scott insisted that Patti promise to marry him. ⁶When a surprised Patti refused, Scott's mild mannered personality changed dramatically. ⁷He began to call Patti frequently as many as twenty times a day to tell her that she belonged to him. ⁸Patti who was really a kind person hated to hurt his feelings. ⁹But Scott's scary personality change made her want to do just one thing get away. ¹⁰Eventually she moved and took a job in another state she left no forwarding address.

1. _nice-looking_____

2. _town (where she'd moved only recently) so____

3. _activities: playing_____

4. _company; however_____

5. _met—only four weeks after their first date—Scott_

6. _mild-mannered_____

7. _frequently—as many as twenty times a day—to_

8. _Patti (who was really a kind person) hated____

9. _thing: get_____

10. _state; she_____

12 Homonyms

Seeing What You Know

In the following sentences, underline each correct word in parentheses. Then read the explanations below.

1. (You're, Your) the only student (who's, whose) always (hear, here) on time.

2. (Its, It's) difficult to (break, brake) the habit of smoking.

3. I never (knew, new) that (there, they're) could be such a problem as having (too, to) little money to get through the month.

4. The Fergusons found that (their, there) dog had eaten the (hole, whole) ham.

5. The (plane, plain) had (two, too) engines, and one of them caught on fire.

Understanding the Answers

1. **You're** the only student **who's** always **here** on time.

   You're is the contraction of the words *you* and *are*. *Who's* is the contraction of the words *who is*. *Here* means "in this place."

2. **It's** difficult to **break** the habit of smoking.

   It's is the contraction of the words *it* and *is*. *Break* means "end."

3. I never **knew** that **there** could be such a problem as having **too** little money to get through the month.

   Knew is the past tense of *know*. *There* is used with forms of the verb *to be—is, are, was, were*, and so on. *Too* means "extremely."

4. The Fergusons found that **their** dog had eaten the **whole** ham.

   Their means "belonging to them." *Whole* means "entire."

5. The **plane** had **two** engines, and one of them caught on fire.

   Plane means "airplane." *Two* is the spelling of the number 2.

135

This chapter looks at a number of words that are mistaken for one another because they are **homonyms:** words that are pronounced the same (or almost the same) but are spelled differently and are different in meaning.

THE BIG FOUR

Of all frequently confused homonyms, the following four groups cause writers the most trouble:

its   *belonging to it*
it's   contraction of *it is*

If the house doesn't get **its** roof repaired soon, **it's** going to be full of water. (If the house doesn't get the roof *belonging to it* repaired, *it is* going to be full of water.)

It's a shame that the new restaurant lost **its** license. (*It is* a shame that the new restaurant lost the license *belonging to it.*)

their   *belonging to them*
there   (1) *in that place;* (2) used with *is, are, was, were,* and other forms of the verb *to be*
they're contraction of *they are*

The coach told the players that **there** was no excuse for **their** unprofessional behavior; **they're** going to run extra laps as punishment. (The coach told the players *there was* no excuse for the unprofessional behavior *belonging to them; they are* going to run extra laps as punishment.)

Their bodies were discovered over **there** in a shallow grave; tomorrow **there** will be an autopsy to determine the cause of death. (The bodies *belonging to them* were discovered over *in that place* in a shallow grave; tomorrow *there will be* [form of *to be*] an autopsy to determine the cause of death.)

to   (1) used before a verb, as in *to say;* (2) *toward*
too   (1) *overly* or *extremely;* (2) *also*
two   *the number 2*

It would be **too** confusing **to** name the baby Lucy; her mother and **two** of her aunts are named Lucy **too.** (It would be *overly* confusing *to name* [verb] the baby Lucy; her mother and *2* of her aunts are named Lucy *also.*)

Let's go **to** the mall **to** look for clothes, unless you are **too** tired. (Let's go *toward* the mall *to look* [verb] for clothes, unless you are *overly* tired.)

your   *belonging to you*
you're   contraction of *you are*

If **you're** going out in this downpour, take **your** umbrella. (If *you are* going out in this downpour, take the umbrella *belonging to you.*)

Do you think **your** family will be upset when they learn **you're** moving to Alaska? (Do you think the family *belonging to you* will be upset when they learn *you are* moving to Alaska?)

Practice

Underline the correct homonym in each group.

1. (Its, It's) a shame (its, it's) going to rain today; we won't be able to give the front porch (its, it's) second coat of paint.

2. (Their, There, They're) isn't any good reason to give the twins (their, there, they're) birthday presents early; (their, there, they're) just going to want more presents when the real birthday comes around.

3. Having (to, too, two) read and take notes on (to, too, two) chapters a night is simply (to, too, two) much work.

4. (Your, You're) not serious when you say (your, you're) planning to sell (your, you're) house and live in a tent in the woods, are you?

OTHER COMMON HOMONYMS

brake   (1) *to slow* or *to stop;* (2) *mechanism that stops a moving vehicle*
break   (1) *to cause to come apart;* (2) *to bring to an end*

If you don't **brake** your sled as you go down the icy hill, you could easily **break** a leg.

hear   (1) *to take in by ear;* (2) *to be informed*
here   *in this place*

The music **here** near the band is so loud that I can't **hear** you.

hole   *empty or hollow spot*
whole   *complete* or *entire*

The mechanic examined the **whole** surface of the flat tire before finding a tiny **hole** near the rim.

knew   (past tense of *know*) (1) *understood;* (2) *was or were aware of*
new   (1) *not old;* (2) *recently arrived*

Jay **knew** he needed a **new** bike when his old one broke down again yesterday.

know   (1) *to understand;* (2) *to be aware of*
no   (1) *not any;* (2) *opposite of yes*

I have **no** idea how much other people **know** about my divorce.

passed   (past tense of *pass*) (1) *handed to;* (2) *went by;* (3) *completed successfully*
past   (1) *time before the present;* (2) *by*

As Ben walked **past** Sharon's desk, he **passed** her a Valentine and pleaded, "Let's forget about the **past** and be friends again."

peace   *calmness* or *quiet*
piece   *portion of something*

The usual **peace** of the house was disturbed when my brother discovered that someone had eaten a **piece** of the cake he had baked for his girlfriend's birthday.

plain   (1) *not fancy;* (2) *obvious;* (3) *straightforward*
plane   shortened form of *airplane*

It was **plain** to see that a **plane** had recently landed in the muddy field.

right   (1) *correct;* (2) *opposite of left*
write   *to form letters and words*

I can **write** clearly using my **right** hand; when I use my left, my writing is illegible.

than   word used in comparisons
then   (1) *at that time;* (2) *next*

First Aaron realized he was driving faster **than** the speed limit; **then** he saw the police car behind him.

threw   (past tense of *throw*) *tossed*
through   (1) *into and out of;* (2) *finished*

Yesterday I went **through** my old letters and **threw** most of them away.

wear   *to put on* (as with clothing)
where   *in what place* or *to what place*

Because Samantha was not told **where** her friends were taking her for her birthday, she had trouble deciding what to **wear**.

weather   *outside conditions* (rain, wind, temperature, etc.)
whether   *if*

The **weather** won't spoil my vacation; **whether** it rains or not, my days will be spent on the beach.

who's   contraction of *who is* or *who has*
whose   *belonging to whom*

The boss yelled, "**Who's** responsible for this mistake? **Whose** fault is it?"

Note   Additional information about homonyms appears on pages 222–224.

Name _____ Section _____ Date _____

■ Homonyms: Test 1

In the ten sentences below, underline the correct word in each group of homonyms.

Note   To help you review some of the homonyms in this chapter, use the definitions given in half of the sentences.

1. Did you (here, hear) the old legend about a famous Native American chief who is buried (here, hear)?
   Did you *take in by ear* the old legend about a famous Native American chief who is buried *in this place*?

2. (To, Too) many people wanted tickets for the concert, so the promoters decided (to, too) add a second concert the following night.

3. The stray dog can't make up (it's, its) mind whether to trust me or not, so (it's, its) still sitting in the driveway watching me.
   The stray dog can't make up *the mind belonging to it* whether to trust me or not, so *it is* still sitting in the driveway watching me.

4. Some customers don't (no, know) how to say (no, know) to salespeople.

5. (Their, There, They're) too afraid of spiders to appreciate (their, there, they're) remarkable beauty.
   They are too afraid of spiders to appreciate the remarkable beauty *belonging to them*.

6. My young niece just (threw, through) her soccer ball (threw, through) our neighbors' kitchen window.

7. The loud whistling call of a blue jay about to feed on a (peace, piece) of bread was the only sound to be heard amid the (peace, piece) and quiet.
   The loud whistling call of a blue jay about to feed on a *portion* of bread was the only sound to be heard amid the *calmness* and quiet.

8. Pointing to the chunk of cheese on the table, the little boy said, "Couldn't you afford cheese that was (hole, whole)?" He didn't know that Swiss cheese always has (holes, wholes) in it.

9. The (knew, new) student in Spanish class (knew, new) how to speak the language better than anyone else.
   The *recently arrived* student in Spanish class *understood* how to speak the language better than anyone else.

10. (Your, You're) not supposed to dial 911 unless, in (your, you're) opinion, there's a life-threatening emergency.

To the Instructor   Additional tests on homonyms can be found in the *Instructor's Manual.*

Name _____   Section _____   Date _____

Score: (Number right) _____ × 5 = _____ %

■ Homonyms: Test 2

Underline the correct word in each group of homonyms.

1. I know you are angry about seeing me at Elaine's house, but (their, there, they're) was a good reason for me to go (their, there, they're).

2. If you don't (brake, break) before you go over the speed bump, you're going to (brake, break) the shock absorbers.

3. A large paperback bookstore is opening right (hear, here) on campus, and I (hear, here) it plans to sell computer supplies as well as books.

4. Since you (knew, new) that Suki's car was (knew, new), you should have been especially careful with it.

5. (Its, It's) easy to see from your face that your day has had (its, it's) bad moments.

6. On the celebrity tour, we drove (passed, past) several movie stars' homes; we also (passed, past) the restaurant where many Hollywood people have lunch.

7. The two brothers have not had any (peace, piece) ever since they began arguing over a small (peace, piece) of property their father left them.

8. (Whose, Who's) shoes are these in the middle of the floor, and (whose, who's) been messy enough to leave crumbs all over the table?

9. The teacher told Richard to (right, write) the assignment on the (right, write) side of the blackboard.

10. (Wear, Where) in this store might I find something appropriate to (wear, where) to a job interview?

Name _____   Section _____   Date _____

Score: (Number right) _____ × 10 = _____%

■ Homonyms: Test 3

Each short paragraph below contains **two** homonym errors. Find these errors and underline them. Then write the correct words in the spaces provided.

Note   To help guide your work, one error in each group is indicated.

1. If its sunny tomorrow, our English class will meet outside. Unfortunately, we can't know in advance what the whether will be. Even if we meet inside, though, our teacher has promised us an unusual class.

   a. _____ it's _____   If *it is* sunny tomorrow

   b. _____ weather _____

2. There are to many wild and hungry cats loose in this town. It's the fault of the summer visitors. When their ready to leave town, many of them just leave their cats behind. The poor cats get wild and hungry.

   a. _____ too _____   *Overly* many cats

   b. _____ they're _____

3. It's important to provide an adequate and safe supply of drinking water. Not having enough water to drink is more dangerous then having to little food. Humans will die of thirst long before they die of hunger.

   a. _____ than _____   Not having water to drink is *being*

   b. _____ too _____   *compared with* not having food to eat.

4. After experiencing a tragedy in her life, my aunt began to talk to a counselor. "I can't change the passed," she said, "but it's plane to me that talking can help me cope with it better."

   a. _____ past _____   She can't change what happened in

   b. _____ plain _____   the *time before the present.*

5. Most people no the swastika as a symbol of Nazi Germany. However, the swastika, or "hooked cross," existed long before Hitler came to power. Ancient Norsemen and Native Americans new it as a symbol of the sun's journey through the sky.

   a. _____ know _____   Most people *are aware of* the swastika.

   b. _____ knew _____

Name _____   Section _____   Date _____

Score: (Number right) _____ × 10 = _____%

■ Homonyms: Test 4

Each short paragraph below contains **two** homonym errors. Find these errors and underline them. Then write the correct words in the spaces provided.

1. Because my family is so large, the hole family rarely drives anywhere together. Usually four of the children will drive with one parent, and five with the other. There are always arguments among the youngest children about who's turn it is to ride in the front seats.

    a. _____ whole _____

    b. _____ whose _____

2. The doctor spoke sternly to Donald at his last checkup. "Your overweight and you almost never exercise," the doctor warned. "I'm telling you in plane language that you're asking for a heart attack."

    a. _____ You're _____

    b. _____ plain _____

3. Some parents try to limit the amount of television their children watch. They believe that more then an hour a day of television interferes with schoolwork. They also don't like much of the language that kids here on TV shows.

    a. _____ than _____

    b. _____ hear _____

4. Medical researchers have found that if your often in a bad mood, its more likely you will die of a stress-related disease such as high blood pressure, heart disease, or stroke. To live longer, they advise, take the steps needed to achieve inner peace.

    a. _____ you're _____

    b. _____ it's _____

5. The legend of the vampire Dracula is based on the story of a real-life Romanian prince named Vlad, who lived more than five hundred years ago. Vlad was a bloodthirsty madman who may have killed as many as 100,000 people during his six years in power. His favorite method of killing was two run a stake threw his victims. Vlad was finally killed in 1476.

    a. _____ to _____

    b. _____ through _____

Name _____ Section _____ Date _____

■ Homonyms: Test 5

Underline the correct homonym in each of the following sentences. Then, in the spaces provided, write an explanation for the answer you chose.

Note   To help you review some of the homonyms in this chapter, use the hints given for half of the homonyms.

[1](Weather, Whether) or not animals can use language is a question that interests many scientists. [2]We don't (no, know) if animals "talk" to each other in the wild. [3]However, (their, there, they're) have been fascinating experiments done with animals in captivity. [4]One of the most famous of those experiments involves a gorilla named Koko, (whose, who's) vocabulary in American Sign Language exceeds six hundred words. [5]A human trainer shows Koko the (right, write) way to sign a word. [6](Than, Then) the trainer watches Koko carefully to see if she uses the sign to communicate her needs. [7]If Koko uses the sign correctly, she has learned (its, it's) meaning. [8]It is (plain, plane) from Koko's correct use of her signs that she understands the words she uses. [9]What is more remarkable (than, then) that is that Koko uses her vocabulary to create new words. [10]For example, in the (passed, past) she has come up with the terms "finger bracelet" to describe a ring and "eye hat" for a mask.

Wording of explanations may vary.

1. "Whether" means "if."   The question is if animals can use language or not.

2. "Know" means "be aware of."

3. "There" is used before forms of "be."   *Have been* is a form of the verb *to be*.

4. "Whose" means "belonging to." The vocabulary belongs to Koko.

5. "Right" means "correct."   A human trainer shows Koko the *correct* way to sign a word.

6. "Then" means "next." Next, the trainer watches Koko carefully.

7. "Its" means "belonging to it."   The gorilla has learned the meaning *belonging to* the sign.

8. "Plain" means "obvious."

9. "Than" is used in comparisons.   Koko's ability to create new words is *being compared with* her correct use of signs.

10. "Past" refers to a time before the present.

Name _____   Section _____   Date _____

Score: (Number right) _____ × 10 = _____%

■ Homonyms: Test 6

Underline the correct homonym in each of the following sentences. Then, in the spaces provided, write an explanation for the answer you chose.

[1]"(Who's, Whose) résumé is this?" asked the career counselor. [2]Jamila raised her hand, wondering (weather, whether) the counselor thought her résumé was especially good or especially bad. [3]"Let's go (threw, through) this with the class as we discuss what makes a résumé work," said the counselor.

[4]"The biggest problem is that Jamila's entries are (to, too, two) brief," he said. [5]"(Hear, Here), for instance, it says she was a secretary for three years. [6]Surely that doesn't tell the (hole, whole) story of what she did on the job. [7]I'd like to see Jamila (right, write) down every responsibility she had. [8]If she wrote her boss's letters, used a computer, supervised another employee, or planned business meetings, her résumé should let us (know, no) that. [9]Remember this: Employers only glance at most résumés as they decide if an applicant is the best person for (their, there, they're) position. [10](Your, You're) résumé must quickly provide specific information about what you are qualified to do."

Wording of explanations may vary.

1. "Whose" means "belonging to whom."

2. "Whether" means "if."

3. "Through" means "into and out of."

4. "Too" means "overly."

5. "Here" means "in this place."

6. "Whole" means "complete."

7. "Write" means "form letters and words."

8. "Know" means "be aware of."

9. "Their" means "belonging to them."

10. "Your" means "belonging to you."

13 Capital Letters

Seeing What You Know

Place capital letters on the words that need them in the following sentences. Then check your answers by reading the explanations below.

1. the coach growled, "if i see you drop one more pass, ed, you're off the team."
   - T above "the"; I above "if"; I above "i"; E above "ed"

2. At bronx community college in new york, students can take night courses in hispanic literature and asian cooking as well as english.
   - B above "bronx"; C above "community"; C above "college"; N above "new"; Y above "york"; H above "hispanic"; A above "asian"; E above "english"

3. Did you know that thanksgiving is always the fourth thursday in november?
   - T above "thanksgiving"; T above "thursday"; N above "november"

4. At breakfast I often read the latest issue of *people* while eating wheat-ies sprinkled with raisins and toast spread with skippy peanut butter.
   - P above "people"; W above "wheat-"; S above "skippy"

Understanding the Answers

1. **The** coach growled, "**If I** see you drop one more pass, **Ed,** you're off the team."
   The first word of a sentence, the first word of a quoted sentence, the pronoun *I,* and people's names are capitalized. *Coach* and *team,* which are general terms (not specific names), are not capitalized.

2. At **Bronx Community College** in **New York,** students can take night courses in **Hispanic** literature and **Asian** cooking as well as **English.**
   Capital letters are used for names of specific places. Names of races, nationalities, and languages are also capitalized. *Students, night courses, literature,* and *cooking* are general terms that are not capitalized.

3. Did you know that **Thanksgiving** is always the fourth **Thursday** in **November?**
   The names of holidays, days of the week, and months are always capitalized.

4. At breakfast I often read the latest issue of ***People*** while eating **Wheaties** sprinkled with raisins and toast spread with **Skippy** peanut butter.
   Titles of magazines and brand names of products are capitalized. General words like *raisins, toast,* and *peanut butter* are not capitalized.

Capital letters have many uses, the most common of which appear in this chapter.

THE FIRST WORD IN A SENTENCE OR DIRECT QUOTATION

Sentences begin with capital letters. The first word of a quoted sentence is also capitalized.

My sister said, "**D**on't forget Nick's surprise party. **I**t's Friday at 8 P.M."

"**L**et's hope," **I** replied, "that nobody tells Nick about it."

In the second sentence, the word *that* is not capitalized because it does not start a sentence. It is part of the sentence that begins with the words *Let's hope.*

THE WORD "I" AND PEOPLE'S NAMES

"**T**oday **I** got a call from an old high school friend, **D**ick **H**ess," **S**andy said.

Note   A title that comes before someone's name is treated as part of the name.

Next week **U**ncle **D**ave and **A**unt **G**loria are seeing **D**r. **M**endell for checkups.
But: My uncle and aunt go to the best doctor in town.

NAMES OF SPECIFIC PLACES AND LANGUAGES

In general, if something is on a map (including a street map), capitalize it.

Frankie graduated from **K**ennedy **H**igh **S**chool on **M**ain **S**treet, left her home in **A**ltoona, **P**ennsylvania, moved to **N**ew **Y**ork, and took a job as a waitress in a **G**reenwich **V**illage restaurant.

Note   Places that are not specifically named do not require capital letters.

Frankie graduated from high school, left her home in a small town, moved to the big city, and took a job as a waitress in a neighborhood restaurant.

The names of languages come from place names, so languages are also capitalized.

Inez, who was born in Spain, speaks fluent **S**panish as well as **E**nglish.

NAMES OF SPECIFIC GROUPS (RACES, RELIGIONS, NATIONALITIES, COMPANIES, CLUBS, AND OTHER ORGANIZATIONS)

Although Barbara is **L**utheran and Mark is **J**ewish, and she is his boss at the local **H**ome **D**epot store, their marriage seems to work very well.

The robbery suspect is a six-foot-tall **C**aucasian male with a **G**erman accent.

The **A**merican **C**ivil **L**iberties **U**nion supports the **K**u **K**lux **K**lan's right to demonstrate.

Practice 1

Place capital letters on the words that need them in the sentences below.

1. as we watched the movie, doug leaned over and whispered, "don't you think this is pretty boring?"
   <small>A — D — D</small>
2. st. mary's seminary in baltimore, maryland, has trained catholic priests for more than two hundred years.
   <small>S M S — B — M — C</small>
3. we decided to hold the retirement dinner for professor henderson at the florentine, the new italian restaurant on lake street.
   <small>W — P — H — F — I — L S</small>
4. some of the most expensive shops in the world are found along rodeo drive in beverly hills, california.
   <small>S — R D — B H C</small>
5. "when I was a kid," the comedian rodney dangerfield told his audience, "my parents moved a lot—but i always found them."
   <small>W — R D — I</small>

CALENDAR ITEMS

Basically, everything on a calendar—including names of days of the week, months, and holidays—should be capitalized. The only exceptions are the names of the seasons (*spring, summer, fall, winter*), which are not capitalized.

Since Joy was born on **D**ecember 26, her family celebrates her birthday on **C**hristmas **D**ay.

Next **M**onday, which is **L**abor **D**ay, all government offices will be closed.

Stan watches baseball on television in the spring and summer, football in the fall, and basketball in the winter.

PRODUCT NAMES

Capitalize the copyrighted brand name of a product, but not the kind of product it names.

Pilar won't buy presweetened cereals for her children. She prefers less sugary brands such as **C**heerios and **W**heat **C**hex.

Our cats have refused to eat any more **F**riskies or **N**ine **L**ives cat food. They insist on eating **S**tarkist tuna—right off our plates.

TITLES

The titles of books, television or stage shows, songs, magazines, movies, articles, poems, stories, papers, and so forth are capitalized.

The book *Shoeless Joe* was made into the movie *Field of Dreams*.

I'd much rather read *Newsweek* than the *New York Times*.

Professor Martin praised Aisha's term paper, "The Social Impact of the Industrial Revolution," but he suggested that she revise one section.

Note   The words *the, of, a, an, and,* and other short, unstressed words are not capitalized when they appear in the middle of a title.

FAMILY WORDS THAT SUBSTITUTE FOR NAMES

When I was a little girl, **G**randma was my favorite baby-sitter.

I'll ask **D**ad if he'd like to go to the movie with us.

Capitalize a word such as *grandma* or *dad* only if it is being used as a substitute for that person's name. Do not capitalize words showing family relationships when they are preceded by possessive words such as *my, her,* or *our.*

Did you know that my grandmother goes to the racetrack every week?

SPECIFIC SCHOOL COURSES

Capitalize the names of specific courses, including those containing a number.

To graduate, I need to take **A**dvanced **B**iology, **S**peech 102, and **L**iterature of **O**ther **C**ultures.

But the names of general subject areas are not capitalized.

To graduate, I still need to take a biology course, a speech course, and a literature course.

Practice 2

Place capital letters on the words that need them in the sentences below.

1. Our student body is about 50 percent caucasian, 30 percent african-american, and 10 percent each hispanic and asian.
2. Elvis Presley's hit song "all shook up" was inspired by a bottle of pepsi.
3. Rashid heard that introduction to statistics was impossible to pass, so he signed up for a psychology course instead.
4. The second monday in october is celebrated as columbus day.
5. "But, mommy, it *hurts!*" the boy whimpered as his mother dabbed solarcaine lotion on his sunburn.

Note   Additional information about capital letters appears on page 225.

Name _____ Section _____ Date _____

Score: (Number right) _____ × 4 = _____ %

■ Capital Letters: Test 1

Underline the words that need to be capitalized. Then write the words correctly in the spaces provided. The number of spaces shows how many capital letters are missing in each sentence.

Note   To help you master capitalization, explanations are given for half of the sentences.

1. when dad shouted, "don't move!" I froze in fear.

   ____When____   ____Dad____   ____Don't____

   Capitalize the first word of a sentence and of a direct quotation. Also capitalize a word used instead of a person's name.

2. A story about my disabled boss, ted, once appeared in *sports illustrated.*

   ____Ted____   ____Sports____   ____Illustrated____

3. My uncle, dr. lopez, works at southside clinic.

   ____Dr.____   ____Lopez____   ____Southside____   ____Clinic____

   Capitalize people's names, titles that come before names, and names of specific places.

4. The speaker at parkside college's graduation was senator holland.

   ____Parkside____   ____College's____   ____Senator____   ____Holland____

5. Every january, renee's grandparents travel to florida for a winter vacation.

   ____January____   ____Renee's____   ____Florida____

   Capitalize the name of a month, of a particular person, and of a particular place.

6. When the door opened, aunt sarah whispered, "bring in the birthday cake now; then start singing."

   ____Aunt____   ____Sarah____   ____Bring____

7. Most british people who attend church belong to the church of england.

   ____British____   ____Church____   ____England____

   Capitalize names of nationalities. Also capitalize names of religions. Short, unstressed words in the middle of a name are not capitalized.

8. The television show *60 minutes* is Fran's favorite; she's writing a paper about one of its stories for sociology 101.

   ____Minutes____   ____Sociology____

To the Instructor   Additional tests on capital letters can be found in the *Instructor's Manual.*

Name _____ Section _____ Date _____

Score: (Number right) _____ × 2.5 = _____ %

■ Capital Letters: Test 2

Underline the words that need to be capitalized. Then write the words correctly in the spaces provided. The number of spaces shows how many capital letters are missing in each sentence.

1. The city of new orleans is famous for its celebration of the holiday mardi gras.

   _____New_____   _____Orleans_____   _____Mardi_____   _____Gras_____

2. Years ago i knew a guy named andy who lived on forest avenue.

   _____I_____   _____Andy_____   _____Forest_____   _____Avenue_____

3. In one of his best-remembered speeches, president john kennedy said, "ask not what your country can do for you; ask what you can do for your country."

   _____President_____   _____John_____   _____Kennedy_____   _____Ask_____

4. Since you're going to the supermarket, could you get me a carton of tropicana orange juice, a box of tide, and a can of maxwell house coffee?

   _____Tropicana_____   _____Tide_____   _____Maxwell_____   _____House_____

5. *Interview with the vampire,* a book by anne rice, is about a vampire named louis.

   _____Vampire_____   _____Anne_____   _____Rice_____   _____Louis_____

6. The teenagers cruised down grant drive and then headed over to concord mall.

   _____Grant_____   _____Drive_____   _____Concord_____   _____Mall_____

7. Many people in hollywood told arnold schwarzenegger he would never succeed as an actor because of his austrian accent.

   _____Hollywood_____   _____Arnold_____   _____Schwarzenegger_____   _____Austrian_____

8. I last saw grandpa and aunt rhoda at my cousin's wedding in march.

   _____Grandpa_____   _____Aunt_____   _____Rhoda_____   _____March_____

9. The high school choir performed some african-american spirituals as well as a piece by franz schubert.

   _____African_____   _____American_____   _____Franz_____   _____Schubert_____

10. A popular ad campaign for chevrolet featured the song "the heartbeat of america."

    _____Chevrolet_____   _____The_____   _____Heartbeat_____   _____America_____

Name _____ Section _____ Date _____

■ Capital Letters: Test 3

Underline the two words that require capital letters in each group of sentences below. Then write the words (with capital letters) in the spaces provided.

Note   To help you master capitalization, explanations are given for half of the sentences.

1. I don't know my way around <u>chicago</u> well. If I get too far away from the downtown area known as the <u>loop</u>, I become hopelessly lost. All the streets look the same to me.

   a. _____Chicago_____   Names of specific places are capitalized.

   b. _____Loop_____

2. Winter is my favorite season. However, my brother says, "<u>what</u> moron likes to be cold and wet all the time? Warm, beautiful <u>june</u>, the beginning of summer, is the best time of year."

   a. _____What_____   Capitalize the first word of a quoted sentence.

   b. _____June_____

3. Lillian, who is Methodist, had never visited a <u>catholic</u> church before. She went with her friend Henry to attend an <u>easter</u> service there. Afterward they stayed for a meal in the church's fellowship hall.

   a. _____Catholic_____   Names of religions are capitalized.

   b. _____Easter_____

4. Jasmin's husband teaches an evening class once a week. Since he comes home late on <u>wednesdays</u>, Jasmin often takes the children out for supper on that night. This week the kids have asked to eat at Burger <u>king</u>.

   a. _____Wednesdays_____   Days of the week are capitalized.

   b. _____King_____

5. My cousin is studying to be a teacher. For a course called Introduction to <u>teaching</u>, she was asked to read a book by Jonathan Kozol called *Savage inequalities,* which criticizes public schools. She now wants to be a public school teacher and help inner-city children get the best education possible.

   a. _____Teaching_____   Names of specific school courses are capitalized.

   b. _____Inequalities_____

Name _____   Section _____   Date _____

Score: (Number right) _____ × 10 = _____%

Capital Letters: Test 4

Underline the two words that require capital letters in each group of sentences below. Then write the words (with capital letters) in the spaces provided.

1. Karen stayed after class to talk over her grade with professor Hartzler. Although she enjoyed her french classes, she wasn't doing very well. Her professor suggested that Karen get some extra tutoring in the language.

   a. _____Professor_____

   b. _____French_____

2. Is your uncle going to come to the party? I'd like him to meet aunt Lydia. They're both single and active in the democratic party. Maybe they would like each other.

   a. _____Aunt_____

   b. _____Democratic_____

3. Although grandpa lives in New England for most of the year, he travels to a warmer climate for the winter. He says, "when the snow flies, so do I."

   a. _____Grandpa_____

   b. _____When_____

4. Amanda visited New mexico last summer. She was fascinated by the mix of Native American and spanish cultures there. She is reading everything she can find about this region and hopes to go back again someday.

   a. _____Mexico_____

   b. _____Spanish_____

5. Now that Betsy has small children to take along, she no longer enjoys trips to the mall. It's easier for her to buy from catalogs or online. Last week, she ordered clothing from the coldwater creek catalog and computer supplies from two different Web sites.

   a. _____Coldwater_____

   b. _____Creek_____

Name _____ Section _____ Date _____

■ Capital Letters: Test 5

Each sentence in the passage below contains one or more words that require capitalization. Underline these words; then write the words (with capital letters) on the lines below. The number of spaces shows how many capital letters are needed in each sentence.

Note   To help you master capitalization, explanations are given for half of the sentences.

   ¹last summer my husband jerry and i decided to take a vacation. ²As we discussed where we should go, I jokingly said, "you know, we never got to niagara falls on our honeymoon." ³Next thing we knew, we had a house full of road maps and literature from the niagara chamber of commerce. ⁴On the second monday in july, we hopped into our car and headed for the canadian border. ⁵It was a long drive, so we took turns driving and passed some time singing old songs like "home on the range." ⁶When jerry drove, I often read the recent issues of *time* that I'd brought along to catch up on the news. ⁷finally we arrived at our destination, a hotel full of interesting people, including lots of japanese tourists. ⁸There was also a lively convention of people belonging to the american association of retired persons. ⁹That very night, after sending picture postcards to mom and dad, we went out to get our first look at the falls in the dark. ¹⁰Although I'd grown up looking at pictures of the falls on boxes of nabisco cereals, nothing could have prepared me for the majestic beauty of the real thing.

1. ____Last____   ____Jerry____   ____I____
   Capitalize the first word of a sentence, people's names, and the word *I*. Names of seasons are not capitalized.

2. ____You____   ____Niagara____   ____Falls____

3. ____Niagara____   ____Chamber____   ____Commerce____
   Names of particular organizations are capitalized.

4. ____Monday____   ____July____   ____Canadian____

5. ____Home____   ____Range____
   Capitalize song titles. Do not capitalize short, unstressed words in the middles of titles.

6. ____Jerry____   ____Time____

7. ____Finally____   ____Japanese____
   Capitalize the first word of a sentence and the names of nationalities.

8. ____American____   ____Association____   ____Retired____   ____Persons____

9. ____Mom____   ____Dad____
   Capitalize names of relatives used in place of their actual names. The word *falls* is used here as a general term, so it is not capitalized.

10. ____Nabisco____

Name _____   Section _____   Date _____

Score: (Number right) _____ × 4 = _____%

■ Capital Letters: Test 6

Each sentence in the passage below contains one or more words that require capitalization. Underline these words; then write the words (with capital letters) on the lines below. The number of spaces shows how many capital letters are needed in each sentence.

[1]Probably few friends spend as much time arguing as my friends and <u>i</u> do. [2]We're all seniors at Eliot <u>high</u> <u>school</u>, we're all taking the same <u>english</u> and history courses, and we get together almost every <u>friday</u> night. [3]But becoming head of a big corporation like <u>general</u> <u>motors</u> would be easier than getting us to agree on anything—for instance, where to eat. [4]Raquel is so crazy about the food at the <u>asian</u> <u>dragon</u> <u>cafe</u> that she'd probably go there for <u>christmas</u> dinner. [5]Tasha, on the other hand, likes the vegetarian restaurant on <u>chestnut</u> <u>street</u>. [6]We usually end up going to <u>pizza</u> <u>hut</u>. [7]Later, when it's time to rent a movie, Paul is so proud of his heritage that he wants only movies with <u>stallone</u>, <u>pacino</u>, and other <u>italian</u> actors. [8]But I prefer exciting comedies like <u>*freaky friday*</u>. [9]If we try to watch a war movie, there will usually be an argument between Randy, who is a <u>quaker</u> and doesn't believe in serving in the military, and Alan, who is planning to join the <u>marine</u> <u>corps</u>. [10]<u>sometime</u> during the course of the evening, someone will usually announce, "<u>if</u> you guys weren't my best friends, I couldn't stand any of you."

1. _____I_____			
2. __High__	__School__	__English__	__Friday__
3. __General__	__Motors__		
4. __Asian__	__Dragon__	__Cafe__	__Christmas__
5. __Chestnut__	__Street__		
6. __Pizza__	__Hut__		
7. __Stallone__	__Pacino__	__Italian__	
8. __Freaky__	__Friday__		
9. __Quaker__	__Marine__	__Corps__	
10. __Sometime__	__If__		

14 Word Choice

Seeing What You Know

Imagine that the following sentences appeared in a business or school report. Check the sentence in each pair that is worded more appropriately. Then read the explanations below.

1. _____ At this point in time we have not yet scheduled the date of the exam.

   _✓_ We have not yet scheduled the exam.

2. _____ Fred wishes the office manager would get off his case.

   _✓_ Fred wishes the office manager would stop criticizing him.

3. _____ The first-grade children have been busy as bees all day, but they still seem fresh as daisies.

   _✓_ The first-grade children have been active all day, but they still seem energetic.

Understanding the Answers

1. **The second sentence is more direct.**
   The first sentence is longer than necessary because of the wordy expressions *at this point in time* and *scheduled the date*.

2. **The second sentence is more businesslike.**
   The slang expression *get off his case* in the first sentence is too informal for school or business writing.

3. **The second sentence is less stale.**
   The first sentence is weakened by the clichés *busy as bees* and *fresh as daisies*.

155

Not all writing problems involve grammar. A sentence may be grammatically correct yet fail to communicate effectively because of the words that the writer has chosen. Wordiness, slang, and clichés are three enemies of effective communication.

WORDINESS

Which of the following signs would help the campus cafeteria run more smoothly?

____ Due to the fact that our plates and our silverware are in short supply, the management kindly requests all patrons of this cafeteria, when they have finished their meals, to place all used plates and silverware on a cart before leaving the cafeteria so that they may be washed.

✓
____ Please put your used plates and silverware on a cart.

Wordy writing is writing that—like the first sign above—uses more words than necessary to get a message across. Such writing both confuses and irritates the reader, who resents having to wade through extra words.

To avoid wordiness, edit your writing carefully. Remove words that have the same meaning as other words in the sentence.

Wordy: In my opinion, I think that job quotas in the workplace are unfair.

Revised: I think that job quotas are unfair.

In general, work to express your thoughts in the fewest words possible that are still complete and clear. Notice, for example, how easily the following wordy expressions can be replaced by single words:

Wordy Expression	*Single Word*
at this point in time	now
came into the possession of	obtained
due to the fact that	because
during the time that	while
each and every day	daily
few in number	few
in order to	to
in the event that	if
in the near future	soon
in this day and age	now
made the decision to	decided
on account of	because
postponed until later	postponed
small in size	small

Practice 1

Cross out the wordy expressions and unnecessary words in the sentences that follow. Then rewrite each sentence as clearly and concisely as possible.

1. ~~Due to the fact that~~ the judge's hair is prematurely gray ~~at an earlier age than most women~~, people think she is much older than ~~her~~ thirty-eight ~~years of age.~~

   Because the judge's hair is prematurely gray, people think she is much older
   than thirty-eight.

2. I ~~just~~ can't understand why there are, ~~in this day and age~~, so many poor ~~and needy~~ people ~~in number~~ in this country ~~of ours~~.

   I can't understand why there are now so many poor people in this country.

3. ~~In the event of~~ weather that is ~~problematic, officials will make the decision to~~ postpone the baseball game ~~until a later point in time~~.

   If the weather is bad, the baseball game will be postponed.

SLANG

Which of the following would be appropriate to print in a newspaper?

✓ The police just captured a local criminal who posed as a utility serviceman and stole from several trusting senior citizens.

___ The police just busted a local criminal who posed as a utility serviceman and ripped off several trusting senior citizens.

Slang expressions (like *busted* and *ripped off*) are part of our everyday language. They are lively and fun to use. But while slang may be appropriate in casual conversation, it generally does not belong in formal writing. Slang, by nature, is informal.

Even in less formal writing, slang is often inappropriate because not all readers understand it. Slang is frequently used by limited social groups, and it changes rapidly. When we read slang expressions from the 1960s like *groovy* or *far out,* they sound out-of-date or meaningless. Your use of slang might have the same effect on someone older (or younger) than you. For example, when you write about someone who seems confused or not very bright, "The lights are on, but nobody's home," you may know exactly what you mean. Your reader may not.

Use slang only when you have a specific purpose in mind, such as being humorous or communicating the flavor of an informal conversation.

Practice 2

Rewrite the two slang expressions (printed in *italics*) in each sentence.

Answers
may vary.

1. If you want to *ace* your courses, don't *ditch* too many classes.

    do very well in . . . deliberately miss

2. I really *lucked out.* Five people in the office were *sacked,* but I kept my job.

    was fortunate . . . fired

3. Jesse finally *crashed* after *pulling an all-nighter* to finish his report.

    fell asleep . . . working all night

CLICHÉS

Which of the following belongs in a nurse's daily report?

    ___   The patient in 201 slept like a log until the crack of dawn.

    ✓   The patient in 201 slept deeply until 6:30 A.M.

A **cliché** is a commonplace, boring expression. Once, it might have been fresh, vivid, even funny. But too many people used it, so it has become stale. Don't be lazy and use other people's worn-out sayings. Find original ways to say what you mean.

Here are just a few of the many other clichés to avoid in your writing:

avoid like the plague	drive like a maniac	old as the hills
busy as a bee	easier said than done	pretty as a picture
cold as ice	in the nick of time	short and sweet
couldn't care less	it goes without saying	sigh of relief
crazy like a fox	last but not least	tried and true
dog-tired	light as a feather	without a doubt

Practice 3

Rewrite the two clichés (printed in *italics*) in each sentence.

Answers
may vary.

1. Hiroshi was *as sick as a dog* yesterday, but he looks *fit as a fiddle* today.

    very sick . . . healthy

2. My sister was *down in the dumps* because she was *fighting a losing battle with her math course.*

    depressed . . . not doing well in

3. The news of the president's resignation, which came *like a bolt from the blue, spread like wildfire* across campus.

    unexpectedly . . . traveled quickly

Note   Additional information about word choice appears on page 226.

Name _____ Section _____ Date _____

■ Word Choice: Test 1

Each sentence below contains one or two examples of ineffective word choice. Underline each error. Then, in the space provided, write *W, S,* or *C* to indicate wordiness, slang, or cliché. Finally, use the answer line to rewrite each faulty expression, using more effective language.

Note   To help you develop skill in choosing words effectively, suggestions are given for half of the answers.

Corrections may vary.

_____S_____ 1. I really <u>blew up</u> when Helen called me a liar.

   got angry
   _____
   Correct the slang.

_____S_____ 2. All the critics <u>trashed</u> the new Kevin Costner film.

   condemned
   _____

_____W_____ 3. <u>Due to the fact that</u> it rained, the game was <u>postponed until later</u>.

   Since . . . postponed
   _____
   Correct the two cases of wordiness.

_____W_____ 4. Some students were late to class <u>on account of</u> their bus was delayed.

   because
   _____

_____C_____ 5. The course was supposed to be hard, but it was <u>easy as pie</u>.

   very easy
   _____
   Correct the cliché.

_____C_____ 6. The explosion <u>made enough noise to wake the dead</u>.

   was extremely loud
   _____

_____W_____ 7. <u>In my opinion, I don't think</u> there is any excuse for world hunger <u>at this point in time</u>.

   I don't think . . . now
   _____
   Correct the two cases of wordiness.

_____W_____ 8. Over fifty invitations were <u>sent out in the mail</u>, but only <u>a total of twelve</u> people responded.

   mailed . . . twelve
   _____

To the Instructor   Additional tests on word choice can be found in the *Instructor's Manual.*

Name _____ Section _____ Date _____

Score: (Number right) _____ × 10 = _____ %

■ Word Choice: Test 2

Each sentence below contains one or more examples of ineffective word choice. Underline each error. Then, in the space provided, write *W*, *S*, or *C* to indicate wordiness, slang, or cliché. Finally, use the answer line to rewrite each faulty expression, using more effective language.

Corrections may vary.

_____C_____ 1. The job applicant wore a suit that had seen better days.

was shabby _____

_____S_____ 2. The horror movie was too gross for me.

disgusting _____

_____W_____ 3. In the event that I'm not back by three o'clock, would you put the roast in the oven?

If _____

_____S_____ 4. Because my neighbor is not exactly the sharpest knife in the drawer, I didn't take his story seriously.

not especially intelligent _____

_____S_____ 5. The competing singers were forced to sweat it out while the judges made their decision.

wait anxiously _____

_____W_____ 6. The new client has not called at this point in time but is expected to do so in the very near future.

yet . . . soon _____

_____C_____ 7. When the computer screen went blank as I was writing my report, I realized I would have to start from scratch.

begin again _____

_____S_____ 8. The whole class freaked out when the teacher announced a surprise test.

was outraged _____

_____W_____ 9. Owing to the fact of the teachers' strike, school has not yet opened.

Because _____

_____C_____ 10. Velma said her boyfriend treated her like dirt, so she told him to take a hike.

treated her badly . . . not to see her again _____

Name _____   Section _____   Date _____

■ Word Choice: Test 3

Each sentence below contains **two** examples of ineffective word choice. Underline each error. Then, in the space provided, write *W, S,* or *C* to indicate wordiness, slang, or cliché. Finally, use the answer line to rewrite each faulty expression, using more effective language.

Note   To help you develop skill in choosing words effectively, suggestions are given

Corrections for the first answer in each group.
may vary.

1. I was pleased as punch when I learned someone would be working with me today. Being in the shop alone would have been a bummer.

    _C_ a. _happy_ _____   Correct the cliché.

    _S_ b. _boring_ _____

2. It's too bad that dress is too large in size for Jen. The style and color both suit her to a T. I wonder if it could be taken in to fit her better.

    _W_ a. _large_ _____   Correct the wordiness.

    _C_ b. _are perfect for her_ _____

3. There's never a dull moment in the Doyles' house! Yesterday the children emptied the sand that was in their sandbox onto the lawn, poured shampoo into the fish tank, and fed chocolate cake to the dog.

    _C_ a. _Something is always going wrong at_ ___   Correct the cliché.

    _W_ b. _emptied their sandbox_ _____

4. Although Sheila's friends warned her that Mark was just a player, she didn't listen to them. She was head over heels about Mark. When he suddenly had no time for her, Sheila realized her friends were right.

    _S_ a. _someone who uses women_ _____   Correct the slang.

    _C_ b. _very much in love with_ _____

5. Tired to the bone, the couple returned home after a long day's work. They were especially ticked off to find a sink full of dirty dishes left by their children.

    _C_ a. _Thoroughly exhausted_ _____   Correct the cliché.

    _S_ b. _annoyed_ _____

■ Word Choice: Test 4

Each sentence below contains **two** examples of ineffective word choice. Underline each error. Then, in the space provided, write *W, S,* or *C* to indicate wordiness, slang, or cliché. Finally, use the answer line to rewrite each faulty expression, using more effective language.

Corrections may vary.

1. Tyrell is messing with you when he says he can't be at your party. Don't listen to his teasing—he wouldn't miss that party for the world.

    __S__ a. joking _____

    __C__ b. really wants to go to that party _____

2. As Alex wrote his penalty check, he wondered why the IRS bothered with small potatoes like him. Why didn't they go after the big shots who regularly cheated the government out of millions of dollars in taxes?

    __S__ a. ordinary people _____

    __S__ b. rich people _____

3. You can't believe anything that woman says. She's full of baloney. During the time that I've known her, I've heard her tell many lies.

    __S__ a. always exaggerating _____

    __W__ b. Since _____

4. The workers wondered if their boss was leveling with them when she told them the company wasn't doing well. They thought she might be saying that due to the fact that she didn't want to give any raises.

    __S__ a. telling them the truth _____

    __W__ b. because _____

5. My uncle has been down on his luck lately. His situation took a turn for the worse when he got sick and then lost his apartment.

    __C__ a. unlucky _____

    __C__ b. worsened _____

Name _____ Section _____ Date _____

■ Word Choice: Test 5

Each sentence in the following passage contains an example of wordiness, slang, or a cliché. Underline each error. Then, in the space provided, write *W, S,* or *C* to indicate wordiness, slang, or cliché. Finally, use the answer line to rewrite the faulty expression, using more effective language.

Note   To help you develop skill in choosing words effectively, suggestions are given for half of the answers.

Corrections may vary.

[1]My sister, Elaine, never had good luck with her boyfriends, even though she's dated some <u>hunks</u>. [2]She always broke up with them <u>on account of the fact that</u> all they cared about was their gorgeous selves. [3]Then <u>it dawned on her</u> that she might get along better with very studious types. [4]So she started going out with <u>nerds</u>. [5]But she would <u>return back home again</u> from those dates complaining that the smart ones weren't much fun. [6]I hated to see my sister <u>in the dumps</u>. [7]I kept saying, "Don't lose hope—someday you'll find someone as <u>awesome</u> as Jeff." [8]Jeff, my boyfriend, was good-looking, did well in school, and was <u>as sweet as pie</u>, too. [9]<u>During the time that</u> Elaine was having boyfriend problems, Jeff and I often discussed her. [10]Maybe I mentioned Jeff and Elaine to each other too often; anyway, they're getting <u>hitched</u> this June.

1. _S_ very attractive men _____ Correct the slang.

2. _W_ because _____

3. _C_ she realized _____ Correct the cliché.

4. _S_ intelligent men _____

5. _W_ return _____ Correct the wordiness.

6. _C_ sad _____

7. _S_ wonderful _____ Correct the slang.

8. _C_ sweet _____

9. _W_ While _____ Correct the wordiness.

10. _S_ married _____

Name _____   Section _____   Date _____

Score: (Number right) _____ × 10 = _____ %

■ Word Choice: Test 6

Each sentence in the following passage contains an example of wordiness, slang, or a cliché. Underline each error. Then, in the space provided, write *W, S,* or *C* to indicate wordiness, slang, or cliché. Finally, use the answer line to rewrite the faulty expression, using more effective language.

Corrections may vary.

¹In this day and age of ours not many people remember the book *Beautiful Joe.* ²That is too bad due to the fact that it is a terrific story. ³It begins with a creep named Jenkins who is cruel to animals. ⁴At the point in time when the story opens, his dog has had a litter of puppies. ⁵Instead of loving the puppies, Jenkins loses his cool one day and chops off a puppy's ears and tail. ⁶The puppy is rescued from death in the nick of time by a young man.

⁷A sweet young thing named Laura adopts the puppy and names him Beautiful Joe. ⁸Joe grows up in a happy household with a large number of many other pets. ⁹His owners are really cool people who want to see all animals treated well. ¹⁰Readers breathe a sigh of relief when Jenkins eventually receives the punishment he deserves.

1. W   Today _____

2. W   because _____

3. S   disgusting person _____

4. W   When _____

5. S   loses his temper _____

6. C   just in time _____

7. C   nice young woman _____

8. W   many _____

9. S   fine _____

10. C   are relieved _____

15 Misplaced and Dangling Modifiers

Seeing What You Know

What do you think the writer was trying to say in each of the following sentences? Underline the part of each sentence that does not seem clear. Then read the explanations below.

1. We looked at <u>twenty-five sofas shopping on Saturday</u>.

2. <u>Thrown in a heap on the closet floor, Jean</u> found her son's dirty laundry.

3. <u>Carrying in the main course, the roast</u> slid off its platter.

4. <u>While taking notes in class, Jerome's thoughts</u> were elsewhere.

Understanding the Answers

1. *Twenty-five sofas shopping on Saturday* is the unclear part of the sentence. The intended meaning is that we saw twenty-five sofas while *we* (not the twenty-five sofas) were shopping on Saturday. A better way to say so would be *Shopping on Saturday,* we looked at twenty-five sofas.

2. *Thrown in a heap on the closet floor, Jean* is the unclear part of the sentence.
It sounds as if *Jean* was thrown on the closet floor when she found her son's laundry. The writer means, however, that Jean found *her son's dirty laundry* thrown in a heap on the closet floor.

3. *Carrying in the main course, the roast* is the unclear part of the sentence. The sentence seems to say that the *roast* was carrying in the main course. Actually, the roast *was* the main course; a person (not the roast) was carrying it. To make the intended meaning clear, rewrite the sentence to show who that person was: *As Stacy was* carrying in the main course, the roast slid off its platter.

4. *While taking notes in class, Jerome's thoughts* is the unclear part of the sentence.
It sounds as if *Jerome's thoughts* were taking notes in class. The sentence needs to be rewritten like this: While *Jerome was* taking notes in class, *his* thoughts were elsewhere.

A **modifier** is one or more words that describe other words. Two common errors involving these descriptive words are misplaced modifiers and dangling modifiers.

MISPLACED MODIFIERS

When a modifier is in the wrong place, the reader may not know just what it is meant to describe. Misplaced modifiers can lead to misunderstandings—some of which are unintentionally humorous.

To correct a misplaced modifier, place it as close as possible to what it is describing, so that its meaning will be clearly understood.

Misplaced modifier: The Bensons watched the parade of high school bands sitting in chairs on their lawn.
(It sounds as if *the high school bands* were sitting in chairs, rather than the Bensons.)

Corrected version: **Sitting in chairs on their lawn, the Bensons** watched the parade of high school bands.

Misplaced modifier: Please take this book to Mrs. Bey's house which she lent to me.
(Did Mrs. Bey lend her *house* to the speaker?)

Corrected version: Please take **this book, which Mrs. Bey lent to me,** to her house.

Misplaced modifier: The holdup man ran into the bank carrying a gun.
(The *bank* was carrying a gun?)

Corrected version: **The holdup man, carrying a gun,** ran into the bank.

Practice 1

Underline the misplaced modifier in each sentence. Then rewrite the sentence, placing the modifier where it needs to go to make the meaning clear.

1. The young man gave his driver's license to the officer <u>with shaking hands.</u>

   With shaking hands, the young man gave his driver's license to the officer.

2. We were surprised to hear a siren <u>driving down the country road.</u>

   Driving down the country road, we were surprised to hear a siren.

3. Gina got badly sunburned after spending a day at the beach <u>on her face and back.</u>

   Gina got badly sunburned on her face and back after spending a day at the beach.

4. The registrar will post the schedule for final exams <u>on the Web site.</u>

   The registrar will post on the Web site the schedule for final exams.

5. Stan bought a sports car from a fast-talking salesman <u>with wire wheels.</u>

   Stan bought a sports car with wire wheels from a fast-talking salesman.

SINGLE-WORD MODIFIERS

Pay special attention to single-word modifiers, such as *almost, only,* and *nearly.* For their meaning to be correctly understood, they should be placed directly in front of the word they describe.

Misplaced modifier: Sean won the pole vault event when he almost jumped sixteen feet.
(Did Sean think about jumping sixteen feet, but then not jump at all?)

Corrected version: Sean won the pole vault event when he **jumped almost sixteen feet**.
(The intended meaning—that Sean's winning jump was not quite sixteen feet—is now clear.)

Misplaced modifier: Tanya nearly earned a thousand dollars last summer.
(Tanya had the chance to make a lot of money but didn't take advantage of it?)

Corrected version: Tanya **earned nearly a thousand dollars** last summer.
(Now we see—she earned close to a thousand dollars.)

Practice 2

Underline the misplaced single-word modifier in each sentence. Then rewrite the sentence, placing the modifier where it will make the meaning clear.

1. My sister <u>nearly</u> spends all evening on the telephone.
   My sister spends nearly all evening on the telephone.

2. Carlos must have <u>almost</u> answered a hundred ads before he found a job.
   Carlos must have answered almost a hundred ads before he found a job.

3. I <u>only</u> asked the instructor for one day's extension, but she refused.
   I asked the instructor for only one day's extension, but she refused.

DANGLING MODIFIERS

A modifier that starts a sentence must be followed right away by the word it is meant to describe. Otherwise, the modifier is said to be dangling, and the sentence takes on an unintended meaning. Look at this example:

Staring dreamily off into space, the teacher's loud voice startled me.

The modifier *staring dreamily off into space* is followed by *the teacher's loud voice,* giving the impression that the voice was staring off into space. However, this is not what the author intended. The modifier was meant to describe a word that is missing: *I.*

There are two ways to correct a dangling modifier:

1   Add a subject and verb to the opening word group, and revise as necessary.

As I was staring dreamily off into space, the teacher's loud voice startled me.

2   Place the word or words being described immediately after the opening word group, and revise as necessary.

Staring dreamily off into space, **I was startled by** the teacher's loud voice.

Here are more examples of dangling modifiers and ways they can be corrected:

Dangling modifier: When pulling out of the driveway, the hedge blocks Tracy's view.
(Is the *hedge* pulling out of the driveway?)

Corrected versions: **Whenever Tracy pulls** out of the driveway, the hedge blocks **her** view. *Or:* When pulling out of the driveway, **Tracy finds that** the hedge blocks **her** view.

Dangling modifier: Delighted with the movie, conversation over coffee ended our evening.
(Was the *conversation* delighted with the movie?)

Corrected versions: **We were** delighted with the movie **and** ended our evening **with** conversation over coffee. *Or:* Delighted with the movie, **we** ended our evening **with** conversation over coffee.

Practice 3

In each sentence, underline the dangling modifier. Then, on the line provided, rewrite the sentence so that the intended meaning is clear. Use both methods of fixing dangling modifiers.

Answers may vary.

1. While taking a shower, a mouse ran across my bathroom floor.
    While I was taking a shower, a mouse ran across my bathroom floor.

2. Sitting on the front porch, mosquitoes became annoying.
    Sitting on the front porch, we were annoyed by mosquitoes.

3. While eating at the restaurant, Kareem's coat was stolen.
    While Kareem was eating at the restaurant, his coat was stolen.

4. Ill from the heat, the finish line finally came into the runner's view.
    Ill from the heat, the runner finally saw the finish line come into view.

5. Hoping to catch a glimpse of the band, the parking lot was full of fans.
    Hoping to catch a glimpse of the band, fans filled the parking lot.

Name _____ Section _____ Date _____

Score: (Number right) _____ × 12.5 = _____ %

■ **Misplaced and Dangling Modifiers: Test 1**

In each sentence, underline the one misplaced or dangling modifier. (The first four sentences contain misplaced modifiers; the second four sentences contain dangling modifiers.) Then rewrite each sentence so that its intended meaning is clear.

Note   To help you correct misplaced and dangling modifiers, explanations are given for half of the sentences.

Answers may vary.

1. Kwan returned the overdue book to the librarian behind the desk <u>with apologies</u>.

   With apologies, Kwan returned the overdue book to the librarian behind the desk.

   The sentence suggests that the desk had apologies. The modifier *with apologies* needs to be placed next to *Kwan.*

2. A group of students talked about fishing with live bait <u>in shop class</u>.

   In shop class, a group of students talked about fishing with live bait.

3. The shipwrecked sailors <u>almost</u> went without food and water for a week.

   The shipwrecked sailors went without food and water for almost a week.

   The sentence suggests that the sailors were in danger of going without food and water but avoided this danger. The writer actually means that the sailors *did* go without food and water—for just under a week.

4. Invitations to graduation exercises were <u>nearly</u> sent out to five hundred people.

   Invitations to graduation exercises were sent out to nearly five hundred people.

5. <u>Jumping at a sudden noise</u>, the razor nicked Dean's face.

   Jumping at a sudden noise, Dean nicked his face with the razor.

   Dean, not the razor, was the one who jumped at a sudden noise.

6. <u>Just before leaving for home</u>, the secretary's telephone rang.

   Just before the secretary left for home, her (or his) telephone rang.

7. <u>While hiking through the state park</u>, many animals can be seen.

   While hiking through the state park, people can see many animals.

   People—not animals—are the ones who are hiking through the state park.

8. <u>Tossing trash out the window</u>, the teenagers' car was stopped by the police.

   Because the teenagers were tossing trash out the window, the police stopped their car.

To the Instructor   Additional tests on misplaced and dangling modifiers can be found in the *Instructor's Manual.*

■ ## Misplaced and Dangling Modifiers: Test 2

In each sentence, underline the one misplaced or dangling modifier. (The first four sentences contain misplaced modifiers; the second four sentences contain dangling modifiers.) Then rewrite each sentence so that its intended meaning is clear.

Answers may vary.

1. The instructor told the students to sit down <u>in a loud voice</u>.
    In a loud voice, the instructor told the students to sit down.

2. The children placed their soup on the windowsill, <u>which was too hot to eat</u>.
    The children placed their soup, which was too hot to eat, on the windowsill.

3. After her husband's death, the widow <u>almost</u> refused all invitations to go out.
    After her husband's death, the widow refused almost all invitations to go out.

4. Residents of the burning house were carried out by firemen <u>wearing only pajamas</u>.
    Residents of the burning house, wearing only pajamas, were carried out by firemen.

5. <u>Involved in a noisy game of Monopoly</u>, the summer evening together was enjoyable for us.
    Involved in a noisy game of Monopoly, we enjoyed the summer evening together.

6. <u>Growing thinner every day</u>, Albert's diet is really working.
    Since Albert is growing thinner every day, his diet is really working.

7. Whining and twitching, the <u>dog's dream must have been</u> about chasing rabbits.
    Whining and twitching, the dog must have been dreaming about chasing rabbits.

8. <u>Unable to read yet</u>, my mother explained that the sign said, "No children allowed."
    As I was unable to read yet, my mother explained that the sign said, "No children allowed."

Name _____ Section _____ Date _____

■ Misplaced and Dangling Modifiers: Test 3

Each group of sentences contains one misplaced and one dangling modifier. Underline these errors. Then, on the lines provided, rewrite the parts of the sentences that contain the errors so that the intended meanings are clear.

Note To help you correct misplaced and dangling modifiers, explanations are given for the first error in each group.

1. Will was disappointed when he looked in the refrigerator. There had been lots of spaghetti last night. His roommates, however, <u>almost</u> had eaten all of it. <u>Frowning angrily</u>, nothing but a few strands of spaghetti were left.

   a. _had eaten almost all of it._

   The sentence suggests that the roommates *didn't* eat the spaghetti. Actually, they did eat most of it.

   b. _Frowning angrily, he found nothing left but a few strands of spaghetti._

2. Lani stopped to watch the sidewalk artist <u>with amazement</u>. He was drawing a pencil portrait of a little girl. <u>Sketching quickly</u>, the portrait took shape under the artist's careful hand. "What remarkable talent," Lani commented.

   a. _With amazement, Lani_

   Lani, not the artist, is the one who is amazed.

   b. _As he sketched quickly,_

3. I lost my raincoat last fall. I thought I'd looked everywhere for it. Then, yesterday, <u>stuffed under the bed</u>, I spotted it. <u>Wrinkled and dusty</u>, I was still delighted.

   a. _I spotted it, stuffed under the bed._

   The intended meaning is that the *raincoat*—not the speaker—was under the bed.

   b. _Although it was wrinkled and dusty,_

4. The sky was blue and clear when we arrived home. Only minutes later, though, there was a sudden crash of thunder. <u>Rushing like mad</u>, the windows in the bedrooms were closed. Staring out at the downpour, we were glad to be safe inside. Then we remembered our open car windows, <u>groaning with dismay</u>.

   a. _Rushing like mad, we closed the windows in the bedroom._

   Rushing like mad seems to be describing the windows.

   b. _Then, groaning with dismay, we_

Name _____   Section _____   Date _____
Score: (Number right) _____ × 12.5 = _____%

■ Misplaced and Dangling Modifiers: Test 4

Each group of sentences contains one misplaced and one dangling modifier. Underline these errors. Then, on the lines provided, rewrite the parts of the sentences that contain the errors so that the intended meanings are clear.

Answers may vary.

1. Going to camp was a nightmare for me. <u>Being afraid of water</u>, swimming was a frightening experience. I got a terrible case of poison ivy all over my legs, <u>which seemed to be everywhere at the camp</u>. I always remembered my time at camp as the longest week of my life.

   a. _Since I was afraid of water,_____

   b. _poison ivy, which seemed to be everywhere at the camp, all over___

2. Nick couldn't get to sleep. He was still thinking about his biology teacher. He felt sure she would <u>only</u> give him a D for the class. <u>Glaring at him from the front of the room</u>, he remembered her criticism the day before.

   a. _give him only a D_____

   b. _Glaring at him from the front of the room, she had criticized him the day before._

3. "I'd like to meet the girl who works in the snack shop <u>with the red hair</u>," said Vince. "Do you mean my cousin Helen? I can introduce you," his friend Tony replied. <u>Pleased and excited</u>, the meeting was soon arranged.

   a. _the girl with the red hair who works in the snack shop,"____

   b. _Pleased and excited, Tony soon arranged the meeting._____

4. <u>Cold and hungry</u>, the street seemed a cruel place. People passing by ignored the homeless man completely. He watched them talking and laughing, <u>sitting on the sidewalk in his thin sweater</u>. "When I get out of this mess, I'm never going to ignore another street person again," he promised himself.

   a. _Since the homeless man was cold and hungry, . . . People passing by ignored him_

   b. _Sitting on the sidewalk in his thin sweater, he watched_____

Name _____   Section _____ Date _____
Score: (Number right) _____ × 12.5 = _____ %

■ **Misplaced and Dangling Modifiers: Test 5**

Eight of the sentences in the following passage contain a misplaced or dangling modifier. Underline each modifier you believe to be misplaced or dangling, and then rewrite the parts of the sentences that contain the errors so that the intended meanings are clear.

Note   To help you correct misplaced and dangling modifiers, explanations are given for four of the sentences.

Corrections may vary.

Ted and Linda decided to give their friend Garry a surprise birthday party that he would never forget. <u>Working hard to make everything perfect,</u> their menu was planned weeks in advance. They ordered a beautiful cake from a bakery <u>with thirty-five candles.</u> They bought five flavors of ice cream for the party, <u>which they hid in the freezer.</u> They scattered dozens of colorful balloons around the house, <u>which they filled with helium.</u> Finally, <u>excited and pleased with all they had done,</u> the guests were eagerly awaited. Linda saw people starting to arrive <u>through the window.</u> However, Garry was nowhere in sight. Suddenly, with a gasp, Ted realized that he had forgotten to bring the guest of honor. <u>Rushing off in search of Garry,</u> the party finally started—an hour late. "This party was supposed to <u>only</u> be a surprise for Garry," Ted said to the crowd, "but it turned out to be surprising for us as well."

1. _perfect, Ted and Linda planned their menu weeks in advance._
   The words *working hard to make everything perfect* apply to Ted and Linda, not to their menu.

2. _They ordered from a bakery a beautiful cake with thirty-five candles._

3. _ice cream, which they hid in the freezer, for the party._
   The writer means that the ice cream—not the party—was hidden in the freezer.

4. _balloons, which they filled with helium, around the house._

5. _done, Ted and Linda eagerly awaited their guests._
   Ted and Linda, not the guests, are the ones who were excited and pleased.

6. _Through the window, Linda saw people starting to arrive._

7. _Ted rushed off in search of Garry, and the party_
   The words *Rushing off in search of Garry* seem to be describing the party, but they really are about Ted.

8. _to be a surprise only for Garry (or: for only Garry)_

Name _____   Section _____   Date _____

Score: (Number right) _____ × 12.5 = _____%

■ Misplaced and Dangling Modifiers: Test 6

Eight of the sentences in the following passage contain a misplaced or dangling modifier. Underline each modifier you believe to be misplaced or dangling, and then rewrite the parts of the sentences that contain the errors so that the intended meanings are clear.

Corrections may vary.

Spending the evening together recently, a group of friends got talking about their most embarrassing moments in grade school. Pauline volunteered to tell hers first. "We were having gym class," she said. "Bouncing on the trampoline, my shorts fell down and completely off my feet."

"While taking a test, I was caught cheating," remembered Lin. "I had written the answers to the test on my fingernails. I was asked to write 'I will never cheat again' one hundred times on the board by the teacher. All my classmates almost looked at me as if I were a criminal."

Finally Karen told a story about a classmate, Marta. "Since Marta had just moved from another state, none of us knew her," she said. "Being taller than any of us and gawky, we found her weird, and we didn't make friends with her. Going out to recess one day, it began to snow. As usual, Marta asked if she could play with us, and this time we said 'yes.' While tying her to the swings, Marta asked what game this was. We told her she was a prisoner and we'd come to rescue her later, but then the recess bell rang. So we left her tied to the swings with evil laughs. The teachers found her pretty soon, and we all got in big trouble. I saw Marta again recently," Karen continued. "Still tall, she's now also gorgeous and rich—and a top model in New York."

1. _While I was bouncing on the trampoline,_____
2. _On my fingernails, I had written the answers to the test._____
3. _I was asked by the teacher to write_____
4. _classmates looked at me almost as if_____
5. _Since she was taller than any of us and gawky,_____
6. _When we were going out to recess one day,_____
7. _While we were tying her to the swings,_____
8. _So, with evil laughs, we left her tied to the swings._____

16 Parallelism

Seeing What You Know

Underline the part of each sentence that is not in balance with other parts of the sentence. Then read the explanations that follow.

1. The manager is competent, good-natured, and <u>offers help</u>.

2. <u>To lick water off the shower curtain</u>, climbing up the side of the house, and sleeping in the kitchen sink are some of my cat's strange habits.

3. The expensive restaurant served overcooked fish, <u>clam chowder that was cold</u>, and half-melted ice cream.

4. No matter what his doctor tells him, Grady still smokes cigars, drinks heavily, and <u>is staying out late at night</u>.

Understanding the Answers

1. *Offers help* is the unbalanced portion of the sentence.
   Change it to *helpful* to match *competent* and *good-natured*.

2. *To lick water off the shower curtain* is out of balance.
   Change it to *Licking water off the shower curtain* to match *climbing up the side of the house* and *sleeping in the kitchen sink*.

3. *Clam chowder that was cold* is the nonparallel part of the sentence.
   Change it to *cold clam chowder* to give it the same form as the other two dishes—*overcooked fish* and *half-melted ice cream*.

4. *Is staying out late at night* is the unbalanced portion of the sentence.
   Change it to *stays out late at night* so that it has the same form as the other two parts of the list: *smokes cigars* and *drinks heavily*.

175

Two or more equal ideas should be expressed in **parallel,** or matching, form. The ideas will then read smoothly and naturally.

CORRECTING FAULTY PARALLELISM

Faulty parallelism is jarring and awkward to read. Consider this example:

Not parallel: The bowl was filled with **crisp apples, juicy oranges,** and **bananas that were ripe**.

In *crisp apples* and *juicy oranges,* the descriptive word comes first and the word being described comes second. In *bananas that were ripe,* the order is reversed.

To achieve parallelism, give the nonparallel item the same form as the others:

Parallel: The bowl was filled with crisp apples, juicy oranges, and **ripe bananas**.

Now, the listed items are expressed in parallel form: *crisp apples, juicy oranges,* and *ripe bananas.*

Here are additional examples of problems with parallelism and explanations of how to correct them:

Not parallel: My neighbor likes **to plant a garden, watering it,** and even **to weed it**.

    To plant a garden and *to weed it* are similar in construction, but *watering it* is not. For parallel construction, another *to* is needed.

Parallel: My neighbor likes to plant a garden, **to water it,** and even to weed it.

Not parallel: Would you prefer to spend the morning **playing basketball, watching television,** or **at the mall**?

    The word groups *playing basketball* and *watching television* both are *-ing* constructions, so *at the mall* needs an *-ing* word.

Parallel: Would you prefer to spend the morning **playing basketball, watching television,** or **shopping at the mall**?

Not parallel: The moviegoers **talked** and **were rattling** popcorn boxes during the film.

    Talked, an *-ed* construction, is not parallel to *were rattling.* The problem could be corrected by changing either word group.

Parallel: The moviegoers **talked** and **rattled** popcorn boxes during the film.

Also parallel: The moviegoers *were talking* and *were rattling* popcorn boxes during the film.

Practice 1

Cross out the one item in each list below that is not parallel in form to the other two items. Then, in the space provided, write the parallel form for that item.

1. to gather information
   to write several drafts
   ~~typing the report~~
   to type the report

2. couple argued
   neighbors listened
   ~~crying baby~~
   baby cried

3. wide-brimmed hat
   ~~sunglasses that are dark~~
   protective sunscreen
   dark sunglasses

4. ~~managing an office~~
   sales representative
   telephone operator
   office manager

5. selfish
   impatient
   ~~lacking kindness~~
   unkind

6. teaches social studies
   ~~is coach of the track team~~
   runs the teachers' union
   coaches the track team

Practice 2

The part of each sentence that is not parallel is italicized. On the line, rewrite this part to make it match the other items listed.

1. The young boy, who is very talented, can sing, dance, and _knows how to play the piano._ _play the piano_

2. The most popular items on the buffet table were _shrimp that were steamed,_ barbecued wings, and marinated steak tips. _steamed shrimp_

3. Fall styles include wide-legged pants, short-cropped jackets, and _boots with high heels._ _high-heeled boots_

4. Their intelligence, playfulness, and _being friendly_ make dolphins appeal to people of all ages. _friendliness_

5. The crane's claws cradled the telephone pole, lifted it high overhead, and _were depositing it in the deep hole._ _deposited it in the deep hole_

WHEN TO USE PARALLELISM

Parallelism always applies to two or more _equal_ ideas. Here are some writing situations in which parallelism is appropriate:

1   Presenting a series of items.

Popular summer vacation activities include **visiting** relatives, **hiking** in state parks, and **spending** time at the beach.

2   Offering choices.

The instructor announced that each student in the class could either **write a ten-page report** or **take the final exam.**

3   Making a point effectively. Many famous speeches and pieces of writing feature skillful parallelism. The balance of their words and phrases helps make them memorable. For example,

"Ask not what your country can do for you; **ask what** you can do for your country." —*President John F. Kennedy*

Would Kennedy's speech have had the same ring if he'd said, "Don't ask what your country can do for you. Instead, you should be asking what you can do for your country"?

In his famous "I Have a Dream" speech, Dr. Martin Luther King, Jr., said he hoped that someday America would judge his children not **"by the color of their skin** but **by the content of their character."**

Dr. King's words gain power because they balance "the color of their skin" with "the content of their character." They would have been much less forceful if he had said instead, "Not by the color of their skin but according to how good a person each one is."

Practice 3

In the space provided, complete each list by adding a parallel item.

Answers will vary. Some possibilities are given.

1. Three household tasks that most people could do without are washing dishes, dusting furniture, and ___scrubbing floors___.

2. To get the best buy on an appliance, compare brands, visit several stores, and ___wait for sales___.

3. At the adult evening school, I could sign up for a course in ballroom dancing, aerobic exercising, or ___creative writing___.

4. "I still need a number of volunteers," the park director said, "to rake leaves, pick up trash, and ___plant flowers___."

5. Members of the work crew spent their lunch break eating sandwiches, napping on the grass, and ___reading newspapers___.

Name _____   Section _____   Date _____

Score: (Number right) _____ × 12.5 = _____%

■ Parallelism: Test 1

Underline the part of each sentence below that upsets the sentence's parallelism. Then, in the space provided, rewrite the nonparallel item so that it matches the other item or items listed.

Note   To help you master the technique of parallelism, directions are given for half of the sentences.

1. Hawaii is famous for its beaches that are beautiful, warm climate, and exotic atmosphere.

   beautiful beaches
   _____

   Beaches that are beautiful is the unbalanced part of the sentence. It needs to be changed to the same form as *warm climate* and *exotic atmosphere*.

2. Before leaving for work, Teresa exercises, eats breakfast, and the dog is fed.

   feeds the dog
   _____

3. A wrecked car and breaking a collarbone were the results of the accident.

   a broken collarbone
   _____

   Breaking a collarbone should be made parallel to *A wrecked car.*

4. Their father's gentleness and the sense of humor of their mother were two things that the children missed after they left home.

   their mother's sense of humor (or: The gentleness of their father)
   _____

5. Although the boss is smart, has good looks, and wealthy, he is coldhearted.

   good-looking
   _____

   Has good looks upsets the sentence's parallelism. It needs to be changed to the same form as *smart* and *wealthy.*

6. Even though Laila and Omar both loved to dance, enjoyed similar movies, and they shared some of the same friends, their blind date was not a success.

   shared some of the same friends
   _____

7. Three remedies for an upset stomach are antacid pills, a diet that is bland, and flat ginger ale.

   a bland diet
   _____

   A diet that is bland is out of balance. It needs to match *antacid pills* and *flat ginger ale.*

8. With her long legs, movements that are graceful, and pulled-back hair, the young woman looks like a ballerina.

   graceful movements
   _____

To the Instructor   Additional tests on parallelism can be found in the *Instructor's Manual.*

Name _____   Section _____   Date _____

Score: (Number right) _____ × 10 = _____%

■ Parallelism: Test 2

Underline the part of each sentence below that upsets the sentence's parallelism. Then, in the space provided, rewrite the nonparallel item so that it matches the other item or items listed.

Answers will vary.

1. At the International Food Festival, visitors tasted tortillas, snacked on suki-yaki, and <u>were munching on manicotti</u>.

   munched on manicotti

2. Having little money and <u>because he owed a great deal</u>, the discouraged inventor decided to file for bankruptcy.

   owing a great deal (or: Because he had little money)

3. The ragged woman said she needed a meal, <u>to have warm clothes</u>, and a job.

   warm clothes

4. You'll always be happy if you have your health, a loving family, and <u>your work is satisfying</u>.

   satisfying work

5. The Harborside Restaurant offers delicious food, good service, and <u>prices that are reasonable</u>.

   reasonable prices

6. Making promises is easy; <u>to keep them</u> is hard.

   keeping them (Or: To make promises)

7. The public relations position includes handling customers' complaints, keeping in touch with clients, and <u>to write marketing material</u>.

   writing marketing material

8. Because she missed her friend and <u>wanting her to visit</u>, Juanita telephoned her with an invitation.

   wanted her to visit (Or: Missing her friend)

9. Every year at the family barbecue, we choose teams and <u>are playing</u> touch football.

   play

10. The professor suggested dropping the course or <u>to get extra tutoring</u>.

    getting extra tutoring

Name _____ Section _____ Date _____

Score: (Number right) _____ × 10 = _____ %

■ Parallelism: Test 3

Each group of sentences contains **two** errors in parallelism. Underline these errors. Then, on the lines below, rewrite the unbalanced portion to make it parallel with the other listed items in the sentence.

Note   To help you master the technique of parallelism, hints are provided for half of the sentences.

1. The police officers have been setting up roadblocks, stopping traffic, and they have questioned drivers for days. They are looking for a young man who tied up, beat, and was robbing an elderly store owner last week.

    a. _questioning drivers_   (*They have questioned drivers* must parallel

    b. _robbed_   *setting up roadblocks* and *stopping traffic.*)

2. Good teachers, a modern facility, and students who are hardworking have all given the high school an excellent reputation. The school replaced two smaller schools that were known as places where teachers were third-rate, shabby described the buildings, and students were frustrated.

    a. _hardworking students_   (*Students who are hardworking* must parallel

    b. _buildings were shabby_   *good teachers* and *a modern facility.*)

3. My sister is a terrific athlete. She enjoys tennis, plays volleyball, and even rock climbing. I, on the other hand, find it challenging enough to climb stairs, walk around the block, or running for a bus.

    a. _volleyball_   (*Plays volleyball* must parallel *tennis* and

    b. _run for a bus_   *rock climbing.*)

4. With her long black hair, eyes that are sparkling and dark, and tall, slim body, Regina looks like a fashion model. But she worries that no one notices her intelligence and hard work. Regina wants people to know that a woman can have beauty, ambition, and be intelligent, too.

    a. _sparkling dark eyes_   (*Eyes that are sparkling and dark* needs to

    b. _intelligence_   parallel *long black hair* and *tall, slim body.*)

5. Working conditions at the factory were poor: loud machinery, conversations that were shouted, and blaring radios. Workers also complained about the low pay and the hours were long.

    a. _shouted conversations_   (*Conversations that were shouted* must

    b. _long hours_   parallel *loud machinery* and *blaring radios.*)

■ Parallelism: Test 4

Each group of sentences contains **two** errors in parallelism. Underline these errors. Then, on the lines below, rewrite the unbalanced portion to make it parallel with the other listed items in the sentence.

1. Everything seemed to go wrong on Tuesday. My car broke down, <u>my girlfriend not calling</u>, and I locked myself out of my apartment. Besides, I had a sore throat, a headache, and <u>my stomach ached</u>.

   a. _my girlfriend didn't call_____

   b. _a stomachache_____

2. I never spend money on fancy wrapping paper. When people get a present, they generally want to rip off the paper and <u>be looking</u> at what's inside. So I wrap my gifts in either plain brown grocery bags or <u>Sunday comics that are colorful</u>.

   a. _look_____

   b. _colorful Sunday comics_____

3. The symptoms of diabetes often include extreme thirst, hunger, and <u>losing weight</u>. The need to urinate frequently can also be a sign of the disease. If untreated, diabetes can lead to kidney and heart failure, <u>the person going into a coma</u>, and death.

   a. _weight loss_____

   b. _coma_____

4. My New Year's resolutions are to stop smoking, to study harder, and <u>getting more involved in campus activities</u>. On the other hand, my wife has resolved to eat more chocolate, <u>exercising less</u>, and to spend more time insulting my friends.

   a. _to get more involved in campus activities_____

   b. _to exercise less_____

5. The woman had ordered a large head of lettuce, <u>green beans that were fresh</u>, and ripe strawberries. The delivery man arrived with a <u>head of cabbage that was tiny</u>, frozen yellow beans, and sour red cherries.

   a. _fresh green beans_____

   b. _a tiny head of cabbage_____

Name _____ Section _____ Date _____

■ Parallelism: Test 5

Ten of the sentences in the passage below contain errors in parallelism. Underline the errors and write in the numbers of the sentences that contain the errors. Then rewrite the nonparallel portion of each sentence in the space provided.

Note   To help you master the technique of parallelism, directions are given for half of the sentences.

¹One summer Lynn worked as a student intern at her city's newspaper. ²Although she was young, didn't have much experience, and nervous, she did well at her job. ³Her cheerful attitude, willingness to work hard, and having the ability to get along with her coworkers impressed her editor. ⁴Lynn did some of everything: she wrote up traffic accidents and weddings, was covering a few meetings, and even helped the photographer in the darkroom.

⁵One day her editor said, "Lynn, our police reporter needs an assistant. ⁶Why don't you spend a few days following him around and see how you like it?" ⁷Ozzie, the police reporter, explained to Lynn that he spent much of his time talking with police officers, visited crime scenes, and interviewing victims and witnesses. ⁸Since she had always been interested in police work and liking Ozzie, Lynn was pleased with her new assignment. ⁹At first she just trailed Ozzie around, took notes, and was asking a lot of questions. ¹⁰One evening at home, however, as Lynn was straightening up her apartment and her plants were watered, Ozzie appeared at her door. ¹¹"Grab your notebook and camera—we're going on a raid," he yelled.

¹²Lynn dropped everything and was racing for Ozzie's car. ¹³Soon they were speeding toward the address Ozzie had: a campground that had been closed for years. ¹⁴Expecting a drug raid, the reporters were surprised to find dozens of police officers there breaking up an illegal cockfight operation. ¹⁵Lynn and Ozzie began photographing the dead and wounded roosters and to question the gamblers. ¹⁶As they drove back to the newspaper office late that night, Lynn said to Ozzie, "My college courses can teach me how to write, how to take pictures, and interviewing people. ¹⁷But they could never prepare me for a crazy night like this."

1. Sentence __2__: inexperienced   (Parallel *young* and *nervous*)

2. Sentence __3__: ability to get along with her coworkers

3. Sentence __4__: covered a few meetings   (Parallel *wrote up* and *helped*)

4. Sentence __7__: visiting crime scenes

5. Sentence __8__: she liked Ozzie   (Parallel *she had always been interested*)

6. Sentence __9__: asked a lot of questions

7. Sentence __10__: watering her plants   (Parallel *straightening up her apartment*)

8. Sentence __12__: raced for Ozzie's car

9. Sentence __15__: questioning the gamblers   (Parallel *photographing the dead and wounded roosters*)

10. Sentence __16__: how to interview people

■ Parallelism: Test 6

Ten of the sentences in the passage below contain errors in parallelism. Underline the errors and write in the numbers of the sentences that contain the errors. Then rewrite the nonparallel portion of each sentence in the space provided.

¹Dinosaurs and other ancient reptiles seem to fascinate almost everyone. ²Some were huge, some were fierce, peaceful ones lived also; but they all hold our interest millions of years after they died out.

³One ancient sea creature, the plesiosaur, was enormous, sharp-toothed, and moved slowly. ⁴Its tremendously long neck could flash out and catch a fish many feet away. ⁵Some people who have studied, sighted, and even did photograph the "Loch Ness monster" believe it to be a surviving plesiosaur.

⁶Many people's favorite dinosaurs are the immense brontosaurs, creatures that measured sixty feet long and weighing thirty or forty tons. ⁷Brontosaurs were plant-eaters—huge, frightening, but they were also peaceful. ⁸Wading into deep water and to let only their nostrils stick out of the water was their best defense against enemies.

⁹Other plant-eaters were better armed. ¹⁰The triceratops, for example, had two long horns above its eyes, a short horn above its mouth, and a hard, bony shield was around its neck. ¹¹On the basis of a study of its bones, which are often broken and with scars, scientists theorize that it was a fierce fighter.

¹²But the dinosaur that interests and is frightening people most of all is *Tyrannosaurus rex*. ¹³With its enormous jaws, six-inch teeth, and claws that were sharp, the tyrannosaur was the most ferocious meat-eater of all time. ¹⁴When it attacked, it was like a slicing, ripping, killing machine.

1. Sentence __2__: some were also peaceful
2. Sentence __3__: slow-moving
3. Sentence __5__: photographed
4. Sentence __6__: weighed
5. Sentence __7__: also peaceful
6. Sentence __8__: letting only their nostrils stick out (Or: To wade....)
7. Sentence __10__: a hard, bony shield around its neck
8. Sentence __11__: scarred
9. Sentence __12__: frightens
10. Sentence __13__: sharp claws

Part Two

Extending the Skills

Preview

Part Two presents some topics not included in Part One:

It also includes additional information about many of the topics presented in Part One:

17 PAPER FORM

Your instructor will probably give you specific directions for how your paper should look. However, the following guidelines normally apply:

1 Use 8.5- by 11-inch white paper.

2 Write or type on only one side of the paper.

3 Leave margins on all four sides of each page (1 to 1.5 inches is standard).

4 Put your title on the top line of the first page. Center it. Do not use quotation marks or underline your title. Capitalize the first word of the title as well as its other important words. (In the middle of a title, do not capitalize *a, an, the,* or prepositions of up to five letters: *of, in, on, for, from, about,* and so on.) Skip a line between the title and the first sentence of your paper.

5 Ideally, prepare your paper on a computer. But if you are writing by hand,

    a Use blue or black ink—never pencil.

    b Use wide-lined paper, or write on every other line of narrow-lined paper.

    c Leave spaces between words. Also, leave a bit more space between sentences.

    d Make punctuation marks and capital letters clear and easy to read.

    e Write as neatly and legibly as you can.

6 Indent the first line of each paragraph one-half inch from the left-hand margin. Do not indent when starting a new page—unless you are also starting a new paragraph.

7 If a word will not fit at the end of a line, hyphenate it (divide it with a hyphen) only between syllables. Do not divide a one-syllable word.

8 Make sure your pages are in the correct order, numbered (except for page 1), and fastened.

9 Put your name, the date, the course number, and, if required, your instructor's name where you have been told to put them—either at the top of page 1 or on a separate title page.

10 Proofread your paper carefully before handing it in. Neatly correct any errors you find. Recopy or print a new copy of the paper if you discover a great many errors.

Practice

Following are the title and the first paragraph of a paper. Copy the title (adding capital letters where needed) and as much of the paragraph as will fit into the model of lined paper below. Use the guidelines above.

Information for the paper:

Title: the importance of national service

In his inaugural address, President John F. Kennedy urged Americans to discover what they could do for their country. Many people, inspired by his words, support national service for America's youth. The idea is a good one for several reasons. National service would bring a sense of community back to American life. It would provide many needed social programs. Finally, it would give young people a sense of purpose.

	The Importance of National Service
	In his inaugural address, President John F. Kennedy
	urged Americans to discover what they could do for their
	country. Many people, inspired by his words, support national
	service for America's youth. The idea is a good one for several

18 SPELLING

The following hints will help even a poor speller become a better one.

1   **Use spelling aids.** These include a dictionary, a spelling-checker on a computer or electronic typewriter, and pocket-size electronic spell-checkers.

2   **Keep a personal spelling list.** Write down every word you misspell. Include its correct spelling, underline the difficult part of the word, and add any hints you can use to remember how to spell it. You might even want to start a spelling notebook that has a separate page for each letter of the alphabet. Here's one format you might use (another is on the inside back cover of this book):

How I spelled it	Correct spelling	Hints
recieve	rec<u>ei</u>ve	I before E except after C.
seperate	sep<u>a</u>rate	There's A RAT in sepARATe.

Study your list regularly, and refer to it whenever you write or proofread a paper.

3   **Learn commonly confused words.** Many spelling errors result from confusing words like *to* and *too, its* and *it's, where* and *were.* Study carefully the pairs of words on pages 136–138 and 222–224.

4   **Apply basic spelling rules.** Here are four rules that usually work. The first rule will help you spell *ie* and *ei* words. The last three rules refer to adding endings.

I before E rule: I before E except after C
                     Or when sounded like A, as in *neighbor* and *weigh.*

Examples: believe, chief, receive, ceiling, their
Exceptions: either, leisure, seize, science, society, foreign

Silent E rule: If a word ends in a silent (unpronounced) *e*, drop the *e* before an ending that starts with a vowel. Keep the *e* before an ending that begins with a consonant.

Examples: hope + ed = hoped   guide + ance = guidance
              confuse + ing = confusing love + ly = lovely
              fame + ous = famous   care + ful = careful

Exceptions: peaceable, truly, argument, judgment

Y rule: Change the final *y* of a word to *i* when

            a The last two letters of the word are a consonant plus *y.*
            b The ending being added begins with a vowel or is *-ful, -ly,* or *-ness.*

But: Keep a *y* that follows a vowel. Also, keep the *y* if the ending being added is *-ing.*

Examples: fly+ es = flies   happy + ness = happiness
              try + ed = tried   destroy + s = destroys
              beauty + ful = beautiful display + ed = displayed
              lucky + ly = luckily   carry + ing = carrying

Exceptions: paid, said, laid, daily

Doubling rule: Double the final consonant of a word when

            a The last three letters of the word are a consonant, a vowel, and a consonant (CVC).
            b The word is only one syllable (for example, *stop*) or is accented on the last syllable (for example, *begin*).
            c The ending being added begins with a vowel.

Examples: stop + ed = stopped   hot + er = hotter
              begin + ing = beginning red + est = reddest
              control + er = controller occur + ence = occurrence

Note   With amazing frequency, students misspell the words *a lot* and *all right*. In each case they incorrectly combine the words to form one word: *alot* and *alright*. Remember that both *a lot* and *all right* are two words!

Practice

Use the preceding rules to spell the ten words that follow.

1. (Add the ending)   party + s =   _____parties_____
2. (Add the ending)   refer + ed =   _____referred_____
3. (Add the ending)   write + ing =   _____writing_____
4. (Add the ending)   definite + ly =   _____definitely_____
5. (Write *ie* or *ei*)   dec__ei__ve
6. (Add the ending)   employ + er =   _____employer_____
7. (Add the ending)   admit + ance =   _____admittance_____
8. (Add the ending)   marry + ing =   _____marrying_____
9. (Write *ie* or *ei*)   fr__ie__ndly
10. (Add the ending)   pity + ful =   _____pitiful_____

19 PARTS OF SPEECH: A REVIEW

Words—the building blocks of sentences—can be divided into eight parts of speech. **Parts of speech** are classifications of words according to their meaning and use in a sentence. This chapter will explain the eight parts of speech:

nouns	prepositions	conjunctions
pronoun	adjectives	interjections
verbs	adverbs	

Nouns

A **noun** is a word that is used to name something: a person, a place, an object, or an idea. Here are some examples of nouns:

woman	**city**	**pancake**	**freedom**
Oprah Winfrey	**alley**	**diamond**	**possibility**
actor	**island**	**box**	**love**
Brad Pitt	**Chicago**	**Corvette**	**mystery**

Most nouns begin with a lowercase letter and are known as **common nouns.** These nouns name general things. Some nouns, however, begin with a capital letter. They are called **proper nouns.** While a common noun refers to a person or thing in general, a proper noun names someone or something specific. For example, *woman* is a common noun—it doesn't name a particular woman. On the other hand, *Oprah Winfrey* is a proper noun because it names a specific woman.

Singular and Plural Nouns

Singular nouns name one person, place, object, or idea. **Plural** nouns refer to two or more persons, places, objects, or ideas. Most singular nouns can be made plural with the addition of an *s*.

Some nouns, like *box, city, leaf,* and *woman,* have irregular plurals. You can check the plural of nouns you think may be irregular by looking up the singular form in a dictionary.

Singular:	pancake	alley	freedom	box	city	leaf	woman
Plural:	pancakes	alleys	freedoms	boxes	cities	leaves	women

For more information about nouns, see "Subjects and Verbs," pages 19–22.

Pronouns

A **pronoun** is a word that stands for a noun. Pronouns eliminate the need for constant repetition. Look at the following sentences:

After the phone rang eight times, Bill answered the phone.

Lisa met Lisa's friends in the record store at the mall. Lisa meets Lisa's friends there every Saturday.

The waiter rushed over to the new customers. The new customers asked the waiter for menus and coffee.

Now look at how much clearer and smoother the sentences sound with pronouns:

After the phone rang eight times, Bill answered **it.**
(The pronoun *it* is used to replace the word *phone.*)

Lisa met **her** friends in the record store at the mall. **She** meets **them** there every Saturday.
(The pronoun *her* is used to replace the word *Lisa.* The pronoun *she* replaces *Lisa.* The pronoun *them* replaces the words *Lisa's friends.*)

The waiter rushed over to the new customers. **They** asked **him** for menus and coffee.
(The pronoun *they* is used to replace the words *the new customers.* The pronoun *him* replaces the words *the waiter.*)

There are a number of types of pronouns. For convenient reference, they are described briefly in the box below.

Types of Pronouns

Personal pronouns can act in a sentence as subjects, objects, or possessives.

Singular: I, me, my, mine   you, your, yours   he, him, his; she, her, hers; it, its

Plural: we, us, our, ours   you, your, yours   they, them, their, theirs

Relative pronouns refer to someone or something already mentioned in the sentence.

who, whose, whom, which, that, whoever, whomever, whichever, whatever (These words begin dependent-word groups.)

Interrogative pronouns are used to ask questions.

who, whose, whom, which, what

Demonstrative pronouns are used to point out particular persons or things.

this, that, these, those

Note   Do not use *them* (as in *them* shoes), *this here, that there, these here,* or *those there* to point out.

Reflexive pronouns are those that end in *-self* or *-selves*. A reflexive pronoun is used as the object of a verb (as in *Cary cut **herself***) or the object of a preposition (as in *Jack sent a birthday card to **himself***) when the subject of the verb is the same as the object.

Singular: myself, yourself, himself, herself, itself

Plural: ourselves, yourselves, themselves

Intensive pronouns have exactly the same forms as reflexive pronouns. The difference is in how they are used. Intensive pronouns are used to add emphasis. (*I **myself** will need to read the contract before I sign it.*)

Indefinite pronouns do not refer to a particular person or thing.

One words: anyone, someone, everyone, no one, one, none
Body words: anybody, somebody, everybody, nobody
Thing words: anything, something, everything, nothing
Other indefinite pronouns: each, either, both, several, any, most, all

Reciprocal pronouns express shared actions or feelings.

each other, one another

For more information about pronouns, see "Pronouns," pages 83–86, and "Pronoun Types," pages 198–202.

Verbs

Every complete sentence must contain at least one verb. There are two types of verbs: **action verbs** and **linking verbs.**

Action Verbs

An **action verb** tells what is being done in a sentence. For example, look at the following sentences:

Mr. Jensen **swatted** at the bee with his hand.
Rainwater **poured** into the storm sewer.
The children **chanted** the words to the TV commercial.

In these sentences, the verbs are *swatted, poured,* and *chanted.* These words are all action verbs; they tell what is happening in each sentence.

Note   Action verbs can also be classified as **transitive** and **intransitive.** Transitive verbs have a direct object—something that receives the action: The bee **stung** Mr. Jensen. Intransitive verbs do not have a direct object: The sewer **overflowed.**

Linking Verbs

Some verbs are **linking verbs.** These verbs link (or join) a noun to something that is said about it. For example, look at the following sentence:

The clouds **are** steel gray.

In this sentence, *are* is a linking verb. It joins the noun *clouds* to words that describe it: *steel gray.* Other common linking verbs include *am, is, was, were, will be, appear, become, feel,* and the "sense verbs" *look, seem,* and *sound. Smell* and *taste* can also be used as linking verbs: The stew **smells** good. It **tastes** good, too.

Helping Verbs

Sometimes the verb of a sentence consists of more than one word. In these cases, the main verb will be joined by one or more **helping verbs.** Look at the following sentence:

The basketball team **will be leaving** for their game at six o'clock.

In this sentence, the main verb is *leaving.* The helping verbs are *will* and *be.*

Other helping verbs include *am, are, is, was, were, being, been, has, have, having, had, do, does, did, can, could, may, might, must, shall, should, will,* and *would.*

For more information about verbs, see "Subjects and Verbs," pages 19–22; "More about Subjects and Verbs," pages 208–209; "More about Verbs," pages 29–34; and "Even More about Verbs," pages 209–211.

Prepositions

A **preposition** is a word that connects a noun or a pronoun to another word in the sentence. For example, look at the following sentence:

A man in the bus was snoring loudly.

In is a preposition. It connects the noun *bus* to *man*.

Here is a list of common prepositions:

about	around	beside	for	off	under
above	at	between	from	on, onto	until
across	before	by	in, into	over	up
after	behind	down	inside	through	upon
along	below	during	like	to	with
among	beneath	except	of	toward	without

The noun or pronoun that a preposition connects to another word in the sentence is called the **object** of the preposition. A group of words that begins with a preposition and ends with its object is called a **prepositional phrase.** The words *in the bus,* for example, are a prepositional phrase.

Now read the following sentences and explanations:

An ant was crawling **up the teacher's leg.**
The noun *leg* is the object of the preposition *up. Up* connects *leg* with the word *crawling.* The prepositional phrase *up the teacher's leg* describes *crawling.* It tells just where the ant was crawling.

The man **with the black mustache** left the restaurant quickly.
The noun *mustache* is the object of the preposition *with.* The prepositional phrase *with the black mustache* describes the word *man.* It tells us exactly which man left the restaurant quickly.

The plant **on the windowsill** was a present **from my mother.**
The noun *windowsill* is the object of the preposition *on.* The prepositional phrase *on the windowsill* describes the word *plant.* It describes exactly which plant was a present.

There is a second prepositional phrase in this sentence. The preposition is *from*, and its object is *mother.* The prepositional phrase *from my mother* explains *present.* It tells who gave the present.

For more information about prepositions, see "Subjects and Verbs," pages 20–21, and "Subject-Verb Agreement," page 42.

Adjectives

An **adjective** is a word that describes a noun (the name of a person, place, or thing). Look at the following sentence:

The dog lay down on a mat in front of the fireplace.

Now look at this sentence when adjectives have been inserted:

The **shaggy** dog lay down on a **worn** mat in front of the fireplace.
The adjective *shaggy* describes the noun *dog;* the adjective *worn* describes the noun *mat.*

Adjectives add spice to our writing. They also help us to identify particular people, places, and things.

Adjectives can be found in two places:

1   An adjective may come before the word it describes (a **damp** night, the **moldy** bread, a **striped** umbrella).

2   An adjective that describes the subject of a sentence may come after a linking verb. The linking verb may be a form of the verb *be* (he *is* **furious,** I *am* **exhausted,** they *are* **hungry**). Other linking verbs include *feel, look, sound, smell, taste, appear, seem,* and *become* (the soup *tastes* **salty,** your hands *feel* **dry,** the dog *seems* **lost**).

Note   The words *a, an,* and *the* (called **articles**) are generally classified as adjectives.

For more information about adjectives, see "Adjectives and Adverbs," pages 202–203.

Adverbs

An **adverb** is a word that describes a verb, an adjective, or another adverb. Many adverbs end in the letters *ly.* Look at the following sentence:

The canary sang in the pet-store window as the shoppers greeted each other.

Now look at this sentence after adverbs have been inserted:

The canary sang **softly** in the pet-store window as the shoppers **loudly** greeted each other.

The adverbs add details to the sentence; they tell how the canary sang and how the shoppers greeted each other. They also allow the reader to contrast the singing of the canary to the noise the shoppers are making.

Look at the following sentences and the explanations of how adverbs are used in each case:

The chef yelled **angrily** at the young waiter.
The adverb *angrily* describes the verb *yelled.* It tells how the chef yelled.

My mother has an extremely **busy** schedule on Tuesdays.
The adverb *extremely* describes the adjective *busy.* It tells how busy the schedule is.

The sick man spoke **very faintly** to his loyal nurse.

The adverb *very* describes the adverb *faintly*. *Faintly* tells how the sick man spoke; *very* tells how faintly he spoke.

Some adverbs do not end in *-ly*. Examples include *very, often, never, always,* and *well.*

For more information about adverbs, see "Subjects and Verbs," page 22, and "Adjectives and Adverbs," pages 203–204.

Conjunctions

Conjunctions are words that connect. There are two types of conjunctions, coordinating and subordinating.

Coordinating Conjunctions (Joining Words)

Coordinating conjunctions join two equal ideas. Look at the following sentence:

Kevin **and** Steve interviewed for the job, **but** their friend Anne got it.

In this sentence, the coordinating conjunction *and* connects the proper nouns *Kevin* and *Steve.* The coordinating conjunction *but* connects the first part of the sentence, *Kevin and Steve interviewed for the job,* to the second part, *their friend Anne got it.*

Following is a list of all the coordinating conjunctions. In this book, they are simply called joining words.

for   and   nor   but   or   yet   so

One good way to remember all seven coordinating conjunctions is with a catchword made from their first letters: FANBOYS.

For more information about coordinating conjunctions, see information on joining words in "Sentence Types," page 53; "Run-Ons," pages 74–76; "Comma," pages 95–96; and "More about the Comma," page 216.

Subordinating Conjunctions (Dependent Words)

Subordinating conjunctions join two ideas of unequal importance. When a subordinating conjunction is added to a word group, the words can no longer stand alone as an independent sentence. They are no longer a complete thought. For example, look at the following sentence:

Karen fainted in class.

The word group *Karen fainted in class* is a complete thought. It can stand alone as a sentence.

See what happens when a subordinating conjunction is added to a complete thought:

When Karen fainted in class

Now the words cannot stand alone as a sentence. They are dependent on other words to complete the thought:

When Karen fainted in class, **we put her feet up on some books.**

Below are some subordinating conjunctions. In this book, they are called **dependent words,** and the word groups containing them are called **dependent word groups.**

after	before	if	though	where, wherever
although	even if	in order that	unless	whether
as	even though	since	until	while
because	how	so that	when, whenever	

Here are some more sentences with subordinating conjunctions:

After she finished her last exam, Joanne said, "Now I can relax."
After she finished her last exam is not a complete thought. It is dependent on the other part of the sentence, *Joanne said, "Now I can relax,"* to be a complete sentence.

Lamont listens to books on tape **while** he drives to work.
While he drives to work cannot stand by itself as a sentence. It depends on the rest of the sentence, *Lamont listens to books on tape,* to make up a complete thought.

Since apples were on sale, we decided to make an apple pie for dessert.
Since apples were on sale is not a complete sentence. It depends on *we decided to make an apple pie for dessert* to complete the thought.

Note   Do not confuse the preposition *like* with the subordinating conjunction *as.* Use *like* before a noun: That coffee tastes **like** mud. Use *as* or *as if* before a subject and verb: That coffee tastes **as if** it could power a diesel engine. Still, nothing wakes me up as quickly **as** coffee does.

For more information about subordinating conjunctions, see information on dependent words in "Sentence Types," page 54; "Fragments," pages 62–63; and "Run-Ons," pages 75–76.

Correlative Conjunctions

Correlative conjunctions are pairs of words that join two equal items: *either/or, neither/nor, both/and, not only/but also.* They are often found in compound subjects and in sentences using parallel structure:

Neither the coach **nor** the players could figure out why they had lost the game.

I am allergic **not only** to fish **but also** to shellfish.

For more examples of the use of correlative conjunctions, see "Parallelism," pages 176–178, and "More about Subject-Verb Agreement," pages 212–213.

Interjections

Interjections are words that can stand independently and are used to express emotion. They are often followed by an exclamation point. Examples are *oh, wow, ouch*, and *oops*. These words are usually not found in formal writing.

"**Hey!**" yelled Maggie. "That's my bike."

Oh, we're late for class.

A Final Note

A word may function as more than one part of speech. For example, the word *dust* can be a verb or a noun, depending on its role in the sentence.

I **dust** my bedroom once a month, whether it needs it or not. *(verb)*

The top of my refrigerator is covered with an inch of **dust**. *(noun)*

20 PRONOUN TYPES

Subject Pronouns

Subject pronouns function as subjects of verbs. These are the subject pronouns:

I	you	he	she	it	we	they

Here are some examples of subject pronouns in sentences:

He can resolve the problem. (*He* is the subject of the verb *can resolve*.)

You and **she** had a fight. (*You* and *she* are the ones who had a fight.)

It was **I** who called you.
(Use a subject pronoun after a form of the verb *be—am, are, is, was, were, has been*, etc.)

I'm as hungry as **they**.
(This means, "I'm as hungry as they *are*." *They* is the subject of the suggested verb *are*.)

Object Pronouns

Object pronouns serve as the objects of verbs (receivers of the verbs' action) or of prepositions (the last words in prepositional phrases). Here is a list of object pronouns:

me	you	him	her	it	us	them

Here are examples of object pronouns in sentences:

The children had wandered away, but their father finally found **them**. (*Them* receives the action of the verb *found.*)

The teacher gave a retest to José and **me**. (*Me* is the object of the preposition *to.*)

Hint   If a sentence is about two people and you aren't sure which pronoun to use, try using each pronoun by itself. Then choose the pronoun that sounds correct. For example, you would say, "The teacher gave a retest to me," not "to I."

Possessive Pronouns

Possessive pronouns show ownership or possession. Here are the possessive pronouns:

Singular:	**my, mine**	**your, yours**	**his**	**her, hers**	**its**
Plural:	**our, ours**	**your, yours**		**their, theirs**	

Here are examples of possessive pronouns in sentences:

José got an A on **his** retest, but I got only a B on **mine**. (*His* refers to José's test; *mine* refers to my test.)

There are two points to remember about possessive pronouns:

1   Possessive pronouns never contain an apostrophe.

The book Alice lent me is missing **its** cover (not *it's cover*).

2   Do not use a subject or object pronoun where a possessive is needed.

Could I borrow **your** notes (not *you notes*) before the exam?
My refrigerator (not *me refrigerator*) is out of order.

Relative Pronouns

Relative pronouns refer to someone or something already mentioned in the sentence. Relative pronouns include the following:

who	**whose**	**whom**	**which**	**that**

Here are some examples of relative pronouns in sentences:

A cousin **whom** I've never met is coming to visit me. (*Whom* refers to *cousin.*)
The drill **that** you want is in the basement. (*That* refers to *drill.*)
Dick saw an old classmate **whose** name he had forgotten. (*Whose* refers to *classmate.*)

Here are some rules to remember about relative pronouns:

1   *Whose* means *belonging to whom.* Don't confuse it with *who's,* which means *who is.*

2   The pronouns *who* and *whom* refer to people. *Whose* usually refers to people but often refers to things ("The tree **whose** branches damaged our roof belongs to our neighbor"). *Which* refers to things. *That* can refer to either people or things.

3   *Who* is a subject pronoun; *whom* is an object pronoun.

    I wonder **who** is at the door. (*Who* is the subject of the verb *is.*)

    The clerk **whom** I asked couldn't help me. (*Whom* is the object of *asked.*)

Note   To determine whether to use *who* or *whom,* find the first verb after the place where the *who* or *whom* will go. Decide whether that verb already has a subject. If it lacks a subject, use the subject pronoun *who.* If it does have a subject, use the object pronoun *whom.*

My parents will accept any person (who, <u>whom</u>) I choose to marry.

Look at the verb *choose.* Does it have a subject? Yes, the subject is *I.* Therefore, the object pronoun *whom* is the correct choice: My parents will accept any person *whom* I choose to marry.

Demonstrative Pronouns

Demonstrative pronouns are used to point out one or more particular persons or things. These are the demonstrative pronouns:

this	**that**	**these**	**those**

This and *these* generally refer to things that are near the speaker; *that* and *those* refer to things farther away.

I like **this** better than **those.**

Don't ever say **that** to me again.

Note 1   Demonstrative pronouns can also be used as adjectives: **this** cake, **those** cookies, **that** word.

Note 2   Do not use *them, this here, that there, these here,* or *those there* to point out.

Reflexive and Intensive Pronouns

Singular:	**myself**	**yourself**	**himself, herself, itself**
Plural:	**ourselves**	**yourselves**	**themselves**

(Remember that the plural of *-self* is *-selves.* There is no such word as *ourself* or *themself.*)

A **reflexive pronoun** is the object of a verb or preposition in sentences in which that object is the same as the subject.

I gave **myself** a birthday present.
(The subject of the verb, *I,* is the same as the object of the verb, *myself.*)

In the shower, Dad talks out loud to **himself**.
(The subject of the sentence, *Dad,* is the same as the object of the preposition *to, himself.*)

An **intensive pronoun** emphasizes a noun or another pronoun.

I **myself** will tell the police what happened.

She has to do her schoolwork **herself**.

Interrogative Pronouns

Interrogative pronouns are used to ask questions. Here are common interrogative pronouns:

who	whose	whom	which	what

Here are examples of interrogative pronouns in sentences:

Who is downstairs?   **Which** road should we take?   **What** is the matter?

There are two points to remember about interrogative pronouns:

1 Choose *who* or *whom* in the same manner as you would for relative pronouns.
Whom should I pick for the team?
(*I* is the subject of *should pick,* so use *whom.*)
Who tries hardest?
(The verb after *who* is *tries,* which does not have a subject. Therefore, use the subject form of the word, *who.*)

2 *Whose* is the possessive form of *who. Who's* means *who is.*
Whose turn is it?   **Who's** bringing the sodas?

Indefinite Pronouns

Indefinite pronouns do not refer to specific persons or things. Most of them are singular:

one	none	each	either
anyone	someone	everyone	no one
anybody	somebody	everybody	nobody
anything	something	everything	nothing

Some are plural:

both   **several**   **few**   **many**

Some can be either singular or plural:

some   **most**   **any**   **all**

Here are examples of indefinite pronouns in sentences:

> **Somebody** ate the last piece of chocolate cake. **None** of the cake is left.
>
> **Both** of my sisters want to become police officers.
>
> **Most** of the house has been painted. (singular; refers to one thing—the house)
>
> **Most** of the rooms need painting, too. (plural; refers to several things—the rooms)

Practice

Underline the correct pronoun in each pair in parentheses.

1. Everyone else in my family is taller than (<u>I</u>, me).

2. All those dirty clothes on the closet floor are (<u>hers</u>, her's).

3. Today the manager warned two coworkers and (I, <u>me</u>) about personal use of the copy machine.

4. (<u>He</u>, Him) and (<u>I</u>, me) haven't seen each other in months.

5. Are those (you, <u>your</u>) muddy boots on the closet floor?

6. (Them, <u>Those</u>) eggs are rotten.

7. (<u>Who</u>, whom) is going to get a bonus this year?

8. Are you going to eat (<u>these</u>, these here) corn chips?

9. It is (<u>they</u>, them) who will be sorry for what they (themself, <u>themselves</u>) have done.

10. All the people (who, <u>whom</u>) we asked for directions turned out to be just as lost as we were.

21 ADJECTIVES AND ADVERBS

Identifying Adjectives

Adjectives are words that describe nouns (names of people, places, or things). An adjective can be found in two places in a sentence:

1 An adjective comes before the word it describes (a **loud** noise, a **wet** dog, the **oldest** child).

2 An adjective that describes the subject of a sentence may also come after a linking verb (see page 21). The linking verb may be a form of the verb *be* (they are **delicious**, she is **pleased**, I am **sure**). Other linking verbs include *feel, look, sound, smell, taste, appear, seem,* and *become* (it seems **strange,** I feel **sick**, you look **happy**, it tastes **awful**).

Adjectives in Comparisons

Adjectives change form when they are used to make a comparison. Add *-er* to a short (usually one-syllable) adjective when you are comparing two things. Add *-est* when you are comparing three or more things.

This green chili pepper is **hot,** but that red one is **hotter.**

Of all the chili peppers I've ever tasted, that red one is the **hottest.**

With most adjectives that have two or more syllables, however, do not change the form of the adjective at all. Instead, use the word *more* when comparing two things and *most* when comparing three or more things.

To me, David Letterman is **more entertaining** than Jay Leno, but Johnny Carson was the **most entertaining** of all.

Note 1 Do not use both an *-er* ending and *more,* or both an *-est* ending and *most.*

Incorrect: "This is the most happiest day of my life," Denise said.

Correct: "This is the **happiest** day of my life," Denise said.

Note 2 Certain short adjectives have irregular forms:

	Comparing two	*Comparing three or more*
bad	worse	worst
good, well	better	best
little	less	least
much, many	more	most

In my opinion, David Letterman's show is **better** than Jay Leno's, but Johnny Carson's was the **best.**

Identifying Adverbs

Adverbs are words that describe verbs, adjectives, and other adverbs. Most adverbs end in the letters *ly.* The following examples show how adverbs are used:

The clerk spoke to me **rudely.** (The adverb *rudely* describes the verb *spoke.*)

Colleen is **truly** sorry for her angry remark. (The adverb *truly* describes the adjective *sorry.*)

The canary sings **very** sweetly. (The adverb *very* describes the adverb *sweetly.*)

Using Adverbs

Be careful to use an adverb—not an adjective—after an action verb. Compare the following:

Incorrect	*Correct*
The car runs good. (*Good* is an adjective, not an adverb)	The car runs **well**.
Listen careful to the directions. (*Careful* is an adjective)	Listen **carefully** to the directions.
She went to sleep quick. (*Quick* is an adjective.)	She went to sleep **quickly**.

Pay particular attention to the difference between the words *good* and *well*. *Good* is an adjective that often means "talented" or "positive":

Zoe is a **good** guitarist.
We had a **good** time.
Do you feel **good** about yourself?

As an adverb, *well* often means "skillfully" or "successfully":

She plays the guitar **well**.
He does his job **well**.
I did **well** on that project.

As an adjective, *well* means "healthy," as in the question "Are you feeling **well**?"

Practice

Cross out the incorrect adjective or adverb in each of the following sentences. Then write the correction on the line provided.

1. _harder_ Is psychology a more harder subject than sociology?
2. _regularly_ To stay in good shape, exercise regular.
3. _really_ Those three students did real well on the last exam.
4. _greatest_ The most greatest challenge in my life is working and going to school at the same time.
5. _easier_ Of the two computers I tried last week, the Macintosh was easiest for me to use.
6. _softly_ Brenda spoke soft to the frightened puppy.
7. _less_ I use lesser butter and sugar in my cooking than I used to.

8. _____carefully_____ Always proofread the last version of your paper ~~careful~~ before handing it in.

9. _____well_____ Cara didn't go to class today because she didn't feel ~~good~~.

10. _____better_____ After she took aspirin and cold medicine, Cara felt ~~more better~~ than she had before.

22 NUMBERS AND ABBREVIATIONS

Numbers

Here are some guidelines to follow when writing numbers:

1 Spell out a number if it can be written in one or two words. Otherwise, write it in numerals.

The new high school has **three** vice principals, **ninety-five** teachers, and **two thousand** students.

There are **15,283** books in its library.

2 Spell out any number that begins a sentence.

Four hundred ninety-three people were in the first graduating class.

3 Be consistent when you write a series of numbers. If one or more numbers in the series need to be written as numerals, write *all* the numbers as numerals.

The carpenter bought **150** nails, **12** bolts, and **2** drill bits.

4 Use numerals to write dates, times, addresses, percentages, portions of a book, and exact amounts of money that include change.

The attorney asked the witness where she was on September **12, 2005**.

Set the alarm for **5:45** A.M. (When the word *o'clock* is used, however, the time is spelled out, as in *I get up at five o'clock.*)

The cabdriver took me to **418** East **78th** Street.

Only **30** percent of the students voted in the mock presidential election.

The test will cover Chapters **1, 2,** and **3** in your textbook, pages **5–74**.

My monthly car payment is **$348.37**.

Abbreviations

In general, avoid using abbreviations in papers you write for class. The following are among the few abbreviations that are acceptable in formal writing.

1   Titles that are used with proper names (for example, *Mr., Mrs., Dr., Jr., Sr.*):

Mrs. Richardson   **Dr.** Bell   Edwin Sacks, **Jr.**   **Prof.** George Smith

2   Initials in a person's name:

J. Edgar Hoover   Edgar **A.** Poe

3   Time references (A.M., P.M., B.C., A.D.):

After the party, we didn't get to bed until 4 A.M.

4   Organizations, technical words, and trade names referred to by their initials. These are usually written in all capital letters and without periods:

FBI CIA IRS AIDS NAACP UNICEF YMCA

Practice

Cross out the mistake in number or abbreviation in each of the following sentences. Then write the correction on the line provided.

1. _____twelve_____ In the summer, the local library lets readers borrow ~~12~~ books at a time.

2. _____25_____ If only ~~twenty-five~~ percent of every paycheck didn't get taken out for taxes!

3. _____company_____ The ~~co.~~ is taking job applications from 8:00 to 11:00 A.M.

4. _____One hundred fifty_____ ~~150~~ members of the marching band spelled out "Victory!" in front of fifty thousand cheering fans.

5. _____college_____ To earn my degree, I went to ~~coll.~~ for 4 years, took 40 courses, and wrote a 125-page thesis.

6. _____6_____ Why are you setting the alarm for ~~six~~ A.M. if your first class isn't until eight o'clock?

7. _____doctor_____ My ~~dr.~~ just told me that I had to lose fifteen pounds.

8. _____7_____ On June ~~seventh~~, 2009, Rasheed will finally be discharged from military duty.

9. _____professor_____ That ~~prof.~~ doesn't give you an A unless you score 94 percent or above.

10. _____10_____ When Rachel opened the used book she had purchased, she saw that Chapter ~~Ten~~ (pages 89 through 102) had been torn out.

23 USAGE

Here are some common incorrect expressions, together with their correct forms:

Incorrect	*Correct*
anyways, anywheres	anyway, anywhere
being as, being that	because, since
can't help but, cannot hardly, cannot scarcely (*double negatives*)	can't help, can hardly, can scarcely
could of, may of, might of, must of, should of, would of	could have, may have, might have, must have, should have, would have
had ought	ought
irregardless	regardless
kind of a	kind of
nowheres	nowhere
off of	off
suppose to, use to	supposed to, used to
sure and, try and	sure to, try to
the reason is because	the reason is that
ways (meaning "distance")	way

Practice

Cross out the incorrect expression in each sentence. Then, on the line provided, rewrite that part of the sentence to eliminate the error in usage.

1. Every time I see the movie *Titanic,* ~~I can't hardly~~ keep from crying.

   can hardly

2. The instructor asked the class to ~~try and~~ finish the assignment by the following Monday.

   try to

3. Verna used to live a long ~~ways~~ from here, but now she's renting an apartment a few blocks away.

   way

4. The reason students are having trouble in this course is ~~because~~ no one understands the textbook.

   that

5. Nobody ~~could of~~ known ahead of time how different college is from high school.

   could have

6. "Regardless of what you think," the counselor said, "you ~~should of~~ gone to class more often."

   ___should have_____

7. I ~~couldn't help but notice~~ that you're wearing a different kind of cologne.

   ___couldn't help noticing_____

8. ~~Being that~~ he has spent at least ten winters in Indiana, Bob ought to be used to cold weather.

   ___Since (or Because)_____

9. "Take your muddy feet ~~off of~~ my sofa this minute!" Juanita screamed at her son. "You certainly should have known better than to do that!"

   ___off_____

10. The driver pulled over to the curb and asked, "Is there a convenience store ~~anywheres~~ nearby?"

    ___anywhere_____

24 MORE ABOUT SUBJECTS AND VERBS

Sentences with More Than One Subject

A sentence may have a compound subject—in other words, more than one subject.

Ellen and **Karla** have started their own part-time business.

Sentences with More Than One Verb

A sentence may have a compound verb—in other words, more than one verb.

They **plan** parties for other people and also **provide** all the refreshments.

Sentences with More Than One Subject and Verb

A sentence may have both a compound subject and a compound verb.

In the last two weeks, **Ellen** and **Karla arranged** a wedding reception, **catered** a retirement dinner, and **earned** more than five hundred dollars.

Practice

In the sentences below, cross out any prepositional phrases. Then underline each subject once and each verb twice.

1. Tulips, daffodils, and azaleas bloom ~~among the debris in the urban park~~.

2. The car's <u>motor</u> <u>coughed</u> once and <u>refused</u> to start.

3. <u>Accounting</u> and <u>computer</u> <u>science</u> <u>are</u> very practical majors but <u>require</u> a lot ~~of work~~.

4. <u>Lisa</u> <u>tore</u> the wrapping ~~off the present~~, <u>lifted</u> the lid ~~of the box~~, and <u>gasped</u> ~~in delight~~.

5. The <u>author</u> ~~of the popular children's book~~ and her <u>husband</u> <u>attended</u> the book signing, <u>sipped</u> coffee, and <u>chatted</u> ~~with visitors~~.

25 EVEN MORE ABOUT VERBS

Tense

Tense refers to time. The tenses of a verb tell us when the action of the verb took place. The twelve major tenses in English for the regular verb *look* are shown in the box that follows.

Twelve Verb Tenses		
Tense	*Time Referred To*	*Example*
Present	Happens now *or* happens habitually	I **look** good today. Miguel **looks** like his father.
Past	Already happened	Students **looked** the word up in the dictionary.
Future	Is going to happen	Things **will look** better for you in a few days.
Present perfect	Began in past and now completed or continuing in present	Corinne **has looked** much more relaxed since she changed jobs. Corinne **has looked** for a new job before.
Past perfect	Happened before another past action	She **had looked** very tired before she quit her old job.
Future perfect	Is going to happen before some other future action	Her former boss **will have looked** at 350 job applications by the end of the month.
Present progressive	Is in progress	Eli **is looking** for a new apartment right now. His parents **are looking**, too.
Past progressive	Was in progress	He **was looking** in their old neighborhood, but they **were looking** downtown.
Future progressive	Will be in progress	With rents so high, they probably **will be looking** for quite a while.
Present perfect progressive	Was in progress and still is	Flora **has been looking** at soap operas for the last two hours.
Past perfect progressive	Was in progress until recently	She **had been looking** at her study notes.
Future perfect progressive	Will be in progress until a set time in the future	Unless she gets back to work, she **will have been looking** at television until dinnertime.

Voice

Voice refers to the active or passive form of a verb. In the **active voice,** the action of the verb is done *by* the subject:

Active: A police officer **took** the lost child home. (The police officer performed the action.)

In the **passive voice**, the action is done *to* the subject:

Passive: The lost child **was taken** home by a police officer. (The police officer performed the action, which was done to the child.)

In your own writing, you should normally use active verbs, which are more powerful than passive verbs. Use the passive voice, however, in situations where the doer of the action is not known or not important:

Passive: On the morning of Chen's wedding day, his car **was stolen**.

Passive: I **was promoted** last week.

Verbals

Verbals, formed from verbs, are used to name or describe people, places, and things. The three kinds of verbals are shown below.

Verbal	How Formed	Example and Comment
Infinitive	*To* plus a verb	The lost child began **to cry**. (Infinitives are used as adjectives, adverbs, or nouns. In the sentence above, *to cry* functions as a noun—the direct object of the verb *began.*)
Participle	Present: verb plus *-ing* Past: verb + *-ed* or irregular form	The **crying, frightened** child could not be comforted. (Participles are used as adjectives to describe a noun; here the adjectives *crying* and *frightened* describe the child.)
Gerund	verb plus *-ing*	**Crying** is sometimes very healthy. (Gerunds are used as nouns; here the noun *crying* is the subject of the sentence.)

Practice 1

On the line, write the indicated form of each verb in parentheses.

1. (gerund)   *(See)* _____Seeing_____ is *(believe)* _____believing_____.

2. (infinitive)   Peter Pan was determined never *(grow)* ____to grow____ up.

3. (present   That cat *(give)* _____has given_____ birth to five litters of
   perfect)   kittens.

4. (future   In early October, many tourists *(travel)* ___will be traveling___
   progressive)   through New England, just when the trees *(display)*
                    ___will be displaying___ their most magnificent fall colors.

5. (passive)   Since the couple wanted to keep wedding costs low, the bride's
                    gown was homemade, and the groom's tuxedo *(borrow)*
                    ___was borrowed___ from his uncle.

Three Troublesome Pairs of Irregular Verbs

	Basic Form	Past Tense	Past Participle
lie / lay	*Lie* means *rest* or *recline*.	lay	lain
	Lay means *put* or *place* something down.	laid	laid

My father likes to **lie** down and take an afternoon nap. Yesterday he **lay** on the living-room couch for two hours. He has sometimes **lain** there all afternoon without getting up.

Rico **lays** his wet towel anywhere in the house. This morning he **laid** it on a hot radiator. After he **had laid** it there, the towel began to steam.

	Basic Form	Past Tense	Past Participle
sit / set	*Sit* means *rest* or *take a seat*.	sat	sat
	Set means *put* something down or *prepare* something for use.	set	set

LaToya never **sits** down at a table to eat. Monday she **sat** at her desk to eat lunch. She **has sat** in front of the television to eat dinner every night this week.

My sister is the one who **sets** the family dinner table every day. She **has set** it in various ways, depending on what's for dinner. For instance, when we had Chinese food last week, she **set** the table with just napkins and chopsticks.

	Basic Form	Past Tense	Past Participle
rise / raise	*Rise* means *go up.*	rose	risen
	Raise means *lift* something up or *increase* it.	raised	raised

The sun **rises** every morning. Today it **rose** at 6:12 A.M. As soon as it **had risen,** trash trucks began clattering down the street.

Justine **raises** her hand a lot in class. This week, she **raised** her hand every time the instructor asked a question. Maybe she **has raised** her grade this way.

Practice 2

Underline the correct form of each verb in parentheses.

1. You look tired. Why don't you (sit, set) down and rest for a while?

2. Those old magazines have (lain, laid) in piles in our garage for years.

3. The accident victim was in such pain that she couldn't (rise, raise) her head.

4. Everyone in the stadium (rose, raised) to sing the national anthem.

5. The restaurant customer (lay, laid) a five-dollar bill on the table and said to the waiter, "This is yours if you can bring me my food in five minutes."

26 MORE ABOUT SUBJECT-VERB AGREEMENT

When compound subjects are joined by *or, nor, either . . . or, neither . . . nor,* or *not only . . . but also,* the verb agrees with the closer subject.

Either clams or lobster **is** the featured special every Friday at the restaurant. (*Lobster,* a singular subject, is closer to the verb, so the singular form *is* is required.)

Either lobster or clams **are** the featured special every Friday at the restaurant. (*Clams,* a plural subject, is closer to the verb, so the plural verb *are* is used.)

While most indefinite pronouns are always singular (*each, everyone, one, somebody,* etc.—see page 43), a few are not. The pronouns *both, several, many,* and *a few* are always plural and require plural verbs:

Both of my uncles **play** the piano and **sing** professionally. A few of my cousins **are** also performers.

The pronouns *all, any, some,* and *most* are either singular or plural, depending on the words that follow them. If the words after them are singular, they are singular. If the words after them are plural, however, they are plural. Notice the examples.

Some of the birthday cake **is** still on the table. (Since *cake* is singular, *some* is singular in this sentence. A singular verb, is, is needed.)

Some of the party guests **are** not having any dessert. (*Guests* is plural, making *some* plural in this sentence. The plural verb *are* is appropriate here.)

Practice

Underline the subject or subjects of each sentence. Then fill in the verb in parentheses that agrees with the subject or subjects.

1. *(tastes, taste)* A <u>few</u> of the chocolates in the box _____ taste _____ funny.

2. *(stays, stay)* Either <u>Thelma</u> or her <u>mother</u> _____ stays _____ at home to care for Thelma's grandmother.

3. *(is, are)* Not only <u>Carl</u> but also his <u>friends</u> _____ are _____ to blame for the accident.

4. *(was, were)* <u>All</u> of the students in the course _____ were _____ glad when it was over.

5. *(has, have)* Neither the head <u>coach</u> nor his assistant <u>coaches</u> _____ have _____ yet been fired for supplying bodybuilding drugs to players.

6. *(needs, need)* <u>Both</u> of my good shirts _____ need _____ to be ironed.

7. *(has, have)* Either the professor's <u>lectures</u> or the <u>textbook</u> _____ has _____ to be updated.

8. *(Is, Are)* _____ Is _____ <u>any</u> of the lemon chiffon pie still in the refrigerator?

9. *(Is, Are)* _____ Are _____ <u>any</u> of the other desserts still available?

10. *(seems, seem)* Since <u>all</u> of the desserts _____ seem _____ to be gone, I'm going out for ice cream.

27 MORE ABOUT RUN-ONS

Other Methods of Correcting a Run-On

Run-ons may be corrected by putting a **semicolon (;)** between the two complete thoughts. A semicolon is a stronger mark of punctuation than a comma; it can therefore be used to connect two complete thoughts.

Run-on: Carmen has a broken foot she won't be doing any hiking this summer.

Corrected: Carmen has a broken foot**;** she won't be doing any hiking this summer.

Run-on: Our history professor has the flu, half the class is sick as well.
Corrected: Our history professor has the flu; half the class is sick as well.

Note   Use the semicolon only when the connection between the two complete thoughts is obvious.

Or you can use a **semicolon plus a transitional word and a comma** to make the connection between the two complete thoughts even clearer:

Carmen has a broken foot; **therefore,** she won't be doing any hiking this summer.

Our history professor has the flu; **in fact,** half the class is sick as well.

Here are some other transitional words that may be used when correcting a run-on:

Transitional Words		
afterward	however	nevertheless
also	in addition	now
as a result	indeed	on the other hand
besides	instead	otherwise
consequently	meanwhile	then
furthermore	moreover	thus

Words That May Lead to Run-Ons

Pay special attention to your punctuation when you use the following two types of words. Since they often begin a new complete thought, they can be a signal to help you avoid writing a run-on.

1   Personal pronouns—*I, you, he, she, it, we, they.*

Run-on: We were tired of studying, we took a break.
Corrected: We were tired of studying, **so** we took a break.

2   Transitional words such as *therefore, in fact,* and the words in the box above.

Run-on: The air conditioning wasn't working, as a result, many customers left the store.

Corrected: The air conditioning wasn't working; as a result, many customers left the store.

Practice

Correct each of the following run-ons by adding a semicolon. In some cases, the semicolon will take the place of a comma.

1. Traffic leaving the concert was horrible;we finally squeezed out of the parking lot at midnight.

2. The dog was thin and dirty; however, he was obviously a fine purebred animal.

3. The family made sure all doors and windows were locked; moreover, they turned the thermostat down before leaving the house.

4. Pedestrians are treated like royalty in London; cars and buses stop to allow them to cross the street.

5. Many ads talk about new and improved products; nevertheless, the label on the box is often all that is new.

6. Jenny couldn't afford to pay her rent; consequently, she advertised in the paper for a roommate.

7. The waiters served soft drinks to the children; they offered wine to the adults.

8. Chipmunks have dug many holes in our yard; now it looks like a miniature golf course.

9. We will have to leave for the game within ten minutes; otherwise, we will miss the kickoff.

10. Our dog barks too much; as a result, the landlord has refused to renew our lease.

28 MORE ABOUT THE COMMA

Short Introductory Material

Short introductory material need not be followed by a comma.

On my return I found the children had cooked dinner.

Next to the computer a pot of coffee was leaking.

Afterward Martin was glad he had gotten the tattoo.

More about Interrupters

A word group that identifies another word in the sentence is actually not an interrupter. It is needed to make the sentence clear and should not be set off with commas.* For instance, look at the boldfaced words in the following sentences:

The woman **who lives next door to me** just won a million dollars in the lottery.

Alice Adams, **who lives next door to me,** just won a million dollars in the lottery.

*Grammar books sometimes refer to interrupters as "nonrestrictive elements" and essential descriptions as "restrictive elements."

In the first sentence, the boldfaced words are needed to identify the woman. Without them, we would not know who just won a million dollars. Since the words do not interrupt the sentence, we do not use commas. In the second sentence, however, we already know who won the million dollars. (It was Alice Adams.) In that case, the boldfaced words are not essential to the main message of the sentence. So, in the second sentence, *who lives next door to me* is an interrupter and should be set off by commas.

To find out whether a word group is an interrupter and should be set off by commas, try reading the sentence without it. The first sentence above would then read, "The woman just won a million dollars in the lottery." This version makes us ask, "Which woman?" The boldfaced words are needed to give us that information. If we read the second sentence without the boldfaced words, we would not be omitting essential information: "Alice Adams just won a million dollars in the lottery."

Other Joining Words

You already know that when two complete thoughts are combined into one sentence by a joining word like *and, but,* or *so,* a comma is used before the joining word. *Or, nor, for,* and *yet* are also joining words. Put a comma before each of these words when it joins two complete thoughts.

Buyers may pay in advance, **or** they may choose the easy-payment plan.

Alonso did not want to read his paper aloud, **nor** did he want anyone else to read it for him.

All the houseplants died, **for** they hadn't been watered in weeks.

The home team was behind by seven runs, **yet** the fans remained in the stadium.

Other Uses of the Comma

1   Use a comma to set off short expressions (*yes, no, well,* and the like) at the beginnings or ends of sentences.

No, you may not borrow the car.

Would you step aside, please?

2   Use a comma to set off the name of a person spoken to.

Can't you sleep, Barry?

Mom, your skirt is too short.

Hey, mister, you forgot your change.

3   Use commas within a date or an address.

Friday, May 12, 2007, will be the last day of final exams. (Place commas after the day of the week, the date, and the year.)

Send your comments about *English Brushup* to McGraw-Hill, 2 Penn Plaza, New York, NY 10121.

Note   When you write an address in a sentence, place commas after the name (if included), the street address, and the city. Do not place a comma between the state and the ZIP code.

4   Place a comma after the opening and closing of an informal letter.

> Dear Aunt Ruth,   Dear Mr. Ellis,   With love,   Sincerely,

Note   A colon is used after the opening of a business letter.

5   Place a comma between two descriptive words when they are interchangeable (in other words, when reversing their order would make sense).

> Many people dream about taking a vacation from their stressful, demanding jobs. (We could just as easily say "demanding, stressful jobs," so a comma is needed.)

> For some people, a fantasy vacation spot is a small tropical island. (We wouldn't say "a tropical small island," so the words are not reversible. No comma is used.)

Note   Another way to tell if two descriptive words need a comma is to see if the word *and* can be put between them. If so, a comma is used. "Stressful and demanding jobs" makes sense, so the comma is appropriate. "Small and tropical island" does not, so no comma is used.

Practice

Insert commas where needed in each of the following sentences.

1. Vanessa, are you ready to make your report?

2. The letter was mailed on Monday morning, yet it did not arrive until the following Saturday.

3. The official-looking form dated March 8, 2007, said to report for jury duty to the Glendale Courthouse, Front and Orange Streets, Glendale, CA 91208.

4. The confused, angry man seemed to be yelling at nobody.

5. The man who came to the party with Joy says he was kidnapped by aliens.

6. Harvey, who came to the party with Joy, says he was kidnapped by aliens.

7. No, you do not need an appointment to get a haircut.

8. Please wear your dark blue suit to the reception, Sam.

9. I'm going to ask Alice for a loan, for she has plenty of money to spare.

10. Dear Rhett,

I can't wait to see you! I'll be there to greet you when you step off the plane.

With love,
Scarlett

29 MORE ABOUT THE APOSTROPHE

Apostrophes in Special Plurals

Use an apostrophe and *s* to make each of the following plural:

Letters. Bert usually gets **C's** in math and science and **A's** in everything else. How many **e's** are there in *cemetery*?

Numbers. There are three **7's** in the store's telephone number.

Words used as words. The instructor told us not to use so many ***and's*** in our papers.

When Not to Use an Apostrophe: Possessive Pronouns

Do not put an apostrophe in any of these possessive pronouns: *his, hers, its* (meaning *belonging to it*), *ours, yours, theirs.* Since they are already possessive, they do not need an apostrophe.

Incorrect	*Correct*
The baseball jackets are theirs'.	The baseball jackets are **theirs**.
One can sometimes tell a book by it's cover.	One can sometimes tell a book by **its** cover.
Are those car keys his' or your's?	Are those car keys **his** or **yours**?

Practice

Insert apostrophes where needed in each of the following sentences. (Not all of the sentences require the addition of apostrophes.)

1. When I write quickly, my 4's, 7's, and T's look exactly alike.

2. Those packages are ours, but the shopping bags in the corner are hers.

3. Does a student need to have all A's and B's to graduate with honors?

4. Until the freshly varnished table has completely dried, its surface will be sticky.

5. What this world needs is more *please's* and *thank-you's*.

30 MORE ABOUT QUOTATION MARKS

Other Uses of Quotation Marks

1 Use single quotation marks to indicate a quotation within a quotation.

You've learned to use quotation marks to indicate someone's exact words or the title of a short work. When a second group of exact words or the title of a short work appears within a quoted passage, use single quotation marks to set it off.

Cal's boss told him, "If I hear you say 'That's not my job' one more time, you're not going to have any job at all."

"Let's join together and serenade our guest of honor with 'Happy Birthday,'" Enrique said.

2 Use quotation marks to set off words used in a special sense, or words used as words.

The "major hurricane" we had all worried about turned out to be just a little rain and breeze.

Many people misspell the word "separate" as "seperate."

Note   In printed matter, *italics* are often used to indicate a word used as a word: The word *separate* contains the words *a rat.*

Quotation Marks and Other Punctuation

Periods and commas at the end of a quotation always go *inside* the quotation marks.

"Unless you're downstairs in three minutes," Lila said, "I'm leaving without you."

Semicolons and colons at the end of a quotation always go *outside* the quotation marks.

The speaker quoted the famous line from Langston Hughes's poem "Harlem": "What happens to a dream deferred?"

Question marks and exclamation points at the end of a quotation normally go *inside* the quotation marks. They go *outside* the quotation marks only if they apply to the entire sentence, not just the quoted part.

Lila asked, "How much longer are you going to take?" (The question mark applies only to what Lila said.)

Did Lila say, "I'm leaving without you"? (The question mark applies to the entire sentence.)

Practice

On the lines provided, rewrite each sentence, inserting quotation marks where needed.

1. For our next class, please read the short story The Yellow Wallpaper and write a journal entry about it, the instructor said.

   "For our next class, please read the short story 'The Yellow Wallpaper' and

   write a journal entry about it," the instructor said.

2. Look out for the green slime monster hiding in your closet! my little brother screamed.

   "Look out for the green slime monster hiding in your closet!" my little brother

   screamed.

3. In which of Shakespeare's plays does a character say, To thine own self be true?

   In which of Shakespeare's plays does a character say, "To thine own self be

   true"?

4. One of the longest words in the English language is antidisestablishmentarianism.

   One of the longest words in the English language is

   "antidisestablishmentarianism."

5. Whenever I'm feeling depressed, my father always makes me smile by saying, Life is far too important to be taken seriously, Joanne said.

   "Whenever I'm feeling depressed, my father always makes me smile by saying,

   'Life is far too important to be taken seriously,'" Joanne said.

31 MORE ABOUT PUNCTUATION MARKS

Semicolon

Use a semicolon to set off items in a series when the items themselves contain commas.

> At the family reunion I spent time talking with Uncle Ray, who is a retired train engineer; my cousin Cheryl, who works in publishing; and my nephew Walt, who plays violin in his high school orchestra.

> The radio station invited listeners to choose which of three songs should be named the greatest rock-and-roll classic of all time: "Hey, Jude," by the Beatles; "Satisfaction," by the Rolling Stones; or "Heartbreak Hotel," an Elvis Presley song.

Hyphen

1   Put a hyphen between the two parts of a fraction: one-half, two-thirds.

2   Hyphenate compound numbers from twenty-one to ninety-nine.

Hassan pays his parents eighty-seven dollars, one-fourth of his weekly salary, for room and board.

3   Use a hyphen after the prefixes *all-, ex-,* and *self-.*

Leaders should be self-confident, but they should never think they are all-powerful.

My ex-husband has started therapy to raise his self-esteem.

Dash

Use a dash to signal the end of a list of items.

A three-mile run, forty minutes of weight lifting, and seventy-five push-ups—that's how Grandfather starts his day.

Parentheses

Place parentheses around numbers that introduce items in a list within a sentence.

Grandfather's exercise program consists of (1) jogging, (2) weight lifting, and (3) push-ups.

Underline

Underline the titles of long works: books, magazines, newspapers, movies, plays, television series, and record albums. (Remember, though, that titles of short works are placed in quotation marks. See page 118.)

Students in the current events class must skim <u>USA Today</u> every morning, read both <u>Time</u> and <u>Newsweek</u>, and watch <u>60 Minutes</u> and <u>Meet the Press</u>.

Note   Printed material uses *italics* instead of underlining.

Practice

Insert semicolons, hyphens, dashes, parentheses, or underlines where needed in each of the following sentences.

1. The shipping weight of the computer is thirty-nine pounds.

2. A jar of mustard, a bottle of beer, and half a can of cat food these were the contents of the refrigerator.

3. The latest issue of <u>Reader's Digest</u> includes some interesting articles: "The Town That Wouldn't Die," the story of a Texas suburb that survived an epidemic;"Work Out at Work," a guide to starting an exercise club at the office; and "Fatal Distraction," a first-person account of one man's battle against television addiction.

4. A new couple's budget should cover items such as(1)rent or mortgage,(2)food, (3)car expenses,(4)clothing,(5)entertainment, and, of course,(6)miscellaneous.

5. The most frightening book I ever read was Stephen King's The <u>Tommy-knockers</u>, and the most frightening movie I ever saw was <u>The Fly.</u>

32 MORE ABOUT HOMONYMS

Other Homonyms

all ready   *completely prepared*
already   *previously* or *before*

Those cans of tuna have **already** been stacked too high; they appear **all ready** to fall on an unlucky shopper.

coarse   (1) *rough;* (2) *crass* or *rude*
course   (1) *a unit of instruction;* (2) *a part of a meal;* (3) *certainly* (with *of,* as in *of course*)

The telephone operators are required to take a **course** in phone etiquette to ensure that they do not treat even irritating customers in a **coarse** manner.

lead   *a metal*
led   (past tense of *lead*) (1) *influenced* or *persuaded;* (2) *guided*

The children's poor health **led** the doctor to suspect they were being poisoned by **lead-**based paint in their home.

pair   *a set of two*
pear   *a fruit*

The **pear** tree in the backyard is home this spring to a **pair** of nesting doves.

principal   (1) *main;* (2) *the person in charge of a school*
principle   *a guideline* or *rule*

The **principal** lectured incoming students about drugs. "Our **principle** is a simple one: if you bring drugs to school, you're out of school," she said.

Hint   A trick to remembering one meaning of *principal* is that, ideally, a principal should be a **pal**—the last three letters in the word.

Other Confusing Words

Here are more words that people often have trouble telling apart.

a	*one*—used before a consonant
an	*one*—used before a vowel sound (*a, e, i, o, u,* or silent *h*)

a book	**a d**egree	**a m**istake	**a** surprise	**a y**ard	**a h**ero
an assignment	**an e**gg	**an i**nstructor	**an o**range	**an u**ncle	**an h**onor

Note   The *h* in *hero* is pronounced, but the *h* in *honor* is silent. (The word *honor* is pronounced "ON-er.") Since *honor* begins with a vowel sound, *an* is correct.

accept	(1) *to receive (willingly)*; (2) *to agree to*
except	(1) *to leave out*; (2) *but*

All the workers **except** the part-timers voted to **accept** the new contract.

advice	(rhymes with *nice*) *a suggestion* or *suggestions*
advise	(rhymes with *size*) *to give advice or suggestions to*

Most fortune-tellers' **advice** is pretty worthless; fortune-tellers **advise** their clients to become more and more dependent on them for guidance.

affect	*to influence* or *to have an effect on*
effect	(1) *to cause*; (2) *a result*

The heavy rain the night before did not **affect** the success of the picnic; in fact, the rain had the **effect** of clearing the air and producing a beautiful day.

among	used with three or more
between	used with two

A contest **among** ten candidates who campaigned for the presidency has finally come down to a choice **between** two persons—a man and a woman.

desert	(pronounced DEZ-ert) *a dry and sandy place*
desert	(pronounced de-ZERT) *to leave behind*
dessert	(also pronounced de-ZERT) *the final course of a meal*

Lost in the wasteland of the **desert,** the stranded man dreamed of gallons of ice water and of a cool, refreshing **dessert,** such as orange sherbet.

does	(rhymes with *fuzz*) *present tense of do*
dose	(rhymes with *gross*) *a measured amount of medicine*

Does a double **dose** of cold medicine cure a cold twice as fast?

fewer	*smaller in number*—used with plurals (more than one thing)
less	*smaller in degree, value, or amount*—used with singular words (one thing)

If you work **fewer** hours, you will earn **less** money.

loose   (rhymes with *juice*) (1) *not tight;* (2) *free* or *not confined*
lose   (rhymes with *blues*) (1) *to misplace;* (2) *to get rid of*

It's easy to **lose** a ring that is too **loose** on one's finger.

Hint   Here's one way to remember which is which: *Loose* and *tight* both have five letters; *lose* and *find* both have four letters.

quiet   *silent*
quit   (1) *to give up;* (2) *to stop doing something*
quite   *very*

"This house is **quite** noisy," said the baby-sitter to the children. "If you don't become **quiet** soon, I'm going to **quit** being so patient."

were   (rhymes with *fur*) past tense of *are*
where   (rhymes with *air*) *in what place* or *to what place* (see page 138)

Where did the movie director get all the thousands of people who **were** hired for that immense crowd scene?

Practice

Underline the correct word or words in each group in parentheses.

1. The cocky young man had (all ready, <u>already</u>) decided to (<u>quit</u>, quite, quiet) school, and he refused to (<u>accept</u>, except) his family's (advise, <u>advice</u>) to reconsider.

2. The rich (desert, <u>dessert</u>) had the (<u>effect</u>, affect) of giving several guests a stomachache, so their host gave them each a (does, <u>dose</u>) of Pepto-Bismol.

3. If I'm going to (<u>lose</u>, loose) ten pounds, I'll just have to eat (fewer, <u>less</u>) fattening food, but it'll be worth it for (a, <u>an</u>) opportunity to wear the (<u>pair</u>, pear) of size ten designer jeans that's been hanging in my closet for (<u>a</u>, an) year.

4. Several students' complaints about the (<u>coarse</u>, course) language in the wood-working class (<u>led</u>, lead) the school's (<u>principal</u>, principle) to visit the class and issue a warning.

5. I was (<u>all ready</u>, already) to put my groceries on the counter when I saw the sign reading "Ten Items or (<u>Fewer</u>, Less)."

6. "It's (quiet, quit, <u>quite</u>) difficult to (quiet, <u>quit</u>, quite) smoking," the doctor said, "but I (advice, <u>advise</u>) you to give up cigarettes at once—smoking will (<u>affect</u>, effect) your life span."

7. "Please don't (<u>desert</u>, dessert) me," Kim begged her brother. "I don't know anyone at this party (accept, <u>except</u>) you."

8. In her American Government (coarse, <u>course</u>), Sarita is learning the (principal, <u>principle</u>) of the balance of power—how decision-making is divided (<u>among</u>, between) the three branches of the federal government.

9. Jameer walked up to the desk and said in a (<u>quiet</u>, quit, quite) voice, "What time (<u>does</u>, dose) the library close?"

10. The parents couldn't remember (were, <u>where</u>) the Christmas decorations (<u>were</u>, where) stored until their six-year-old (lead, <u>led</u>) them to the Christmas box stacked (<u>among</u>, between) many other boxes in the attic.

33 MORE ABOUT CAPITAL LETTERS

Other Rules for Capital Letters

1   Capitalize the names of geographic locations.

The **S**outhwest is known for its hot, dry climate, while **N**ew **E**ngland is famous for cold winters.

People from the **S**outh have a reputation for hospitality.

Note   Do not, however, capitalize words that mean directions (not places).

The mountains are **s**outh and slightly **w**est of here.

Drive six blocks **e**ast on Walnut Street and then turn **n**orth onto 23d Street.

2   Capitalize the names of historical periods and well-known events.

The **R**enaissance is a period famous for the art it produced.

The **M**y **L**ai **M**assacre was one of the ugliest incidents of the **V**ietnam **W**ar.

3   Capitalize all words in the opening of a letter and the first word in the closing.

Dear **P**rofessor **C**ross: **D**ear **M**s. **H**ill: **V**ery truly yours,   **W**ith all my love,

4   Capitalize common abbreviations made up of the first letters of the words they represent.

FBI   NAACP   NASA   IBM   NBC   UFO   AIDS

Note   Periods are usually not used in these abbreviations.

Practice

Capitalize words as necessary in the following sentences.

1. After serving in the ^Kkorean ^Wwar, my grandfather wanted a job with the government and ended up working for the ^{CIA}cia.

2. Although we've lived in the northeast for fifteen years, our neighbors do not
   consider us natives because we were born in the midwest.

3. The aids epidemic is often compared to a plague that killed millions during
   the period known as the dark ages.

4. In her dream, Cynthia opened the letter and read, "dear ms. walker, Your
   talents have so impressed us at cbs that we'd like to offer you your own television show."

5. dear sir or madam:

   Please have your store send me a replacement for the defective dvd player I
   bought from you last week.

   yours truly,

   Wanda Stern

34 MORE ABOUT WORD CHOICE

Inflated Words

Keep your writing simple. Overly fancy words may confuse (or unintentionally amuse) a reader. Look at the following example:

The outdoor repast was deferred because of precipitation.

The sentence would communicate more effectively if it were written like this:

The picnic was postponed because of rain.

Here are a few other inflated words and simple replacements for them:

Inflated	Simple	Inflated	Simple
ascertain	learn, find out	facilitate	help
assert	say	finalize, culminate	finish
commence	begin	inquire	ask
commend	praise	manifest	show
compensate	pay	parameters	limits
elucidate	explain	prior to	before
embark upon	begin	replenish	refill
endeavor	try	subsequent to	after

Practice

Cross out the two inflated expressions in each of the sentences below. Then rewrite the faulty expressions on the lines provided, using simpler language. Feel free to consult a dictionary to find the meanings of any of the inflated words.

1. Students must ~~remit~~ 50 percent of their tuition ~~prior to~~ the first day of classes.

   _____pay_____   _____before_____

2. Nobody had ~~ascertained~~ when the next bus would ~~depart~~.

   _____found out_____   _____leave_____

3. Working conditions in that store are good, but the ~~remuneration~~ is ~~insufficient~~.

   _____pay_____   _____too low_____

4. Since the children were being ~~vociferous~~, the baby-sitter ~~endeavored~~ to quiet them.

   _____noisy_____   _____tried_____

5. ~~Subsequent~~ to the mugging, people hurried to help the ~~afflicted~~ man.

   _____After_____   _____injured_____

6. As soon as the game ~~commenced~~, it was clear that the home team would ~~be victorious~~.

   _____began_____   _____win_____

7. "I simply cannot believe any more of your ~~justifications~~," Marva told Rodney. "You've ~~prevaricated~~ entirely too often."

   _____excuses_____   _____lied_____

8. At a fine restaurant, someone will ~~replenish~~ your glass of water as soon as you ~~deplete~~ it.

   _____refill_____   _____empty_____

9. "As soon as you return to your ~~domicile~~," my father said, "please ~~transmit~~ word that you arrived safely."

   _____home_____   _____send_____

10. On Thanksgiving, everyone in my family enjoys a ~~delectable repast~~ at Cousin Miriam's house.

    _____delicious_____   _____meal_____

Part Three
Applying the Skills

Preview

Part Three contains ten combined mastery tests and ten editing tests:

Name _____ Section _____ Date _____

Score: (Number right) _____ × 10 = _____ %

FRAGMENTS AND RUN-ONS

■ Combined Mastery Test 1

Corrections may vary.

In the space provided, indicate whether each item below contains a fragment (F) or a run-on (R-O). Then correct the error.

___R-O___ 1. The little boy liked his new glasses *because* he thought they made him look grown-up. He wanted to wear them all the time, even while he slept.

___F___ 2. Forest fires destroy thousands of acres of woodland every year. Many of them are started through acts of carelessness, *s*Such as tossing a cigarette onto dry leaves.

___F___ 3. Snow piled up in great drifts outside the door, *m*Making it impossible to open. The family actually had to leave the house through a window.

___R-O___ 4. A terrifying scream pierced the night, *T*the friends screamed too and hugged each other. They all agreed it was the best haunted house they'd ever been to.

___F___ 5. Matthew had never been called for jury duty before. He was very nervous as the trial started. But *he soon* found the process fascinating.

___F___ 6. The king's daughter stared in horror at the slimy green frog. *Even if it was an enchanted prince, h*How could she ever bring herself to kiss it? ~~Even if it was an enchanted prince~~.

___R-O___ 7. The juice of the aloe plant is very soothing, *and* it can help heal burns and scrapes. Just break open a piece of the plant and rub the cool juice across your skin.

___R-O___ 8. How can you eat that chili? It is so hot it made my eyes water. I couldn't eat more than a spoonful.

___F___ 9. Christmas comes earlier each year, *b*Because merchants like to stretch out the buying season. Right after Halloween this year, store owners hung colored lights and filled their windows with Christmas decorations.

___R-O___ 10. Darlene walked into the living room. She sat down next to her boyfriend, *and* she held his hand. Then she gently said, "I can't marry you."

Name _____   Section _____   Date _____

Score: (Number right) _____ × 10 = _____%

FRAGMENTS AND RUN-ONS

■ Combined Mastery Test 2

Corrections may vary.

In the space provided, indicate whether each item below contains a fragment (F) or a run-on (R-O). Then correct the error.

F   1. My mother insists that I look good wearing light yellow clothes. I think when I wear yellow, I look as though I had died, ~~s~~everal days ago.

R-O   2. As darkness began to fall, the searchers grew more anxious; ~~t~~hey called the missing child's name again and again. To their great relief, they finally heard the child answer them.

R-O   3. It was clear that someone had been in the cabin while we were gone *because* a window was broken from the outside. Muddy footprints were everywhere, but nothing seemed to be missing.

F   4. When scientists found ancient seashells buried high on the mountain, they became very excited. They realized that the mountain had been below sea level, ~~m~~any years ago.

F   5. Mrs. Morris gazed at her lazy son. *He was asleep* ~~Asleep~~ on the couch for the fourth afternoon in a row. She decided the time had come for him to get a job.

R-O   6. I don't understand why you won't answer the telephone. ~~y~~ou're sitting closer to it than I am. Am I the only one who hears it?

F   7. *Gone with the Wind* was Vivica's favorite book when she was younger. For a few months, she even began speaking with a Southern accent, ~~I~~n imitation of Scarlett O'Hara.

F   8. For years, there have been reports of a strange manlike creature living in northern climates. The creature, whose existence has never been proved, has various names, ~~s~~uch as the Yeti, the Sasquatch, and the Abominable Snowman.

R-O   9. Garlic may smell bad, but it tastes delicious. It has other good qualities as well. Garlic helps lower cholesterol and is also supposed to keep vampires away.

F   10. There are no clocks in Las Vegas gambling casinos. If gamblers don't know what time it is, ~~t~~hey'll stay longer and lose more money.

Name _____   Section _____   Date _____

Score: (Number right) _____ × 10 = _____ %

VERBS

■ Combined Mastery Test 3

Each sentence contains a mistake involving (1) standard English or irregular verb forms, (2) subject-verb agreement, or (3) consistent verb tense. Cross out the incorrect verb and write the correct form in the space provided.

has 1. Each of the sisters in that family ~~have~~ a tattoo.

began 2. The artist picked up a brush, stared hard at the model, and ~~begins~~ to paint.

broke 3. To everyone's surprise, the newest member of the track team ~~breaked~~ the school record for the five-hundred-yard dash.

ran 4. Because so many uninvited people came to the party, we ~~runned~~ out of food.

were 5. Three enormous bags of money ~~was~~ sitting in the trunk of the arrested man's car.

rakes 6. On Saturdays, Jeremy mows the grass, ~~raked~~ the leaves, and pulls the weeds.

saw 7. Just as she was thinking about buying new shoes, Tanya ~~sees~~ a "Sale" sign in the shoe-store window.

are 8. Sleeping on the sunny windowsill ~~is~~ two black-and-white cats.

thought 9. When George first met Lana, he ~~thinks~~ she was the most beautiful girl in the world.

pretended 10. I went to my favorite pizza parlor, where I ran into my ex-boyfriend, who ~~pretends~~ he didn't see me.

Name _____   Section _____   Date _____

Score: (Number right) _____ × 10 = _____ %

VERBS

■ Combined Mastery Test 4

Each sentence contains a mistake involving (1) standard English or irregular verb forms, (2) subject-verb agreement, or (3) consistent verb tense. Cross out the incorrect verb and write the correct form in the space provided.

_is_   1. Although Charlene ~~be~~ teasing you, she doesn't mean to hurt your feelings.

need   2. Several trees in our backyard ~~needs~~ to be cut down.

threw   3. At the first game of our baseball team's season, the oldest man in town ~~throwed~~ the opening pitch.

closed   4. Yvonne opened the refrigerator door, looked hungrily at the chocolate pudding inside, and ~~closes~~ the door again.

keeps   5. The noise of our inconsiderate neighbors ~~keep~~ us awake many nights.

lying   6. The sign said "Beware of the Dog," but the dog ~~laying~~ under the sign did not look very fierce.

Are   7. ~~Is~~ there any bagels left for breakfast?

told   8. At the party Donny flirted with all the girls, ~~tells~~ all his best jokes, and danced up a storm.

ridden   9. I was amazed when my friends described how far they had ~~rode~~ on their bicycles.

plays   10. My little cousin is only eleven, but she already ~~play~~ the piano better than I ever will.

Name _____ Section _____ Date _____

Score: (Number right) _____ × 10 = _____ %

FAULTY MODIFIERS AND PARALLELISM

■ **Combined Mastery Test 5**

Corrections may vary.

In the spaces at the left, indicate whether each sentence contains a misplaced modifier (MM), a dangling modifier (DM), or faulty parallelism (FP). Then correct the errors in the space between the lines.

DM   1. Arriving *As Sam arrived* for the job interview, the nervous lump in Sam's *his* throat made it difficult for him to swallow.

FP   2. My father always said coffee should be strong as sin, sweet as love, and it should be as hot as blazes.

MM   3. Making a loud grating sound, Michelle stopped the car *, which was making a loud grating sound,* to see what was wrong.

MM   4. *With a sense of dread,* Bob noticed a police officer driving behind him with a sense of dread.

DM   5. Hitting *As I was hitting* the "snooze" button on my alarm clock, my eyes just wouldn't open.

FP   6. Playing cards, to watch *watching* football, and working in the garden are my grandfather's favorite activities.

DM   7. While trying on an old pair of blue jeans, Marvin's *Marvin found that the* waistband wouldn't close.

FP   8. Gina uses her computer to send e-mail, get *write* school papers written, and search the Internet.

MM   9. "Don't you feel well? You're hardly eating *eating hardly* anything!" June said to her teenage son.

FP   10. I couldn't find my car keys, even though I searched in my coat pockets, on the kitchen shelf, and looked inside every drawer in the house.

Name _____   Section _____   Date _____

Score: (Number right) _____ × 10 = _____ %

FAULTY MODIFIERS AND PARALLELISM

■ Combined Mastery Test 6

In the spaces at the left, indicate whether each sentence contains a misplaced modifier (MM), a dangling modifier (DM), or faulty parallelism (FP). Then correct the errors in the space between the lines.

Corrections may vary.

_____FP_____   1. Cleaning the bathroom, doing the laundry, and ~~to scrub~~ ^{scrubbing} the kitchen floor are among my least favorite chores.

_____DM_____   2. ^{Since Ron and Helen were glaring} Glaring angrily at each other, it was easy to tell that ~~Ron and Helen's~~ ^{their} argument was serious.

_____MM_____   3. ^{Sitting on his father's shoulders, the} ~~The~~ little boy stared in wonder at the elephant ~~sitting on his father's shoulders~~.

_____MM_____   4. ^{I was surprised the trees, bending} Bending almost double in the strong wind, ~~I was surprised the trees~~ didn't break.

_____DM_____   5. Without a word of good-bye, ^{Teron} ~~the car~~ sped off ~~with Teron at the wheel~~ ^{in the car.}

_____FP_____   6. High fever, a hacking cough, and muscles ~~that ache~~ ^{aching} are all symptoms of the flu.

_____MM_____   7. Denzel ~~almost received~~ ^{received almost} fifty e-mails yesterday.

_____FP_____   8. Nelson never keeps a girlfriend long, because of his hot temper, his jealousy, and ~~the fact that he is dishonest~~ ^{his dishonesty.}

_____MM_____   9. We enjoyed the delicious barbecue that our neighbors had prepared ~~with hearty appetites~~ ^{with hearty appetites}.

_____DM_____   10. ^{Although I clicked} ~~Clicking~~ all the buttons on the remote control, my search for something good to watch on TV was unsuccessful.

Name _____   Section _____   Date _____

Score: (Number right) _____ × 10 = _____ %

CAPITAL LETTERS AND PUNCTUATION

■ **Combined Mastery Test 7**

Each of the following sentences contains an error in capitalization or punctuation. Refer to the box below and, in the space provided, write the letter identifying the error. Then correct the error.

a.	missing capital letter
b.	missing apostrophe
c.	missing quotation marks
d.	missing comma

_____c_____ 1. During my haircut, it made me very nervous to hear my barber say,"Oops".

_____b_____ 2. Most of the town's citizens agree that the mayor is doing a fine job.

_____a_____ 3. My math class is not too difficult, but my english class is driving me crazy.

_____d_____ 4. "Please close your books and put away your notes," said Mrs. Shoup. "It is time for a quiz."

_____b_____ 5. If you know you can't keep a secret, you should warn your friends not to tell you any.

_____b_____ 6. Everyone knows that my uncle's hair isn't real, but we all pretend to think it is.

_____c_____ 7. "I tell you, my whole life has been tough," said the comedian."When I was a kid, I had to tie a pork chop around my neck so the dog would play with me."

_____d_____ 8. Even though we told him the four o'clock party began at three o'clock, my brother still showed up two hours late.

_____a_____ 9. If you drive forty miles north of here, you will reach the michigan line.

_____d_____ 10. *Rebecca,* a wonderful novel by Daphne du Maurier, is about a woman who is haunted by her husband's former wife.

Name _____   Section _____   Date _____

Score: (Number right) _____ × 10 = _____%

CAPITAL LETTERS AND PUNCTUATION

■ Combined Mastery Test 8

Each of the following sentences contains an error in capitalization or punctuation. Refer to the box below and, in the space provided, write the letter identifying the error. Then correct the error.

> a. missing capital letter
>
> b. missing apostrophe
>
> c. missing quotation marks
>
> d. missing comma

__b__   1. If you've got time before school, would you take the trash out to the curb?

__d__   2. Almost nine hundred people showed up to audition for a part in the movie, but only two were chosen.

__a__   3. My mother always insisted on using ~~c~~risco shortening in her pie crust, but I use any brand I happen to have on hand.

__c__   4. "On my first date with your mother," my father told me, "her little brother came along to make sure I behaved myself."

__d__   5. A real banana split should contain a banana, three scoops of ice cream, whipped cream, peanuts, and a cherry.

__a__   6. As I carefully eased open the front door, I heard my mother's stern voice say, "you missed your curfew."

__a__   7. For the Bradshaw family, it's a tradition to watch the movie *It's a wonderful Life* at least once during the holiday season.

__d__   8. Although Jimmy claims to hate tomatoes, he loves spaghetti sauce and pizza.

__b__   9. My sister's boyfriend gave her a ring that quickly turned her finger green.

__c__   10. "I'm giving you three weeks to work on this project," announced Mrs. Smith-field, "so I don't expect anyone to ask for extra time."

Name _____   Section _____ Date _____

Score: (Number right) _____ × 5 = _____ %

HOMONYMS AND SPELLING

■ Combined Mastery Test 9

Each of the following groups of sentences contains two errors. The errors involve either homonym mistakes or misspelled words. Underline the two errors and write the correct forms of the words in the spaces provided.

1. It seems really <u>wierd</u> to me that I have to take algebra. I don't see how I will ever use that <u>coarse</u> in my daily life.

   _____ weird _____   _____ course _____

2. At the county fair, we saw the <u>fatest</u> pig you can imagine. We also walked <u>threw</u> a barn where cows were being milked.

   _____ fattest _____   _____ through _____

3. <u>Wear</u> my sister is going the weather will be warm, so she is packing light. She is taking just two <u>pears</u> of shorts, two T-shirts, and a sweatshirt.

   _____ Where _____   _____ pairs _____

4. Brad eagerly <u>excepted</u> his aunt's offer of a summer job. He knew the job was a lucky <u>brake</u>, and he was determined to make the most of it.

   _____ accepted _____   _____ break _____

5. Although Maria and Teresa are the best of <u>freinds</u>, they have very different personalities. Maria is <u>quite</u> and shy, while Teresa is talkative and outgoing.

   _____ friends _____   _____ quiet _____

6. I am constantly <u>loosing</u> my house key. I guess I'm just <u>to</u> absentminded. Maybe I should tie it on a string around my neck.

   _____ losing _____   _____ too _____

7. Is the new movie "one of the most <u>exciteing</u> ever made" or "a waste of two hours"? It depends on <u>weather</u> you believe one critic or another.

   _____ exciting _____   _____ whether _____

8. The girl that Paul is <u>begining</u> to date seems to really like him. She has <u>all ready</u> invited him to spend Thanksgiving with her family.

   _____ beginning _____   _____ already _____

Continued

9. I can't believe that you spent fifteen dollars to have <u>you're</u> fortune told. If you ask me, a fortune-teller's <u>advise</u> is just a waste of money.

_____*your*_____   _____*advice*_____

10. "I worked hard <u>prepareing</u> the <u>desert</u> for tonight's dinner," Hannah laughingly told her guests. "I had to drive all the way to the bakery and all the way back again."

_____*preparing*_____   _____*dessert*_____

Name _____ Section _____ Date _____

Score: (Number right) _____ × 5 = _____%

HOMONYMS AND SPELLING

■ ## Combined Mastery Test 10

Each of the following groups of sentences contains two errors. The errors involve either homonym mistakes or misspelled words. Underline the two errors and write the correct form of the word in the spaces provided.

1. If <u>its</u> sunny tomorrow, we are going to go for a long bike ride. But if the <u>whether</u> is bad, we're going to rent videos and watch them all day.

   _____ it's _____   _____ weather _____

2. Nobody knows what the man next door <u>dose</u> for a living. He never seems to go to work, but he's always <u>driveing</u> the nicest car in the neighborhood.

   _____ does _____   _____ driving _____

3. At the school's annual costume party, everyone was amazed <u>too</u> see the most serious teacher of them all arrive. He <u>hoped</u> into the room, dressed as a huge pink rabbit.

   _____ to _____   _____ hopped _____

4. Although many children <u>beleive</u> in Santa Claus, <u>its</u> rather unusual to find an adult who thinks Santa is real. My sister's boyfriend, however, is an unusual guy.

   _____ believe _____   _____ it's _____

5. Larry is one of those people who think the secret of <u>happyness</u> is money. Being rich is more important to him <u>then</u> anything else in the world.

   _____ happiness _____   _____ than _____

6. Sarah looked beautiful at the awards banquet. She was wearing a very <u>plane</u> black dress, but she'd dressed it up with a <u>knew</u> silver necklace and earrings.

   _____ plain _____   _____ new _____

7. Don't you hate it when someone says, "Oh, I don't want dessert," but then wants a <u>peace</u> of whatever you order? In my opinion, <u>their</u> just being rude in doing that.

   _____ piece _____   _____ they're _____

8. The <u>whole</u> in the garage roof is getting larger and larger. <u>Its</u> letting so much rain in that we really have to do something about it soon.

   _____ hole _____   _____ It's _____

Continued

9. Mr. Taylor is <u>to</u> protective of his children. He won't let them ride bicycles, play softball, or roller-skate, believing that <u>there</u> going to get badly hurt.

_____*too*_____   _____*they're*_____

10. Didn't anyone else <u>here</u> that loud party going on last night? I was <u>already</u> to call the police when it finally quieted down at 3 A.M.

_____*hear*_____   _____*all ready*_____

Name _____ Section _____ Date _____

Score: (Number right) _____ × 20 = _____ %

EDITING TEST 1

Identify the sentence-skills mistakes at the underlined spots in the selection that follows. From the box below, choose the letter that describes each mistake and write it in the space provided. Then, in the spaces between the lines, correct each mistake.

a.	run-on
b.	fragment
c.	missing capital letter
d.	missing apostrophe
e.	missing comma

Some corrections may vary.

Every year, on the third Sunday in May, the world's largest footrace is held, it takes
place in San Francisco, California. As many as 100,000 runners participate in the Bay
to Breakers Run, a twelve-kilometer run that begins at the San Francisco Bay and ends
at the Pacific ocean. Although some of the worlds best runners participate in the race,
many others are less serious about winning. Costumed runners dress up as almost anything
imaginable, Including human tacos, palm trees, and even the Golden Gate Bridge. Groups
of thirteen runners tied together compete as human centipedes. Waiters jog along, trying
to balance glasses of champagne resting on trays. The race,which has been held annually
since 1912, is as much fun to watch as it is to participate in.

1. __a__   2. __c__   3. __d__   4. __b__   5. __e__

EDITING TEST 2

Identify the sentence-skills mistakes at the underlined spots in the selection that follows. From the box below, choose the letter that describes each mistake and write it in the space provided. Then, in the spaces between the lines, correct each mistake.

a.	faulty parallelism
b.	inconsistent verb tense
c.	fragment
d.	run-on
e.	missing comma

Some corrections may vary.

If you know the name of Leonardo da Vinci, it is probably as an artist. Leonardo produced some of the world's most famous paintings, including the *Mona Lisa* and *The Last Supper*. But Leonardo was not only an artist. He also deserves to be known as an inventor, a scientist, and ~~he worked in engineering too~~ *an engineer*. Leonardo was born in 1452. He ~~goes~~ *went* to Florence, Italy, to study art when he was a teenager. Although he became an official "court artist," he also found time to dream up dozens of inventions. Some became realities ³ in his lifetime *, but* others were left for the future. Among the many designs that Leonardo came ³ up with were those for flying machines, parachutes, submarines, and underwater breathing ⁴ devices. Although he was a gentle vegetarian, Leonardo also designed many new weapons. By the time he died in 1519, Leonardo was recognized as a genius, *, one* Ǿne of the greatest the ⁵ world had ever produced. ⁵

1. __a__   2. __b__   3. __d__   4. __e__   5. __c__

Name _____ Section _____ Date _____

Score: (Number right) _____ × 20 = _____%

EDITING TEST 3

Identify the sentence-skills mistakes at the underlined spots in the selection that follows. From the box below, choose the letter that describes each mistake and write it in the space provided. Then, in the spaces between the lines, correct each mistake.

a.	fragment
b.	run-on
c.	inconsistent verb tense
d.	homonym mistake
e.	missing quotation mark

Some corrections may vary.

Recently something happened that made me feel like a human dinosaur. I was taking care of my eight-year-old niece for the afternoon. I said I wanted to talk to an old friend of mine who lives in another state. Kate ~~says~~ *said*, "Why don't you e-mail her?" I answered, "Because I don't have a computer, and I don't know how to use e-mail, anyway." Kate stared at me, *A*s if I'd just said I didn't know how to tie my shoes. "How can anybody not know how to use e-mail?" she said. *S*he really didn't seem able to believe it. The next week Kate came over to visit again. This time she had her friend Paige with her. "Paige wanted to meet you," she said. Feeling flattered, I said, "Well, hello, Paige." "Hi," Paige said. "I've never met anyone who couldn't use e-mail before. My brother said you must be one of those people who lives in the ~~passed~~ *past*." I gave them cookies and sent them home. I guess it could be worse. At least Kate didn't take me to school for show-and-tell.

1. __c__   2. __a__   3. __b__   4. __e__   5. __d__

Name _____   Section _____   Date _____
                                          Score: (Number right) _____ × 20 = _____ %

EDITING TEST 4

Identify the sentence-skills mistakes at the underlined spots in the selection that follows. From the box below, choose the letter that describes each mistake and write it in the space provided. Then, in the spaces between the lines, correct each mistake.

a.	fragment
b.	run-on
c.	inconsistent verb tense
d.	homonym mistake
e.	missing apostrophe

Some corrections may vary.

Do you have a memory that makes you burn with shame, even years after the event?

I do. A boy I didn't know very well had walked up to me in the lunchroom, _a ~~And~~ asked me

for a date. I was so surprised that I automatically said yes. Later, though, I *started* ~~start~~ to have
_____   _____
   1   2

second thoughts. I *didn't* think I would have any fun. I began to wish I had said no. And so,
            _____
              3

a few hours before our date, I called him. Trying to sound miserable, I said I was too sick to

                                    all right
go out. He politely said that was ~~alright~~. Feeling much better, I instantly called a girlfriend
                                     _____
                                       4

and arranged to go out for pizza. And you guessed it—there in the pizza parlor was the boy

I had stood up. I'll never forget the disappointed look he gave me. Over the next few years,

I realized that he was a really great guy and that I'd been an idiot not to go out with him.

                                          since
But by then, of course, I'd lost my chance, ^ he never spoke to me again.
_____
                         5

1. __a__   2. __c__   3. __e__   4. __d__   5. __b__

Name _____   Section _____   Date _____

Score: (Number right) _____ × 20 = _____ %

EDITING TEST 5

Identify the sentence-skills mistakes at the underlined spots in the selection that follows. From the box below, choose the letter that describes each mistake and write it in the space provided. Then, in the spaces between the lines, correct each mistake.

a. missing capital letter
b. faulty parallelism
c. homonym mistake
d. run-on
e. fragment

Some corrections may vary.

                                           for

My great-aunt was an unusual woman, she liked animals at least as much as she
                                1

liked humans. She lived in a house with a big backyard that faced a forest. Over the years,
   1

                                                      knew

she took in dozens of wounded or orphaned animals. Visitors never ~~new~~ what they would
                                                             2

find when they stopped by her house. I remember seeing broken-legged blue jays, bullet-
                                      one-eyed owls

wounded squirrels, and ~~owls with one eye~~ living there. She once raised a family of baby
                              3
                                      , a

foxes, feeding them from a bottle. And then returned them to the woods. When my aunt
                                                4

                                                             P

died, she left the little bit of money she had to the Society for the prevention of Cruelty to
                                                                5

Animals.

1. __d__   2. __c__   3. __b__   4. __e__   5. __a__

Name _____   Section _____   Date _____

Score: (Number right) _____ × 10 = _____ %

EDITING TEST 6

Identify the sentence-skills mistakes at the underlined spots in the selection that follows. From the box below, choose the letter that describes each mistake and write it in the space provided. Then, in the spaces between the lines, correct each mistake. (The number in parentheses indicates how many of each mistake occur in the selection.)

a.	fragment (2)
b.	pronoun mistake (2)
c.	apostrophe mistake (2)
d.	homonym mistake (2)
e.	mistake in subject-verb agreement (1)
f.	missing quotation mark (1)

Some corrections may vary.

Many of us are annoyed by ~~telemarketer's~~ *telemarketers* who call ~~you~~ *us* day and night, trying to sell
                              1   2

everything from magazine subscriptions ~~too~~ *to* vacation homes. These electronic intruders
                                         3

~~dont~~ *don't* seem to care how much they are inconveniencing us~~,~~ *, and they* ~~And~~ refuse to take "no" for an
4   5

answer. However, nuisance callers can be stopped if we take charge of the conversation.
5

As soon as one of them asks how we are doing~~,~~ *, we* ~~We~~ should respond, "Fine, and are you
                                                             6

a telephone ~~solicitor?~~ *solicitor?"* This technique puts the caller on the defensive. We then have an
            7

opening to say that we do not accept solicitations over the phone, only ~~threw~~ *through* the mail. This *response*
                                                                         8   9

puts a quick end to the conversation. Of course, anyone who ~~prefer~~ *prefers* not to be called at all
                                                            10

can sign up at the National Do Not Call Registry at **www.donotcall.gov** and be safe from

annoying calls for five years.

1. __c__   2. __b__   3. __d__   4. __c__   5. __a__

6. __a__   7. __f__   8. __d__   9. __b__   10. __e__

Name _____ Section _____ Date _____

Score: (Number right) _____ × 10 = _____ %

EDITING TEST 7

Identify the sentence-skills mistakes at the underlined spots in the selection that follows. From the box below, choose the letter that describes each mistake and write it in the space provided. Then, in the spaces between the lines, correct each mistake. (The number in parentheses indicates how many of each mistake occur in the selection.)

> a. fragment (2)
> b. run-on (2)
> c. missing comma (2)
> d. homonym mistake (2)
> e. mistake in subject-verb agreement (1)
> f. dangling modifier (1)

Some corrections may vary.

Millions of people in this country ~~is~~ (are) terrified of going to the dentist. If you are one
₁

of them, you should know that some dentists specialize in treating people, ~~Who~~ (who) are very
₂

fearful of dental work. These dentists encourage patients to discuss ~~there~~ (their) fears and will
₂ ₃

answer questions in an honest, understanding manner. Even if your dentist does not have

such a ~~specialty you~~ (specialty, you) can arrange to use a ~~signal such~~ (signal, such) as raising your right hand, if you
₄ ₅

experience too much pain. This will give you a feeling of control ~~it~~ (. It) will also guarantee that
₆

the pain—if any—will not go beyond what you can tolerate. You can also try a relaxation
₆

technique. ~~Breathing~~ (If you breathe) deeply before and during appointments, your fears will subside. A
₇ ₈

last good idea is to bring an iPod, ~~you~~ (. You) can then listen to your favorite music in the dental
₈

chair. ~~Its~~ (It's) hard for the brain to register pain, ~~When~~ (when) your favorite song is filling your head.
₈ ₉ ₁₀

1. __e__   2. __a__   3. __d__   4. __c__   5. __c__

6. __b__   7. __f__   8. __b__   9. __d__   10. __a__

Name _____   Section _____ Date _____

Score: (Number right) _____ × 10 = _____ %

EDITING TEST 8

Identify the sentence-skills mistakes at the underlined spots in the selection that follows. From the box below, choose the letter that describes each mistake and write it in the space provided. Then, in the spaces between the lines, correct each mistake.

a. fragment	f. pronoun mistake
b. run-on	g. missing comma
c. irregular verb mistake	h. missing apostrophe
d. mistake in subject-verb agreement	i. missing quotation mark
e. inconsistent verb tense	j. misplaced modifier

Some corrections may vary.

When President Theodore "Teddy" Roosevelt visited the South in 1902, ~~He~~ *, he* was

<u>1</u>

invited to a hunting party. The organizers of the hunt ~~was~~ *were* eager for the President to have a

<u>2</u>

successful hunt. They tied a bear cub to a stake so that the President could not miss ~~it~~ *the bear*. After

<u>3</u>

he realized that the bear could not ~~escape~~ *escape,* Roosevelt refused to fire. A political cartoon was

<u>4</u>

printed in a number of newspapers ~~based on the incident~~. The cartoon, with a drawing of *based on the incident*

<u>5</u>

the small bear, was seen by a shop owner in Brooklyn. The shop owner then ~~maked~~ *made* up a

<u>6</u>

window display version of the little bear in a soft, plush material. Before offering the bear

to customers, the shop owner ~~asks~~ *asked* Roosevelt for permission to sell the new toy as "~~Teddys~~ *Teddy's*

<u>7</u>   <u>8</u>

Bear." The President gave his approval but ~~wrote, I~~ *wrote, "I* don't think my name is worth much to

<u>9</u>

the toy bear cub business." He was clearly wrong, ~~a~~ *. A* bear-buying frenzy swept the country.

<u>10</u>

The teddy bear has been popular ever since.

1. __a__   2. __d__   3. __f__   4. __g__   5. __j__

6. __c__   7. __e__   8. __h__   9. __i__   10. __b__

Name _____ Section _____ Date _____

Score: (Number right) _____ × 10 = _____%

EDITING TEST 9

See if you can locate and correct the ten sentence-skills mistakes in the selection that follows. The mistakes are listed in the box below. As you locate each mistake, write the number of the word group containing it in the space provided. Then, in the spaces between the lines, correct each mistake.

1 fragment ___5___	2 homonym mistakes ___4___
1 run-on ___6___	___9___
1 missing comma ___2___	1 misplaced modifier ___1___
2 apostrophe mistakes ___3___	1 dangling modifier ___7___
___9___	1 faulty parallelism ___4___

Some corrections may vary.

                                                                              from high places
¹Some people believe the superstition that cats have nine lives because they can fall ^

with few, if any, injuries ~~from high places~~. ²They may have minor injuries, such as a

                                   ribs, but   *falls*
bloody nose or cracked teeth or ~~ribs but~~ they recover. ³Cats are able to survive long ~~fall's~~

                                                          their   *low*
because they possess several advantages. ⁴For one thing, ~~there~~ small size and body weight ^

              impact as
~~that is low~~ soften the ~~impact.~~ ⁵As they make contact with the ground. ⁶Also, cats have

                        and   *Since they can quickly adjust*
highly developed inner ears, these give them a keen sense of balance. ⁷~~Quickly adjusting~~ ^

              land
themselves in the air and ~~landing~~ on all four feet, the impact is absorbed by their legs.

⁸Additionally, cats bend their legs when they land. ⁹This cushions and spreads the impact,

                        break   *cat's*
not only through bones that might ~~brake~~ otherwise, but through a ~~cats~~ joints and muscles

as well.

Name _____   Section _____   Date _____

Score: (Number right) _____ × 10 = _____%

EDITING TEST 10

See if you can locate and correct the ten sentence-skills mistakes in the selection that follows. The mistakes are listed in the box below. As you locate each mistake, write the number of the word group containing it in the space provided. Then, in the spaces between the lines, correct each mistake.

1 fragment ___7___	1 missing comma ___4___
1 run-on ___3___	1 missing quotation mark ___8___
1 inconsistent verb tense ___4___	1 missing hyphen ___8___
1 mistake in subject-verb	1 homonym mistake ___4___
agreement ___2___	1 faulty parallelism ___4___
1 missing capital letter ___1___	

Some corrections may vary.

¹One of the top April ~~fool's~~ *Fool's* Day hoaxes of all time was created by Burger King. ²On April 1, a few years ago, Burger King ~~place~~ *placed* a full-page advertisement in *USA Today*. ³The ad stated that an item was being added to their ~~menu it~~ *menu. It* was a "Left-Handed Whopper" specially designed for the 32,000,000 left-handed Americans. ⁴The ~~knew~~ *new* sandwich included the same ingredients as the original Whopper (~~lettuce tomato~~ *lettuce, tomato*, a ~~patty made of hamburger~~ *hamburger patty*, etc.), but all the condiments ~~are~~ *were* rotated 180 degrees for the benefit of their left-handed customers. ⁵Burger King issued a follow-up press release the next day. ⁶According to the press release, although the Left-Handed Whopper was a hoax, thousands of customers had gone into restaurants. ⁷~~T~~*t*o order the new sandwich. ⁸The release went on to add, "Many others requested their own ~~right handed version.~~ *right-handed version."*

Limited Answer Key

Important Note   To strengthen your grammar, punctuation, and usage skills, you must do more than simply find out which of your answers are right and which are wrong. You also need to figure out (with the help of this book, the teacher, or other students) *why* you missed the items you answered incorrectly. By using each of your wrong answers as a learning opportunity, you will strengthen your understanding of the skills. You will also prepare yourself for the chapter tests, for which answers are not given here.

ANSWERS TO THE PRACTICES IN PART ONE

1   SUBJECTS AND VERBS

Practice 1 (p. 21)

1.   *Subject:* Nikki   *Verb:* waited
2.   *Subject:* dog   *Verb:* padded
3.   *Subject:* One   *Verb:* is
4.   *Subject:* kittens   *Verb:* need
5.   *Subject:* I   *Verb:* have

Practice 2 (p. 22)

1.   *Subject:* Everyone
     Verb: is working
2.   *Subject:* child
     Verb: may experience
3.   *Subject:* siren
     Verb: began
4.   *Subject:* shirt
     Verb: should have been put
5.   *Subject:* you
     Verb: must remember

2   MORE ABOUT VERBS

Practice 1 (p. 31)

1.   began
2.   broken
3.   eaten, drank
4.   driven, saw
5.   read, written, taken

Practice 2 (p. 32)

1.   dresses
2.   dropped
3.   looked
4.   hate
5.   manages

Practice 3 (p. 33)

1.   did
2.   has
3.   were
4.   doesn't
5.   was

Practice 4 (p. 34)

1.   realized
2.   disappears
3.   discovered
4.   want
5.   yelled

3   SUBJECT-VERB AGREEMENT

Practice 1 (p. 42)

1.   *Subject:* guys
     Verb: like
2.   *Subject:* women
     Verb: score
3.   *Subject:* noise
     Verb: hurts

4.   *Subject:* bag
     Verb: contains
5.   *Subject:* instructions
     Verb: are

Practice 2 (p. 43)

1.   *Subject:* keys
     Verb: are
2.   *Subject:* hundreds
     Verb: live
3.   *Subject:* people
     Verb: were
4.   *Subject:* geese
     Verb: do
5.   *Subject:* boxes
     Verb: are

Practice 3 (p. 44)

1.   *Subject:* Everything
     Verb: is
2.   *Subject:* Neither
     Verb: works
3.   *Subject:* No one
     Verb: is
4.   *Subject:* Each
     Verb: appears
5.   *Subject:* Everybody
     Verb: knows

Practice 4 (p. 44)

1. *Subject:* cats, dog
   Verb: stay
2. *Subject:* CDs, DVDs
   Verb: Are
3. *Subject:* Staples, Scotch tape
   Verb: hold
4. *Subject:* scratches, dents
   Verb: were
5. *Subject:* course, course
   Verb: require

4 SENTENCE TYPES

Practice 1 (p. 52)

Note Answers will vary. Below are some possibilities.

1. library
2. threw
3. Roast beef . . . Swiss cheese
4. Sylvia . . . jog
5. My aunt . . . uncle . . . ate

Practice 2 (p. 53)

1. Rodrigo is usually cheerful, but he seems quiet and troubled today.
2. All my clothes were dirty this morning, so I'm wearing my husband's shirt.
3. Virginia has learned karate, and she carries a can of self-defense spray.

Practice 3 (p. 54)

1. As the family members were enjoying the wedding, burglars stole the wedding gifts from their home.
2. Jeff broke out in red blotches after he walked through a bank of poison ivy.
3. Although Mei Lin scrubbed for an hour, she could not get the crayon marks off the wall.

5 FRAGMENTS

Note Methods of correction may vary.

Practice 1 (p. 63)

1. <u>When the Wal-Mart discount store opened outside town,</u> stores on Main Street lost a lot of business.
2. <u>Because smoke detectors are so important to a family's safety,</u> their batteries should be checked often.
3. <u>After the children washed the family car,</u> they had a water fight with the wet sponges.
4. Please hang up the damp towel <u>that you just threw on the floor.</u>

Practice 2 (p. 64)

1. Police officers stood near the corner. They were <u>directing people around the accident.</u>
2. The magician ran a sword through the box <u>to prove no one was hiding inside.</u>
3. <u>Sitting quietly on the couch,</u> the dog didn't look as if he'd eaten my sandwich.
4. The restaurant has introduced a new vegetarian menu. Its purpose is <u>to attract diners who prefer not to eat meat.</u>

Practice 3 (p. 65)

1. Television censors watch out for material that viewers might find offensive, <u>such as sexual or racial jokes.</u>
2. The children's toys were everywhere <u>except in the toy chest.</u>
3. All applicants at that company must take a skills assessment test. They must <u>also</u> take <u>a personality profile test.</u>
4. The film class saw every Dustin Hoffman film, <u>including his first one, *The Graduate.*</u>

Practice 4 (p. 66)

1. Greta is friendly to people's faces <u>but criticizes them behind their backs.</u>
2. A mouse's face popped out of a hole near the sink. <u>Then it disappeared quickly.</u>
3. The nurse brought the patient an extra pillow and a glass of water. <u>But she forgot his pain medication.</u>
4. The pot of coffee sat on the burner for hours <u>and became too strong and bitter to drink.</u>

6 RUN-ONS

Note Methods of correction may vary.

Practice 1 (p. 75)

1. It's easy to begin smoking, but it's much harder to quit.
2. Because some people at the office have been laid off, the other workers are nervous.
3. The patient's blood pressure was low. His temperature was low as well.

Practice 2 (p. 76)

1. Hakim was talking on the phone, and he was switching TV channels with his remote control at the same time.
2. I chose the shortest checkout line at the supermarket. Then the one customer in front of me pulled out dozens of coupons.
3. Since the electricity at Jasmin's house went out, she had to write her paper by candlelight.

7 PRONOUNS

Practice 1 (p. 85)

1. she
2. their
3. he or she
4. it
5. him

Practice 2 (p. 85)

1. Rudy
2. the maintenance people
3. the sugar
4. cheating
5. the stores

Practice 3 (p. 86)

1. They
2. his
3. I
4. we
5. you

8 COMMA

Practice 1 (p. 94)

1. newspapers, aluminum,
2. Walking, bicycling,
3. kids, loaded the van,
4. insomnia, inability to concentrate,

Practice 2 (p. 94)

1. course,
2. on,
3. doorway,
4. hours,

Practice 3 (p. 95)

1. Beatles, who originally called themselves the Quarrymen,
2. yogurt, which is relatively low in calories,
3. dieters, on the other hand,
4. building, forty stories high,

Practice 4 (p. 96)

1. house, but
2. glasses, so
3. quickly, but
4. family, and

Practice 5 (p. 96)

1. replied,
2. ends,"
3. women," the mall store owner bragged,
4. do,"

9 APOSTROPHE

Practice 1 (p. 104)

1. you'll, it's
2. I'd, who's
3. What's, that's
4. isn't, aren't
5. didn't, they're

Practice 2 (p. 105)

1. It's, its
2. their, they're
3. Who's, whose
4. your, your
5. It's, their, whose, your

Practice 3 (p. 106)

2. mail carrier's job, that man's vicious dog
3. Everyone's assignment, Monday's class
4. Ben Franklin's inventions, people's ideas
5. Doris's grades, her brothers' grades

Practice 4 (p. 107)

1. officers—plural
   owner's
2. storefront's
   years—plural

3. manager's
   gives—verb
   assignments—plural
4. year's
   shows—plural
   programs—plural
   seasons—plural
5. son's
   coughs—verb
   wheezes—verb
   starts—verb
6. Theo's
   failings—plural
   conclusions—plural
7. Dieters—plural
   glasses—plural
   water's
8. dozens—plural
   elephants—plural
   water holes'
   edges—plural

10 QUOTATION MARKS

Practice 1 (p. 116)

1. "My throat is so sore I can't talk,"
2. "Life's a tough proposition, and the first hundred years are the hardest."
3. "Don't go in that door!"
4. "Parking By Permit Only—Violators Will Be Towed."
5. "After all the trouble the customers at that table have caused," . . . "they'd better leave a decent tip."

Practice 2 (p. 117)

2. Coach Hodges told Lori, "You played an outstanding game."
3. Manuel insisted, "My new glasses haven't improved my vision one bit."
4. The detective exclaimed, "I know the murderer's identity!"
5. I told Dr. Patton, "I haven't been to a dentist since high school."

Practice 3 (p. 118)

1. The Good Food Book . . . "How to Eat More and Weigh Less."
2. "The Garden Party."
3. The Sound of Music, . . . "Climb Every Mountain"
4. "All Gamblers Lose" . . . Newsweek . . . Time.
5. "Will the Circle Be Unbroken?" . . . The Atlantic Monthly

11 OTHER PUNCTUATION MARKS

Practice 1 (p. 126)

1. close?
2. aggressive.
3. birth!
4. run.
5. bins.

Practice 2 (p. 128)

1. black-hatted
2. (I think I've mentioned her to you before)
3. all—if
4. attachments:
5. diet;

12 HOMONYMS

Practice (p. 137)

1. It's, it's, its
2. There, their, they're
3. to, two, too
4. You're, you're, your

13 CAPITAL LETTERS

Practice 1 (p. 147)

1. As, Doug, Don't
2. St. Mary's, Seminary, Baltimore, Maryland, Catholic
3. We, Professor, Henderson, Florentine, Italian, Lake, Street
4. Some, Rodeo, Drive, Beverly, Hills, California
5. When, Rodney, Dangerfield, I

Practice 2 (p. 148)

1. Caucasian, African-American, Hispanic, Asian
2. All, Shook, Up, Pepsi
3. Introduction, Statistics
4. Monday, October, Columbus, Day
5. Mommy, Solarcaine

14 WORD CHOICE

Note Wording of answers may vary.

Practice 1 (p. 157)

1. Because the judge's hair is prematurely gray, people think she is much older than thirty-eight.
2. I can't understand why there are now so many poor people in this country.
3. If the weather is bad, the baseball game will be postponed.

Practice 2 (p. 158)

1. do very well in . . . deliberately miss
2. was fortunate . . . fired
3. fell asleep . . . working all night

Practice 3 (p. 158)

1. very sick . . . healthy
2. depressed . . . not doing well in
3. unexpectedly . . . traveled quickly

15 MISPLACED AND DANGLING MODIFIERS

Note Wording of answers may vary.

Practice 1 (p. 166)

1. With shaking hands, the young man gave his driver's license to the officer.
2. Driving down the country road, we were surprised to hear a siren.
3. Gina got badly sunburned on her face and back after spending a day at the beach.
4. The registrar will post on the Web site the schedule for final exams.
5. Stan bought a sports car with wire wheels from a fast-talking salesman.

Practice 2 (p. 167)

1. My sister spends nearly all evening on the telephone.
2. Carlos must have answered almost a hundred ads before he found a job.
3. I asked the instructor for only one day's extension, but she refused.

Practice 3 (p. 168)

1. While I was taking a shower, a mouse ran across my bathroom floor.
2. Sitting on the front porch, we were annoyed by mosquitoes.
3. While Kareem was eating at the restaurant, his coat was stolen.
4. Ill from the heat, the runner finally saw the finish line come into view.
5. Hoping to catch a glimpse of the band, fans filled the parking lot.

16 PARALLELISM

Practice 1 (p. 177)

1. to type the report
2. baby cried
3. dark sunglasses
4. office manager
5. unkind
6. coaches the track team

Practice 2 (p. 177)

1. play the piano
2. steamed shrimp
3. high-heeled boots
4. friendliness
5. deposited it in the deep hole

Practice 3 (p. 178)

Note Answers will vary. Below are some possibilities.

1. scrubbing floors
2. wait for sales
3. creative writing
4. plant flowers
5. reading newspapers

ANSWERS TO THE PRACTICES IN PART TWO

17 PAPER FORM

Practice (p. 188)

	The Importance of National Service
	In his inaugural address, President John F. Kennedy urged
	Americans to discover what they could do for their country.
	Many people, inspired by his words, support national service for
	America's youth. The idea is a good one for several reasons. . . .

18 SPELLING

Practice (p. 190)

1. parties
2. referred
3. writing
4. definitely
5. deceive
6. employer
7. admittance
8. marrying
9. friendly
10. pitiful

20 PRONOUN TYPES

Practice (p. 202)

1. I
2. hers
3. me
4. He, I
5. your
6. Those
7. Who
8. these
9. they, themselves
10. whom

21 ADJECTIVES AND ADVERBS

Practice (p. 204)

1. harder
2. regularly
3. really
4. greatest
5. easier
6. softly
7. less
8. carefully
9. well
10. better

22 NUMBERS AND ABBREVIATIONS

Practice (p. 206)

1. twelve
2. 25
3. company
4. One hundred fifty
5. college
6. 6
7. doctor
8. 7
9. professor
10. 10

23 USAGE

Practice (p. 207)

1. ~~can't hardly~~ can hardly
2. ~~try and~~ try to
3. ~~ways~~ way

4. ~~because~~ that
5. ~~could of~~ could have
6. ~~should of~~ should have
7. ~~couldn't help but notice~~ couldn't help noticing
8. ~~Being that~~ Since (*or* Because)
9. ~~off of~~ off
10. ~~anywheres~~ anywhere

24 MORE ABOUT SUBJECTS AND VERBS

Practice (p. 208)

1. *Subjects:* Tulips, daffodils, azaleas
   Verb: bloom
2. *Subject:* motor
   Verbs: coughed, refused
3. *Subjects:* Accounting, computer science
   Verbs: are, require
4. *Subject:* Lisa
   Verbs: tore, lifted, gasped
5. *Subjects:* author, husband
   Verbs: attended, sipped, chatted

25 EVEN MORE ABOUT VERBS

Practice 1 (p. 211)

1. Seeing . . . believing
2. to grow
3. has given
4. will be traveling . . . will be displaying
5. was borrowed

Practice 2 (p. 212)

1. sit
2. lain
3. raise
4. rose
5. laid

26 MORE ABOUT SUBJECT-VERB AGREEMENT

Practice (p. 213)

1. *Subject:* few
   Verb: taste
2. *Subjects:* Thelma, mother
   Verb: stays
3. *Subjects:* Carl, friends
   Verb: are
4. *Subject:* All
   Verb: were
5. *Subjects:* coach, coaches
   Verb: have
6. *Subject:* Both
   Verb: need
7. *Subjects:* lectures, textbook
   Verb: has
8. *Subject:* any
   Verb: Is
9. *Subject:* any
   Verb: Are
10. *Subject:* all
    Verb: seem

27 MORE ABOUT RUN-ONS

Practice (p. 214)

1. horrible;
2. dirty;
3. locked;
4. London;
5. products;
6. rent;
7. children;
8. yard;
9. minutes;
10. much;

28 MORE ABOUT THE COMMA

Practice (p. 217)

1. Vanessa,
2. morning,

3. March 8, 2007, Courthouse, Streets, Glendale,
4. confused,
5. no commas needed
6. Harvey, Joy,
7. No,
8. reception,
9. loan,
10. Rhett, . . . With love,

29 MORE ABOUT THE APOSTROPHE

Practice (p. 218)

1. 4's . . . 7's . . . T's
2. no apostrophes needed
3. A's . . . B's
4. no apostrophes needed
5. *please's . . . thank-you's*

30 MORE ABOUT QUOTATION MARKS

Practice (p. 220)

1. "For our next class, please read the short story 'The Yellow Wallpaper' and write a journal entry about it," the instructor said.
2. "Look out for the green slime monster hiding in your closet!" my little brother screamed.
3. In which of Shakespeare's plays does a character say, "To thine own self be true"?
4. One of the longest words in the English language is "antidisestablishmentarianism."
5. "Whenever I'm feeling depressed, my father always makes me smile by saying, 'Life is far too important to be taken seriously,'" Joanne said.

31   MORE ABOUT PUNCTUATION MARKS

Practice (p. 221)

1. thirty-nine
2. food—
3. Reader's Digest ... epidemic; ... office;
4. (1) ... (2) ... (3) ... (4) ... (5) ... (6)
5. The Tommyknockers . . . The Fly

32   MORE ABOUT HOMONYMS

Practice (p. 224)

1. already . . . quit . . . accept . . . advice
2. dessert . . . effect . . . dose
3. lose . . . less . . . an . . . pair . . . a
4. coarse . . . led . . . principal
5. all ready . . . Fewer
6. quite . . . quit . . . advise . . . affect
7. desert . . . except
8. course . . . principle . . . among
9. quiet . . . does
10. where . . . were . . . led . . . among

33   MORE ABOUT CAPITAL LETTERS

Practice (p. 225)

1. Korean War . . . CIA
2. Northeast . . . Midwest
3. AIDS . . . Dark Ages
4. Dear Ms. Walker . . . CBS
5. Dear Sir . . . Madam . . . DVD . . . Yours

34   MORE ABOUT WORD CHOICE

Practice (p. 227)

1. ~~remit~~ pay
   ~~prior to~~ before
2. ~~ascertained~~ found out
   ~~depart~~ leave
3. ~~remuneration~~ pay
   ~~insufficient~~ too low
4. ~~vociferous~~ noisy
   ~~endeavored~~ tried
5. ~~Subsequent to~~ After
   ~~afflicted~~ injured
6. ~~commenced~~ began
   ~~be victorious~~ win
7. ~~justifications~~ excuses
   ~~prevaricated~~ lied
8. ~~replenish~~ refill
   ~~deplete~~ empty
9. ~~domicile~~ home
   ~~transmit~~ send
10. ~~delectable~~ delicious
    ~~repast~~ meal

Index